SOCCERTALK

Life Under the Spell of the Round Ball

PAUL GARDNER

Foreword by Bruce Arena, Head Coach, U.S. National Team

D0932749

MASTERS PRESS

NTC/Contemporary Publishing Group

Library of Congress Cataloging-in-Publication Data

Gardner, Paul, 1930–
        SoccerTalk / Paul Gardner ; foreword by Bruce Arena.
            p.   cm.
        A collection of columns and articles previously appearing in various
    publications.
        Includes index.
        ISBN 1-57028-231-5
        1. Soccer.   2. Newspapers—Sections, columns, etc.—Sports.
    I. Title.   II. Title: SoccerTalk.
    GV943.G294   1999
    796.334—dc21   98-37383
                                                                              CIP

Front-cover photograph copyright © Vera R. Storman/Tony Stone Images
Back-cover photograph copyright © Jon Van Woerden
Cover design by Todd Petersen
Interior design by Impressions Book and Journal Services, Inc.

Published by Masters Press
A division of NTC/Contemporary Publishing Group, Inc.
4255 West Touhy Avenue, Lincolnwood (Chicago), Illinois 60646-1975 U.S.A.
Copyright © 1999 by Paul Gardner
Printed in the United States of America
International Standard Book Number: 1-57028-231-5
99 00 01 02 03 04 MV 19 18 17 16 15 14 13 12 11 10 9 8 7 6 5 4 3 2 1

Also by Paul Gardner

Sports Illustrated Soccer (with Phil Woosnam; 1972)
Pelé: The Master and His Method (1973)
Nice Guys Finish Last: Sport and American Life (1974)
*The Simplest Game: The Intelligent Fan's Guide
    to the World of Soccer* (1976)

For Lyn Fairhurst

Contents

This collection consists of 52 columns and articles that have previously appeared in:

Soccer America
The New York Times
New York Daily News Sunday Magazine
Sports Illustrated
USA Today
The Sporting News
The Village Voice
Soccer Express
'94 Cup Daily
World Sports (London)
World Soccer (London)
The Observer (London)
The Guardian (London)
Official Program for the Bicentennial Cup

Foreword

I have heard it said many times that Paul Gardner is arrogant, opinionated, and knows nothing about soccer. Well, people say that about me, too, and I guess there's some truth in that!

SoccerTalk is an accumulation of Paul Gardner's thoughts on the game. He loves to write and talk about soccer. Most of us have read Paul's columns, traced with humor and cynical verbiage. His use of the English language is remarkable and his views on the sport and the people who play key roles are, at the very least, interesting and controversial. He is critical of acts that he feels have violated the sacred trusts and principles of soccer. He can also be supportive and complimentary, and he truly cares about the game. Regardless of whether we agree or disagree with his views, I think it is safe to say that he is an outstanding writer and is an important voice for soccer. This is why readers of *Soccer America* hastily rush to read his weekly column "Soccer-Talk." Paul entertains us and we savor his next words and thoughts.

Having said that, why is Paul so controversial? I believe it's because he writes about a game that is still relatively unknown and unsophisticated to even the soccer community in our country. At times we are set back by his abruptness on issues. He attacks us and we want to fight back. In retrospect, Paul has a very keen understanding of the game and of the people who play key roles—players, coaches, referees, administrators, and organizations. *SoccerTalk* evokes both emotion and debate, while educating readers about real soccer issues. Paul is without doubt America's foremost writer on the sport of soccer—and he tells it like it is!

I have grown professionally with Paul Gardner. He patiently listened to my thoughts on college soccer in the early 1980s, and then went about educating me on how naive I was to the real game and the shortcomings that college soccer brought to player development. At first I fought back. Eventually I began to appreciate what he had to say and realized the substance behind his writing. His weekly columns have helped me formulate my thoughts on the game, and to this day his words continue to challenge me.

Paul is someone you are afraid to admit you both fear and respect. If you think you play a role in the game (particularly in our country), you are a target for a Paul Gardner article and he holds you accountable for your actions. He challenges us to critically think about important issues. Like it or not, we are all fair game and if we do not do our homework we will end up sitting in the corner wearing the dunce cap. Paul keeps the people in the soccer community back on their heels.

If the game of soccer is to progress in the United States we all need to be put to the test. Coaches, administrators, referees, and so on play a vital role in creating a better soccer environment. In order to develop better players we must create a more competitive soccer environment. Players need to be challenged on a daily basis. A better soccer environment will give us the opportunity to emerge as a real soccer power. This is part of the message Paul tries to convey.

SoccerTalk is the role Paul Gardner plays in helping to develop the game in our country. He critically preaches for a better soccer environment and wants the people involved to get it right. If we all get it right, over time the game will truly emerge in the United States, and we can thank Paul Gardner for the role that he has played.

Bruce Arena
Head Coach, U.S. National Team

Acknowledgments

The writing in this collection covers a mere 30 years. The experience covers twice that period, a lifetime in which soccer has played a prominent role in my life. My thanks go to so many people known and unknown—to adults for the friendship, the support, the knowledge, and the numberless arguments and discussions. And to all those youngsters, the hundreds, nay thousands, of boys whose antics and emotions on the soccer field I have so lovingly watched over so many years. Their glowing delight in this game has been a constant stimulant to my own involvement in it.

Amidst that vast throng there must inevitably be the traditional special-thanks category. As far as this book is concerned, the key man—the "without whom . . ." man—has been Mike Woitalla, executive editor at *Soccer America*. I'm really not at all sure that this would have happened without his ideas, his good humor, and his sympathetic, tireless, and knowing support.

The majority of these pieces appeared in *Soccer America*—where Paul Kennedy has been a most agreeable and helpful managing editor for many years.

Lawrie Mifflin and Dave Hirshey have been two delightfully intelligent companions with whom I've shared soccer frustrations and joys for over a quarter of a century. I know of no clever device, not even in this technological age, that will measure their input into my soccer thinking, but it has been substantial.

There is, too, a huge debt to Brian Glanville, the English soccer writer who in so many important ways blazed a trail for me—and I'm sure for many others—by opening my eyes to the global nature of the sport and showing that soccer journalism could indeed be based on splendid writing.

A sad and wrenching note intruded during the preparation of this book, with the death of Julio Cesar Pasquato, the Argentine journalist who wrote under the pen name Juvenal. Another knowledgeable friend, one who enlightened me so patiently about the history and tradition of South American soccer.

The work of photographer John McDermott, a master craftsman of soccer imagery, has given me much pleasure, as have our many wide-ranging conversations on the sport. And I'd find it difficult to believe that there lives anywhere a person more enthusiastic about soccer than Arnie Ramirez—a valued and trusted friend. Another true friend has been Ted Howard, who has taught me so much about American attitudes to soccer.

Thanking one's editor is always the correct thing to do, of course. But thanking Ken Samelson is no formality. In Ken I have found someone whom I was beginning to doubt I would ever find in this country: an editor who appreciates soccer. An editor whose knowledge of the minutiae of the sport has often astounded me. And that has made everything so much easier, so much more enjoyable. Thanks also to NTC's Julia Anderson, whose cool head and hand navigated the book safely through the perilous production process.

Finally, to rescue just a few of those lively young players from anonymity, thanks to Chris, Joey, Manny, Felipe, Mauro, Leon, Roy, Mitch, David, Joselito, Oscar, Little Dave, Tony, Alfie, Danny, Adam, Gilbert, Ronnie, Steve, Dick, Baba, Ivan, Karl, Russ, Bobby, Felix, Albert, Hugh, Tommy, Philip, Mark, Pudding, Norm, Miguel, Robin, Luis, Salvatore, Eduardo, Vinnie, and all the Johns and all the Josés and all the others for helping me fathom the mysteries of "The Beautiful Game."

Paul Gardner
New York, March 1999

Introduction

It seems to me that things rarely go the way I would like them to. Or even the way I thought they would. If I recall correctly, I had planned at various times to be the greatest trumpet player in the history of jazz, to break the world 880-yard record, to be a crackerjack lawyer, and to reign as Hollywood's most brilliant actor.

Instead, I write about soccer. How did that happen? Something like this, I suppose . . .

. . . As a high school boy in England in the 1940s two passions ruled my life: soccer and writing. I was an outstanding player for my school team, a right halfback of cunning creativity and inexhaustible energy. I was also the apple of my English teacher's eye, who was forever reading aloud my essays so that my entire class would appreciate my talent. The two devotions dovetailed beautifully in later life. I started to write about soccer . . .

That would be a nice, neat beginning, but, alas, I just made it all up. Lies, every word of it. There has been no preordained path to soccer journalism that I have devotedly followed, no carefully thought-out ambition. As far as I can see it has . . . just happened.

My school didn't have a soccer team and I wasn't passionate about anything. The bit about the essay though, that happened just once, an over-written, over-mannered piece about the sadness of being deaf. I kept that woeful composition—I don't know why—along with all my school reports, nearly 50 of them, a comically pompous record of what my elders and betters thought of me between the ages of 7 and 17. "Could do better" is the recurring theme.

The housemaster would write "I am concerned about his casual approach to life. . . ." Underneath, in the stern black ink of authority, the headmaster would add "he must pay attention to what his housemaster says."

I didn't, not because I was a fiery rebel, but because I found it more congenial to get on with what I liked doing. For a start, I resented the school's ban on soccer. It was seen as a common, working-class sport. We played upper-middle-class rugby. Nevertheless, a group of us formed our own team, and we played on raw autumnal Saturday mornings on desolate and bumpy fields. We played, badly, against teams of common, working-class boys who swore and spat profusely, a culture shock that greatly thrilled me.

There was the added excitement of illicit pleasure. The games had to be kept secret. In the afternoon many of us played for the school in rugby or field hockey. Who knows what awful punishment we would have suffered had it got out that we were wasting our adolescent muscle power on soccer only a few hours before school duty called?

So secretive were our games that I cannot now remember whatever name we concocted for our team. I must add that I was a truly awful player, possibly the worst right halfback in the history of soccer. Then again, maybe not. It could be that I was just 15 years ahead of my time. It was in the 1960s that coaches—who had by then begun their gobbledygook-laden rise to power—began to talk of the overriding importance of playing *without* the ball.

I was pretty good at that. Certainly I did all I could to make sure that I saw as little of the ball as possible. It was only when it arrived at my feet, probably as the result of some clumsy miskick by a teammate, that my troubles began.

There was plenty of enthusiasm on our team, though there was a shortage of skill. We always seemed to take the field with only 10, or maybe 9, players. We didn't win very often.

That was the sort of soccer I continued to play, that and any old street game I could get involved in—I loved my abrupt, unexpected involvement in those games, the sudden making of new friends whom I would never see again—until I was 20. By then I was studying pharmacy, which I found time-consuming.

Pharmacy? As I said, I was not passionate about anything in high school. I left (as do most boys, I suspect) without any clear idea what I wanted to do. My father, also a pharmacist, decided for me. I went along, but it was a mistake, of course.

I served a two-year apprenticeship in Wolverhampton in a wonderfully aromatic old pharmacy full of dusty bottles with romantic Latin labels where we happily dispensed bucketsful of amphetamine pills—at that time they were considered ideal appetite suppressants for ladies who simply wanted to lose weight. Innocent days!

Persistently, quietly poking its nose into my life, not quite noticed by me, there was soccer. Mr. Albert Warburton, my boss in the pharmacy, was a great

1931: Ugh!! My aversion to ersatz soccer started here, as I recoiled in horror at a photographer's attempt to pass off a balloon as a soccer ball. Courtesy Paul Gardner

1950: Not my favorite period. The student intellectual in full regalia: beard, pipe, polo-necked pullover—and on the desk the massive typewriter that I affectionately called "The Eiffel Tower." Courtesy Paul Gardner

1947: Spot the author, whose high school shunned working-class soccer in favor of middle-class rugby in baggy shorts. Courtesy Paul Gardner

Wolves fan, a director of the club. Saturday afternoons would find him in a frenzy of frustration. The stadium, Molyneux, was about a 10-minute walk away, but English law is adamant. When the pharmacy was open, he—as the registered pharmacist—had to be on the premises at all times.

Every other Saturday, the same rigmarole. No, Mr. Warburton was not going to the game. But around 10 minutes to 3:00, his face would get decidedly redder, he would start issuing curt instructions to everyone, and would then disappear.

Just before 5:00 he would sweep back into the pharmacy, grab a prescription or two from the waiting clients, and then burst into the dispensary trying to make his two-hour absence seem like a matter of minutes: "Is-the-prescription-for-Malpass-ready-yet-Wolves-three-Tottenham-two-and-she's-*waiting*-for-this-one-Paul," thrusting a prescription into my hand, demanding that it be filled at once, making me feel that I was the one who had been neglecting my duties.

Actually, I was jealous of his trips to Molyneux. Especially when Blackpool, with my soccer hero Stanley Matthews (p. 107), were in town. The Wolves, captained by the legendary Billy Wright, were not at all a bad team in the early 1950s. Wright was the first English player to gain 100 caps, no mean feat in those days when international games were played much less frequently.

Certainly the Wolves were much better than either Nottingham Forest or Notts County, the teams I had to make do with while I was at college. There was one attraction though: County, a third division team, had pulled off a remarkable coup by signing center-forward Tommy Lawton (for a piddling but then-record $100,000 fee). So I saw a lot of Lawton, another of the great names of English soccer, and he never seemed to me to be as good as everyone said he was.

I became a fully-fledged Fellow of the Royal Pharmaceutical Society of Great Britain, but a year of locum pharmacy work in the English midlands confirmed what I'd already known for quite a while. I didn't want to be a pharmacist.

I drifted again. The chance sight of an advertisement sent me to London, where I worked for six years as the assistant editor of a pharmacy journal exotically called *The Alchemist*. Now, by accident it seemed, I was into journalism.

In London I went regularly to watch Arsenal, arriving in style at Highbury on my motorcycle, surrounded as I dismounted by a swarm of grubby little boys with cute faces yelling "Let me watch yer bike, mister," which meant they'd scratch it up or let the tires down if I didn't give them a few pennies.

Arsenal were nothing special in those days, but how I loved those coarse, boisterous afternoons on the terraces at Highbury (p. 172). In 1959 Arsenal

1953: Apothecary at work. The newly-minted Fellow of the Pharmaceutical Society forces a semi-smile—but filling prescriptions was not for me. Courtesy Paul Gardner

1955: London—and to journalistic work as assistant editor of The Alchemist. *Shirtsleeves rolled up, I'm listening to my first—and most treasured—editor, Brian O'Malley.* Courtesy Paul Gardner

A decade of television work between 1976 and 1986 included many games broadcast for ABC alongside Jim McKay (listening patiently in this 1979 picture as I make some vital but long-forgotten point). McKay may not have known soccer, but he was an amazingly quick learner and an ultra-professional. I eventually got too ancient for ABC, who told my agent in 1993 that they were "looking for somebody younger." Courtesy Paul Gardner

rather surprisingly won the championship, and later that same year I emigrated to the States.

Possibly there was a connection, but I don't think so. My move was yet another random act in my life; I really cannot recall what my motive was other than a vague desire for change. Clearly, it had nothing to do with soccer. I mean, who in 1959 would have come to the United States in search of a career in soccer?

And so to New York, where I have lived—apart from a two-year break in Italy—since 1959. I worked on a medical magazine in New York and Montreal. To my surprise I found some soccer in New York. All those ethnic leagues and—during the summers—Bill Cox's International Soccer League.

My view of the game was considerably widened from the narrow English perspective that I had brought with me. I went off to Italy in 1964 and returned to New York in 1966 ready to resume my career as a medical journalist.

This time soccer, which had been whispering and beckoning in the wings of my life, moved center stage. And, as always, I was taken by surprise. Enjoying myself in Italy, I had been unaware of the sudden American interest in pro soccer, of the coming birth of not one, but two, pro leagues.

While I set about looking for a real job, I also made some contacts in this odd new world of American pro soccer, a world where either nobody or everybody was an expert. Being English apparently qualified me as an expert. (I was not—still am not—happy about the type of American snobbery that bows down to the English accent, though I have to admit it has been helpful to me.) I edited the National Professional Soccer League's first yearbook, and I never did get that real job. It's been freelance soccer stuff ever since: articles, columns, books, films, and television (though not lately—too old, ABC told my agent in 1993).

Evidently, soccer has cast some sort of spell over me, a seductive spell that I was slow to recognize. I have given some thought to the nature of that spell, and this is what I have come up with. I find in soccer what I have found in life: unpredictability, constant surprises, and a fascinating contrariness. It is an activity that suggests it has a mind of its own, one that will tease and disappoint as much as it rewards. A little world where players don't do things you were quite certain they would do, and other players do things you never thought they were capable of. A world where planning goes astray and experts are repeatedly confounded.

As for the writing part, I'd like to think that things have gotten better since the affectations of that early essay. Science has undoubtedly improved the mechanics of the writing process, which were always something of a curse to me. Among my other contrarinesses, I grew up solidly left-handed in a right-handed world, a world that still used pen and ink. For a left-hander, writing from left to right meant scratchily pushing a pen, not gracefully drawing it forward. The nib would catch in the paper, little blotches of ink would splatter merrily all over the place. My left hand, laboriously following the protesting nib, was always likely to smudge the slow-to-dry ink. And there was the annoying position of the inkwell, top right in the school desks. The ink-charged pen had to be borne aloft from the well, right across the shining white paper on the desk. Great drops would fall, great blots would spread. Relief for the left-handers came with the ballpoint pen, but it arrived too late to disturb my reputation as an inky-fingered, messy writer.

I always read a great deal, rapidly devouring detective stories (a habit I still indulge), and ransacking the local library for books by P. G. Wodehouse. I loved his humor and became so familiar with his novels that I started to mark up the library books, pointing out when he had used a particular phrase in other books with chapter-and-verse notations in the margins.

When I was still quite young my father had given me a typewriter. Another random event, I must conclude. For my father had no interest in the arts, and seemed hopelessly puzzled when I eventually meandered into a full-time journalist's life.

The typewriter—a Royal, I think—was a huge, heavy, metallic brute that I dubbed "The Eiffel Tower," on which I pecked out delicate poems. Luckily, I discovered George Orwell when I was 17 and immersed myself in his essays, in particular "Why I Write." Good prose, said Orwell, "is like a window pane." It lets you see what's beyond without getting in the way, without distorting the image.

It was perfect advice for me, and it finished my efforts to sound like a romantic poet. Sturdy, masculine prose would be the thing for me. Choosing the right words, and not too many of them, became important. Which was fine, for words had always fascinated me. Orwell said he "suddenly discovered the joy of mere words" when he was 16, but I think I was ahead of him there. For as long as I can remember I have been a devoted doer (though not always a solver) of crosswords. Wordplay intrigues me, and my mind is forever at work spelling words backward or turning them into anagrams, or rhyming them, or finding homonyms, or working on obscure puns.

If I had to settle now for a favorite author it would be Vladimir Nabokov for his matchless magic with "mere words"; as it happens—is this coincidence?—Nabokov played soccer (like Albert Camus, he was a goalkeeper) and the sport crops up repeatedly in his works. Short, offhand references full of the vigor and beauty of the sport itself:

> The pale, sweaty, tensely distorted face of a player depicted from top to toe preparing at full speed to shoot with terrible force at the goal. Tousled red hair, a burst of mud on his temple, the taut muscles of his bare neck. A wrinkled, soaking wet, violet singlet, clinging in spots to his body, comes down low over his spattered shorts, and is crossed with the wonderful diagonal of a mighty crease. He is in the act of hooking the ball sideways; one raised hand with wide-splayed fingers is a participant in the general tension and surge. But most important, of course, are the legs: a glistening white thigh, an enormous scarred knee, boots swollen with dark mud, thick and shapeless, but nevertheless marked by an extraordinarily precise and powerful grace. The stocking has slipped down one vigorously twisted calf, one foot is buried in rich mud, the other is about to kick—and how!—the hideous tar-black ball—and all this against a dark gray background saturated with rain and snow. (*The Gift*)

Nabokov is describing a painting. Looking at the picture, he says "one could *already* hear the whizz of the leather missile, *already* see the goalkeeper's desperate dive." But his words, his wonderful words, are as full of action and excitement as any painting could ever be.

For me, Nabokov and Orwell lead the pack (odd running mates, I know—Nabokov considered Orwell mediocre). Galloping hard on their heels come Charles Dickens, a feast of words tumbling over each other in rich profusion; Evelyn Waugh, quite the opposite, his words so carefully chosen and polished; the incomparable James Thurber, who displaced Wodehouse in the humor department; Graham Greene for his most subtle, most wonderful way of making words carry action, suspense, and menace; and the free-flowing lyrical invective of yet another writer/goalkeeper, the great French master Céline. (Maybe he solves that positional conundrum: "I had the best position in the football game, I kept goal . . . that gave me a chance to meditate . . . I didn't like to be disturbed. . . .") And, more a pair of favorite books than a favorite author, Lewis Carroll's *Alice in Wonderland* and *Through the Looking Glass.*

Above them all, not part of the pack, on another plane altogether, Shakespeare himself, incapable of penning anything not worth reading, and reading again and again.

It has taken quite a while—over 50 years—for me to assemble my own little pantheon of writers. At the beginning, while reading a lot, I didn't do much writing. Certainly not while I was studying pharmacy. I recall a long essay on Louis Armstrong, laboriously typed (I have never learned how to type properly) that was then delivered to the Nottingham University Rhythm Society, of which I was secretary. Someone stood up at the end and called it "erudite," which I had to look up to make sure I wasn't being insulted.

The writing for a living began in London on *The Alchemist*. I got lucky. My editor was a man of enthusiasm, charm, and encyclopedic knowledge. He taught me about layout and typography and the use of journalistic English and the pictorial value of photographs, and he did more, for he made me enthusiastic about those things. I owe a lot to Brian O'Malley, sadly a smoker, dead far too early from lung cancer.

The pieces collected here were born at different times over the past 30 years. Most of them appeared in *Soccer America* under the column title "SoccerTalk." They never expected to find themselves side by side like this. In many ways, they make an awkward group, but I believe that there are one or two discernible, constant themes: my likes and my dislikes. What I like is really utterly simple, and I don't feel that it needs much explaining. I like soccer played as I think it should be played, certainly as I think it must be played if it is to succeed as a sport here in the United States.

Soccer is a fast-moving, highly athletic game. It involves a lot of contact—tackles and collisions are frequent—and quite often that contact is pretty violent. Yes, soccer must have all of those things. But to me those are incidentals, essential incidentals for sure, but side dishes to the real soccer feast.

The main course here has to be ball skill, and in its more refined form, ball artistry. It is this that gives soccer its aesthetic dimension. Without that artistry, truth be said, soccer can be a *very* dull game.

Such an outlook has led me inevitably to lavish praise on Brazil, the masters of attractive, attacking soccer (see pp. 16, 59). And, not incidentally, by far the world's most successful soccer country. Something that tends to get forgotten when the awful realists with their practical, results-are-all-that-matter approach start belittling the "pretty" Brazilian game. I have, too, become increasingly interested in youth soccer, where uninhibited play is more likely than in the coach-dominated professional game. And the team that, for me, has come to represent the boyish joy of soccer is Tahuichi of Bolivia (see pp. 64, 210).

If my likes can be embraced by the general term of "good soccer," my dislikes are much narrower, but they need a bit more explanation. I dislike anything that takes soccer away from its full richness, anything that shrivels it down to a threadbare display of defensive platitudes, anything that features "players" who really do nothing more than charge about all over the field, knocking their opponents down, and whacking the ball 50 yards anytime they get anywhere near it.

As my appreciation of youth soccer has enlarged, my feel for the pro game has ebbed somewhat. It is not only the agglomeration of commercial contracts, and court cases, and silly publicity gimmicks that has jaundiced my view of the pros. The rise of the coach has done the most damage. Or of a certain kind of coach—let us call him Koach.

I spoke earlier of the soccer world having its own logic. I see it as a world like that of cats, those wonderful animals that keep man in his place by refusing to treat him as the center of the universe, by refusing to do what man expects them to do. I'm sure that soccer, like cats, has its own logic—an inscrutable logic, beyond the grasp of man.

But it is not inscrutable to the Koach, it is not beyond *his* grasp, oh no. The Koach believes that he understands the inner workings of the soccer creature, and that he can therefore control the game. It can all be worked out, it can all be planned.

The Koach turns soccer into a kind of chess game. He often talks of the players as though they are inanimate pieces that he can shift around according to his master plans. Naturally, the players he prefers are the automatons, the obedient ones, the *koachable* ones, the ones who will do what they're told, who will play a role. Spontaneity, creativity are suspect to the Koach. He doesn't want unpredictable players, he prefers the runners and the workers.

His approach always emphasizes defense. That part of the game can be planned. I have the feeling that the Koach would have been at home in the German war college, where the ideal was to pose a problem and have everyone come up with the same answer.

The Koach is full of theories and plans and charts and diagrams and set plays. Having to listen to him—so reasonable, so obvious, so *clever*—is bad enough, but it is nothing compared to the tedium of watching his bloodless teams in action.

It would be nice to say that soccer cannot be played in the programmed way so dear to the Koach. But it can. It emerges as a straitjacketed sport, straightforward, totally lacking in artistry and subtlety, a feeble shadow of the rich, sparkling game that is true soccer. Sadly, that sort of soccer can also win games.

My dislike of the Koach and his emphasis on team play and tactics at the expense of individuality and creativity is amply reflected in these pages.

We have more than our fair share of Koaches in this country. Don't we ever. They have been spawned by the system of official coaching schools run by the United States Soccer Federation. Schools that inevitably have fallen into the hands of college coaches, with their academic predilection for giving lectures, conducting clinics, and constructing abstruse theories about how the game should be played.

To my knowledge, no other sport in the United States has lumbered itself with this absurdly inflated structure of pseudo-learning, where coaching licenses—they go all the way from the snobbish A down to the lowly E license—are held to be a sure guide as to whether someone can, or cannot, coach.

The colleges present another huge problem for me (pp. 7, 227). They stand in the way of the development of the game in this country. Not only, or even mainly, because of the eccentric nature of much of the coaching. It is simply that the NCAA's impossibly restrictive conditions—pitifully short schedules, virtually no outside ball—make the college game a joke in terms of player development.

This is a great shame. In soccer we are measuring the development of our players against the rest of the world. By the age of 18 in all the serious soccer countries—Italy, Brazil, Germany, Argentina, England, Spain, France, say—top young talent is already experiencing the rigors of playing at a pro club alongside and against much older, more experienced players. What we like to call wily veterans. While our 18-year-olds enter the lotus fields of college soccer, which is nothing more than a four-year extension of youth soccer. How can we be expected to compete?

My list of soccer distortions includes sociologists (p. 128), noisy goalkeepers (p. 121), and—most emphatically—the type of indoor soccer that is played professionally in this country (p. 177). Indoor soccer with its boards, and its penalty boxes, and its mass substitutions, and its flashing lights, and frenetic announcers. An ugly bastard of a sport that cheapens the majesty of the full game without ever managing to give it any of the thrills that, I am told, enliven hockey.

One further point: I have had a fair amount to say on the rules of the game (the English pompously insist on calling them laws), and have actually accomplished something here. In November 1977, in *World Soccer,* I suggested that the Fédération Internationale de Football Association (FIFA) require numbers on shirtfronts in its competitions. I kept up a one-man campaign on the issue for 13 years. It seemed to be falling on deaf ears until suddenly, in April 1990, I was surprised and gratified to see, in *FIFA News,* that FIFA was about to mandate frontal numbers.

In *Soccer Corner,* in September 1977, I wanted the offside rule changed so that an attacker in line with the last defender would be considered onside— I was one of many voices that eventually (in 1990) got the rule changed. When ejecting a player for a second yellow, I suggested in *Soccer Express,* in October 1979, the referee should hold up the yellow and red cards simultaneously— a system that FIFA adopted in 1992.

More recently, in March 1997, I pointed out to FIFA officials that it was extremely difficult to find in the rules any proof that the referee has the right to eject a coach (that specific authority was, in fact, buried in a separate booklet on "Questions and Answers"). No 13-year wait this time—a month later the 1997 rules appeared, with a new section spelling out the referee's power to expel "team officials."

I suppose that, to paraphrase Robert Frost, I have had—and continue to have—a lover's quarrel with soccer. So here you will find reflections of both love and exasperation. Plenty of praise for Brazil, for Tahuichi, and for the people and players who bring us skillful soccer. Brickbats for the Koach, and for indoor soccer, irritation at the pretensions of the college game.

On top of all, I hope there is detectable a sturdy faith in the real game as I see it. Despite all the depredations of the enemies of soccer (some of them, alas, enemies within), the sport survives, and it thrives.

If I was depressed in the 1970s—and I was—by the fashion for dour, brutal, defensive play, I can now look back and realize that it was nothing more than that—a fashion, a vogue. It has passed, and the sport looks a lot better these days.

I am genuinely hopeful that the twenty-first century will see the demise and interment of the Koach, and that the game will be joyously returned to the players.

Searching for Timeout

NEW YORK—If there is anyone around in these United States who does not know there is a soccer boom going on, he must be the most un-with-it person imaginable. Soccer is the new "in" game, written up in newspapers, magazines, and television, argued about, and—even—an attraction for several thousand spectators each week. While some journalists cannot stand it ("best thing for sleep since pillows," "clumsy basketball played with the feet"), the bulk of the printed comment has been friendly.

There are one or two little things that jar. Its rightful title *football* having been usurped by that padded American version of rugby, soccer gets referred to as *the booting game,* and the players as *booters*—both terms I for one would be happy never to hear again.

Of the two professional leagues that have been battling to launch the sport, it is the unsanctioned National Professional Soccer League (NPSL) that has taken the lead in building up teams, importing the majority of its players from Europe and South America. The standard of NPSL play is patchy; on average the teams would fit into the middle of the English second division, though one or two, the St. Louis Stars and the Pittsburgh Phantoms, for instance, are evidently better than this.

Considering the difficulties involved in starting teams from nothing, using players of goodness knows how many nationalities, most of them transplanted thousands of miles from their homes, it seems churlish to criticize. The language problem alone must have caused many of the coaches to wilt a bit at the knees. But with the help of a *lingua franca* of signs and ges-

Originally published in World Sports *(London) July 1967*

tures, the teams have been knocked into shape. Well, maybe a little more than signs and gestures . . . some of the heated comments heard from players on the field suggest that *goal* is not the only four-letter English word some of them have learned.

The NPSL is being very careful not to do anything that would jeopardize its chances of obtaining official sanction. No snooks have been cocked at FIFA (Fédération Internationale de Football Association) or the United States Soccer Football Association; and Ken Macker, the league commissioner, has been handing out $75–100 fines to players reported for rough play.

The United Soccer Association (USA; they started as the North American Soccer League, but changed titles "to avoid confusion") meanwhile has opened its minileague with each franchised city represented by a foreign team. There has been some holier-than-thou publicity from the USA clubs implying that their league will be providing a better class of soccer than the NPSL.

No doubt they are right, but I would question the assumption that the higher the class of soccer, the more exciting it is to watch. North Korea was certainly not the best team in last year's World Cup, yet created more excitement than all the rest put together. Recent baseball history here underlines the point: the New York Mets, a completely new team formed some five years ago, promptly sunk like lead to the bottom of the league and stayed there. They did everything wrong, became a byword for incompetence, and led their manager to utter a celebrated *cri de coeur,* "Can't anyone here play this game?" They were bad—but the crowds loved them, and it wasn't long before they were outdrawing the winning New York Yankees.

The present New York NPSL team, the Generals, seemed to start out trying to emulate the Mets. On record they are the worst team in the league, with fewer points than any, and fans aren't exactly trampling each other to death to see them. But would the crowds be appreciably bigger if the Generals were a slick, winning team? I think not; what has always brought out the big soccer crowds up until now has been ethnic interest. If the Generals were Inter-Milan, they would get huge crowds of Italian Americans to cheer them on. But if they only play like Inter, the ethnic interest has gone, and most of the fans with it. The Generals most certainly do not play like Inter. When English model Twiggy arrived in New York recently, some were suggesting that the Generals could do a lot worse than to sign her up.

The point is that to build up a following of fans new to the sport, a team has to offer not just top-class soccer, but excitement and entertainment. The NPSL was aware that if anything was likely to ruin things from the start, it would be defensive tactics; hence the league's system offering bonus points for goals scored. The scheme is an attempt to do something about a trend that

1967, Temple University Stadium: Philadelphia Spartans versus New York Generals. The Generals' Warren Archibald gets treatment for an injury—and here comes the referee. To hurry things up? No, quite the opposite—to ask Archibald if he's sure he's OK, to delay the restart so that a TV timeout can run its course without losing any of the game action. *Copyright Paul Gardner*

sees the game only in terms of goal-less draws through defensive 0–0 spectacles, and surely all agree that this is a pernicious trend. The scheme may not work—it is too early yet to tell—but I give the NPSL a thankful B-plus for trying.

Although the NPSL gate receipts at this stage (average crowd—if that is the right word—around 6,400) are not going to make anyone rich, the league has another source of income. This is the money paid by CBS to televise the games, reported to be $1 million for this first season. A set of circumstances that would seem, theoretically at any rate, to give CBS an unholy leverage in the league's affairs. This possibility was widely discussed during the rumpus over fake injury timeouts during televised games.

During one such game between the Toronto Falcons and the Pittsburgh Phantoms, the crowd soon saw that many of the referee's injury calls were bogus, and catcalls and hoots of derision resulted. The referee admitted later that he was equipped with some sort of receiver strapped to his back and was given a signal whenever a commercial was due. At the next foul or stoppage, he would deliberately delay the restart, usually by waving the trainer onto the field.

The Toronto referee, in letting the cat out of the bag, said he visited the dressing rooms before the game and asked the players to cooperate by feigning injury or protest. He denied that he had called any false fouls. I am sure he did not, but the point is that after getting his signal he was looking for a reason to stop play quickly; he may thus have called a foul he might otherwise have ignored—which would certainly make a mockery of the advantage rule—or he may have penalized a team by preventing a quickly taken free kick. Either way, his decisions must have interfered with the normal game.

The NPSL commissioner jumped in with unseemly haste to exonerate CBS from any blame in the affair, and accepted "personal responsibility" for what had happened. The week after the Toronto game, the TV transmission went much more smoothly, with the referee evidently having the say on when a commercial break should be made, and waving a red handkerchief to indicate one.

Anyway, the problem is a real one: how to fit commercials into a sport that has no official timeouts, like basketball, or between-inning pauses, like baseball. The fake injury method is obviously crude and could result in a real injury—to the league and to soccer.

Aside from the operatic interludes, the coverage of the games has been good, and is getting better; there are six cameras covering every game, plus instant replay of all the important action. And it is all in color. The viewing figure of 22 percent of the potential Sunday-afternoon audience seems quite a respectable one.

So on we go with two professional leagues when it must be obvious to everyone that, at this stage, there are barely enough spectators to support one. The stupidity of the situation needs no emphasis; talks between the NPSL and the USA were going on but were broken off in April. It is planned to resume them in the autumn when, one hopes, the groundwork will be laid for a merger of the two leagues.

Socko Box Office in New-Style Garden

NEW YORK—During its 91-year history, Madison Square Garden has been the scene of just about every type of sports event—boxing, ice hockey, basketball, six-day bicycle races, track meets, wrestling, dog shows, circuses—you name it and the chances are the Garden has staged it.

Not all in the same building. There have been four different Gardens over the years, new ones opening as old ones were torn down. The latest, opened just two years ago, is an ultramodern circular building with a pillarless main auditorium holding 20,000 people. Last Sunday afternoon it was sold out for something that even the Garden hasn't thought of before: soccer. The World Cup final, live and in color via satellite, on 15 foot × 20 foot screens.

So many people wanted to see it that they had to open up the 5,000-seat Felt Forum, more often used for rock concerts, to sop up the overflow. That was soon filled, so they put it on at the Coliseum as well, and got 4,000 more in there. All this at prices from $5 to $12.50. The World Cup has been socko box office in the States, with sellouts reported from other cities where it was screened across the country.

Now, sitting in Madison Square Garden in a bright-orange upholstered seat, the atmosphere nicely air-conditioned, vendors yelling their beer and popcorn and soda, an unobstructed view of the screen—I ask you, is that any way to watch a soccer game? We-e-e-ll, it's not exactly traditional, I'll give you that, but it was damned exciting. Twenty thousand fans can make a hell of a lot of noise, and they did just that. Mostly Italians, they came with their banners and their flags, and they cheered and whistled and cursed the referee as only Italians know how, and the miracle of satellite TV was complete. This was a live show.

Originally published in The Observer *(London) June 28, 1970. Copyright © The Observer. Reprinted by permission.*

The outnumbered Brazilians made quite a racket too, and 10 minutes before the kickoff they went one up on the Italians. A group of white-uniformed Brazilian sailors—with an eight-piece band, no less—marched in, a beautifully casual entrance that had everyone, Italians too, standing and cheering. They didn't have *that* at the Aztec Stadium. Nor did they have the superb closeups of Jairzinho's prayer after scoring, of Pelé being viciously chopped down by Mario Bertini, or the slow-motion instant replays of the goals.

Almost as soon as the auditorium lights went down and the huge screens lit up, you forgot where you were, you just cheered and gasped and bit your fingernails and leapt to your feet. You watched in the second half as Brazil began to annihilate Italy, run all over them until you even forgot that there were any blue shirts on the screen—and sometimes, in fact, there weren't because the color went a bit off now and then, giving you orange grass and green players. But that was rare; generally, the quality of the picture was superb.

At the end the Brazilians and their Navy band were making all the noise, and when the lights went up we were all Brazilians, swirling round and round the central square of screens, singing songs that many of us had never heard before and quite certainly didn't know the words to, but, oh!, what songs!

"Please make your way quietly to the nearest exit," a heavy mechanical voice floated down from the roof. Lots of luck, mister. Round and round we went, Brah-*zeel*, Brah-*zeel*, the little Navy band playing deliriously, and then out into the streets of unsuspecting Manhattan, five or six hundred of us stopping the traffic as we sambaed up 7th Avenue, Brah-*zeel*, Brah-*zeel*.

We shuffled past cars and waved at their astonished occupants; past dark, grim New York bars where silent-majority faces, drawn momentarily to the window, looked cynically on; past a little porno store whose owner was hastily pushing the steel grill across his shopfront, past an admiring group of hippies ("What's happenin' man? Unbelievable, man"), and past crowds who just stood and smiled and wondered what the hell was going on, and all the time, those lovely, haunting, rhythmic songs.

It took us an hour to cover 11 blocks, a little bit of Rio snaking through midtown Manhattan, but let me tell you that it had been raining most of the afternoon, and the sambaing conditions underfoot were not good, not good at all.

Then, I suppose, exhaustion set in, the band stopped playing, and we all walked quietly down to the Hudson River to put the sailors aboard their frigate. They talked of a party aboard later that evening, but those who returned for the fun found a heavy security force guarding the boat.

It had been just one beautiful afternoon, and I never felt more Brazilian in my life. I think maybe there should be a law that Brazil always wins the World Cup. I mean, just think what New York would have missed if, say, England had won.

U.S. College Soccer
Deserting the St. Louis Style

NEW YORK—The unmolested reign of St. Louis as the soccer capital of the United States is drawing to a close.* The college scene tells the story. In 1973, St. Louis teams captured all four major college titles, while in 1974 they took only one.

This is not a case of St. Louis soccer deteriorating. Rather, the rest of the country is catching up. St. Louis's strength has always been its extensive CYC (Catholic Youth Council) parish leagues, which started back in 1902 and burgeoned out in 1936, and have given St. Louis boys two essentials so lacking everywhere else—an early start in the sport, and a large number of games.

Until comparatively recently that was a unique setup. But it is not anymore. There are now many areas—such as Southern California, Washington state, and Long Island, to name but three—with large Little League soccer programs. Within a few years, substantial numbers of boys from these programs will be entering college, and the likelihood is that there will be among them many better players than their St. Louis counterparts.

Why should this be so? Mainly because, while St. Louis soccer has not deteriorated, it has not been getting any better, either. It has, in short, been stagnating, fossilized perhaps by the inevitable smugness that comes with too much success.

The awkward question is: Can it get better? The question can be answered only after an analysis of the St. Louis style.

It is primarily an off-the-ball style—that is, it involves a good deal of movement and running by players who are not in possession of the ball.

Originally published in The Sporting News *January 28–February 4, 1975. Reprinted by permission of* The Sporting News.

The progress of the ball is accomplished mainly by first-time passing. It is rare to see a St. Louis player dwelling on the ball, or engaging in a protracted dribble. Indeed, one sometimes has the impression that St. Louis players regard the ball as some noxious object to be got rid of as soon as possible.

Individually, the players tend to be well-built and gluttons for work. They shield the ball well and they strike it accurately. The shooting of a St. Louis team is invariably impressive.

Overall teamwork is excellent, and the game is played at a rip-roaring pace, with the emphasis on attack. No one ever accused a St. Louis team of being overly defensive.

Now this is an array of talents that is not to be sniffed at, and when a large dose of pride is added, one can see just why St. Louis teams are so difficult to beat.

What, then, is the problem? Simply that such a style, based so heavily on off-the-ball play, has built-in limitations. To raise its game, St. Louis will have to produce faster players, or stronger players, or players with more stamina—because it is these physical features that so dominate the style.

Obviously, the room for improvement in those categories is marginal. That is why the St. Louis style is near the peak of its possibilities, and why the answer to the question of its getting any better is no, not much.

A change in emphasis is badly needed, a change to the on-the-ball side of the game. In other words, toward individual ball skills, toward developing players who can hold the ball, who can dribble, who can take on opponents and get past them, who can change the pace of a game, who can do the unexpected. All these elements are glaringly absent from the current St. Louis game.

Why they are lacking is debatable. One could, for example, point to the ridiculously short (25-minute halves) high school games, played on small fields in brutally cold weather, all factors that place a premium on running and hustling. But the real blame almost certainly lies with youth coaches who do not encourage the development of ball skills.

Asked what he thought of this year's Quincy College team, a North American Soccer League coach replied, "The usual thing, construction workers." The jibe was extreme, but it contained more than a smattering of truth, for St. Louis players do tend to be solidly built, rather musclebound types. With an infusion of ball skills into the game, one might expect to see a change to a looser, more supple type of player.

On this point, it was interesting during this year's NCAA Division I final to compare the heading work of the opposing defenders. The Howard University centerbacks snapped their lithe bodies forward to power the ball away.

The St. Louis University backs rose stiffly to meet the ball and rarely got anything on it.

The same game also provided a splendid example of the strengths and weaknesses of the St. Louis game. In the first half, the St. Louis passing and running had Howard in a lot of trouble because the Howard players chose, unwisely, to chase the ball.

Once Howard had switched to a zonal defense in front of its goal, everything changed. St. Louis, to break through, now needed a combination of guile and skilled dribblers. Its attack, completely lacking in both, rarely looked dangerous again.

But perhaps the biggest indictment of the St. Louis style is that it is boring to watch. It is almost true to say that when you've seen one St. Louis game, you've seen them all. Individuality, flair, inventiveness, all the things that comprise the magic of soccer, are rarely in evidence.

Meanwhile, the running and the chasing go on unabated, and the players become indistinguishable parts of a well-oiled machine going through mechanical motions.

To reduce the world's most imaginative and exciting game to dullness, and to be satisfied with what one has done, is no mean crime. In the United States, where soccer is trying to attract new fans, it is tantamount to treason.

The verdict on St. Louis is . . . guilty. The sentence is . . . five years' probation. That ought to be enough time for St. Louis, by discovering that soccer is played on the ball as well as off it, to produce teams that not only win, but are worth watching while they do so.

Notes:

* A prophecy that raised the blood pressure of the *St. Louis Globe-Democrat*'s sports guru Robert L. Burnes. On January 29, 1975, he devoted a column to excoriating "someone named Paul Gardner," and finished with: "We'll put it this way, Mr. Gardner. Come back in five years. If, in these intervening five years, St. Louis has not produced twice as many college championships as all the other schools in the country (with foreign-bred talent), we'll listen to you."

Alas for Mr. Burnes, my prophecy proved remarkably accurate. In the five years that he allowed me (1975 through 1979), there was a total of 25 national championships in the five college categories: NCAA Divisions I, II, and II; NAIA; and NJCAA. Of these, St. Louis schools won only two, both at the NJCAA level. Even including Southern Illinois University and Quincy College, which certainly play, or played, the St. Louis style, the total reaches only seven, with SIU's 1979 Division I title the only NCAA championship. When U.S. national team coach Steve Sampson announced his team for the 1998 World Cup in France, only one player was a St. Louis product.

The Night They Brought
Calcio Storico to Brooklyn

BROOKLYN—Years and years ago I saw a Danny Kaye film where he's traveling on a bus and he suddenly becomes hysterical when they tell him the bus is going to Brooklyn. He leaps up and shrieks: "But I don't want to go to Brooklyn, I don't *want* to go to Brooklyn!" The bus driver just keeps going and snarls out of the corner of his mouth: "Buddy, none of us *wants* to go to Brooklyn, but we all gotta go sometime."

I think of that every time I go there, which is not too often . . . I have to have a special reason, and I think I found one recently. Unique, I should think. At Brooklyn College they were staging a re-creation of the medieval Italian game of *calcio storico*—over 100 participants, all the costumes, the drums, the banners, all brought in from Italy, the real thing. I checked up on it in a book—they used to play in Florence in the seventeenth century, there was a picture of it, a *piazza* full of men in wide-brimmed hats and pantaloons and swinging swords, dozens of them, all over the place.

So I went to Brooklyn, by subway not bus, and I found the college and next to it the field with the lights blazing, and on the ground the hard, smooth look of artificial turf . . . That must be a first, they never played *calcio* on plastic grass in Florence . . . As I walk into the enclosure, the first thing I see is eight young men in blue overalls, written on their backs it says "Brooklyn College Emergency Medical Squad." Are they kidding? For an exhibition?

The field is 80 yards long and about 50 yards wide. At each end, spanning the complete 50 yards, is a sort of fence about four feet high, with a net

Originally published in World Soccer *(London) December 1976. Reprinted by permission.*

stretching another two feet or so above it; to score, you have to get the ball over the fence and into the net. With a goal that big, there should be plenty of scoring. One of the coaches, he's all done up in a track suit, he looks like a genuine coach, tells me there are 27 players on each team. Then he has to go off to instruct the linesmen (recruited college students, I gather) as to what they're supposed to do.

The speeches have started. Someone says the game dates back to before Caesar's time. Someone else insists on calling it *calico* instead of *calcio*. Then at 8:30 we get a marvelous display of flag twirling and throwing by 12 men in brightly colored costumes. Ten minutes of that, then a fanfare from somewhere off the field, over there in the darkness, followed by some deep, gutty thumps on the drums. An exciting noise, immediately marred by the shriek of a police car siren. On comes the parade at the far side of the field, slow-paced, majestic. Helmeted guys with long swords, guards with flags, a man carrying a ball, it certainly looks like a soccer ball. Two very flamboyantly clothed gentlemen, the referees. Then the teams, the Blues and the Whites, over 60 players, pretty hefty-looking specimens some of them. Now the drummers, 17 of them, plus 14 trumpeters. Then some more military-looking types with steel helmets . . . Six dashing swashbucklers gallop past on horseback. The last horse leaves a carefully timed trail of manure as it passes the VIP stand . . . it gets a special cheer. Five men dragging a little toy cannon (it looks like a toy; I can't see anyone laying siege to a castle with that). Lastly, a lovely docile cow with a glistening tapestry draped over it trots past.

Then a proclamation, a sort of *Oyez!* in Italian, followed by a drumroll and a fanfare and an almighty bang! from the cannon. Some toy, that. The players are running all over the field, warming up. They really look like athletes, these guys, stretching and sprinting and jumping. The teams, says the PA voice, will of course play with a 7-7-9 formation, plus the usual four goalkeepers. Maybe it won't be so easy to score after all.

One of the refs throws the ball high into the air and away we go. Quite hectic, this, they look as though they really mean business. They're all wearing rather medieval-looking floppy, striped knickers (though I did spot a zipper on one of them), T-shirts, and sneakers. The game is stopped; there seems to be a fight. (Well, the exhibition has to be realistic.) They're off again, then something else is happening on the other side of the field, play has stopped again, little fights breaking out all over. The crowd, there must be over 1,000 here by now, is roaring with delight, this is just the way it must have been in Florence all those centuries ago.

A player with a ripped T-shirt staggers off the field, the referee is whistling like mad. The action is right in front of me now. I don't know, but that looked like a damn realistic punch someone just threw. Everyone's joining in now. Can this be staged? Lots of shouting among the players, then they're off again. This is mostly rugby; I haven't seen a kick yet, though the ball is being thrown forward.

No throws at the goal yet. After 12 minutes there seems to be total chaos on the other side of the field, players pushing and yelling and, surely, fighting. The coaches and the trainers are all on the field now, none of them seems to be smiling much. Yes, some of the VIPs are walking onto the field; one of them trips gracefully over the restraining rope as he goes. Looks like an appeal for order. A failure, they come off, still no resumption of play, we've been waiting nearly nine minutes now.

Then a sudden sharp voice cuts the cold night air. Somebody in authority evidently, bawling into the PA, telling the players, in Italian, that if the brawling doesn't stop *pronto*, then *lo spettacolo verra cessato immediatamente.* That seems to do it, he must be the guy who signs the checks, within a minute play has restarted. The referee's whistle blasts are hard and long now. Even so, there's still some fighting going on.

After 30 minutes of quite convincing carnage there is no score, but the Whites are coming close. Then they score . . . great exuberance, another blast from the toy cannon as the teams change ends. White scores twice more. Blue reduced to throwing long balls now. I still haven't seen many kicks. The cannon signals the end of the game. "Final score" begins the PA voice—"3 dead and 75 wounded," finishes a boy walking past me.

Well, I have to go down to see what this was all about. Down on the field the first words I hear are: "I think we'll have to get this guy to the hospital." It's one of the emergency medical squad talking; he's looking at one of the Blues who's stretched out along a bench, an icepack on a very swollen knee, face crunched up with pain. A bit farther on I step over a torn T-shirt, spotted with blood, lying on the plastic grass. Another Blue player is sitting down here, also holding an icepack to his knee. And here comes a White, with an icepack on his eye, all puffed and purple. I ask one of the players, "Why so rough?" He looks through me, mutters *"Porca miseria!"* and wanders off. I repeat the question to a man wearing an official's tag and a stunned sort of grin . . . "Ahem, well, ahem, they were supposed to play on Sunday in Central Park, but it was rained out and, ahem, well, I think they were a little keyed up. Ahem."

On the subway going home, I'm thinking of all that pageantry and pomp they used to have in the Middle Ages. The color, the flags, the horses, the noise. Actually, we could do with some of that today, a bit of drama and showmanship. A pregame parade would be fun, though it would have to be a bit quicker than this one, which took six minutes to circle the field. And I'm left with the certain idea that *calcio storico,* if that's what I've been watching, is much more rugby than soccer.

Back home, I turn on the TV for the late show . . . the screen is full of colorful figures in pantaloons and wide-brimmed hats and swinging swords . . . they're rushing all over a courtyard, dragging a protesting figure with them. Lo and behold, it's Danny Kaye, who didn't want to go to Brooklyn! He's a court jester now, but from his dress, he could be a *calcio* player.

Football, Calcio, Futebol

The Different Faces of Soccer

NEW YORK—The English, we are told, invented soccer. A questionable proposition at best. One that ignores the crucial contribution of Scotsmen to English soccer, and one that ignores the very obvious fact that there are a number of different versions of the sport played throughout the world.

What the English did, with some Scottish help, was to invent English soccer (they called it football, of course). A sport not for all seasons, but very definitely for the northern winter, a game in which the weather (usually cold) and the field conditions (often muddy) were major factors.

The result was a vigorous game featuring a good deal of hard running. It was played to the limit in a never-say-die attitude of total commitment. It demanded stamina and strength. It involved much tackling and physical contact (the soft, muddy grounds made falls, if not welcome, at least relatively painless; they also made slide tackling an almost inevitable part of the game). And, in conformity with the English image of straightforwardness, it was a game without frills.

English soccer was, and remains to this day, a relatively unsophisticated game based on stamina, speed, and simplicity. Basic soccer, if you like. Its sheer pace and physical commitment can make it immensely exciting to watch, but these strengths are also its weaknesses.

A high-speed, one-pace game of this sort leaves little room for subtleties. It seems to engender impatience, a rush to get the ball into the opponent's goal mouth. The result, a series of long, high balls lofted into the penalty area,

Originally published in the Official Program for the Bicentennial Cup, *May 1976.*

is a style that puts a premium on heading ability (one of the undoubted strengths of the English game) and gives rapid end-to-end fluctuations in play. But it is also a style that lacks the sophistication and the beauty—to say nothing of the effectiveness—of constructive approach play.

Against ostensibly inferior teams, the English style has proved, time and time again, that it lacks the inventiveness to break through a massed defense.

The English took their game to Italy in the late 1800s, and in no time at all the Italians had taken it away from them and formed their own league. But it was not English-style soccer that they played.

The Italian climate and the Italian temperament produced a new version of the sport. The biggest influence on Italian soccer, or *calcio*, was to come indirectly from Scotland. The Scots had developed a game that, while incorporating all the elements of English soccer, was distinguished by its reliance on short, on-the-ground passing plays. The style caught on in Austria and Hungary, and by the 1920s the Italians had seen enough of it to know that it suited them too.

Calcio became a game with a larger dose of artistry than English soccer, a game with less emphasis on strength and more on ball control. Tackling was less evident in *calcio*, in which a good team gained possession more as the result of interceptions than by physically dispossessing an opponent. *Calcio* also had an acrobatic quality, a touch of Italian bravura, that the English shunned in their own game, suspicious as they have always been of anything that looks like exhibitionism.

The overall pace of *calcio* is certainly slower than that of the English game; the Italians have always professed admiration at the ability of the English players to run inexhaustibly for the full 90 minutes of a game.

Even in its early and most successful days (Italy won the World Cup in 1934 and 1938), *calcio* was built around the strategy of cool, unhurried defense and sudden counterattack. Modern *calcio* has run into criticism for overdoing the defense at the expense of the attack; the development of the *catenaccio* system of play, which often leaves only two players committed to exclusively offensive roles, has brought a torrent of abuse down on the Italians.

Certainly the *catenaccio* system can be—and all too frequently is—a merely negative method of play. But the solid defensive cover that it gives can be viewed as the springboard for launching attacks.

When skilled, offense-minded players are involved (and *calcio*, despite its defensive mentality, has always been able to produce its share of brilliant forwards), then the result can be fascinating and exciting. For there is a fine, pure stylishness about Italian soccer, a neatness and a homogeneity that gives it an aesthetic appeal quite lacking in the English game.

Soccer arrived in Brazil around the turn of the century, and again it was the English residents who were the pioneers. Pioneers without much hope, it seems. "Soccer is not a sport that can hope to flourish in a subtropical climate like that of Brazil"—thus an Englishman wrote in 1912, clearly showing that to him, soccer was a sport for chilly regions. Happily ignorant of this orthodoxy, the Brazilians took soccer, called it *futebol*, and proceeded to do the most marvelous things with it.

If there was an early influence on the Brazilian style, it was Italian. It came, not directly, but through neighboring Argentina, where Italian immigrants were turning their love of *calcio* into a national passion.

Futebol was from the start a game, like *calcio*, in which the importance of ball control outweighed that of physical fitness. But what ball control! The Brazilian players seemed to have an intimate, almost sensuous relationship with the ball—the result, perhaps, of learning to play soccer barefoot on dusty fields or beaches.

In Brazil, soccer found a situation that it had not met before: a population made up of a number of different races, rather than the relatively unmixed stocks of European nations. The Brazilian racial blend gave *futebol* a richness that was not to be found in the European games. In particular, Brazil's black players brought a wonderful, free-flowing agility, an easy flamboyance to the sport.

Brazilian soccer was full of surprises, full of changes of pace—sudden sprints followed by periods when their immaculate ball control allowed the Brazilians to slow the game down to a walk.

But there were problems. The heavily artistic component of *futebol* seemed to give it a fragility that was easily disturbed, particularly by the harder European teams. The Brazilians took a long time to establish themselves on the international soccer scene.

In 1958, when Brazil had so often promised much and accomplished little, the magazine *France Football* summed up the Brazilian player: more of an artist than an athlete, nervous, temperamental, a soldier psychologically unprepared for war. At the beginning of June 1958, it was a fair judgment. A month later, when Brazil had magnificently won the World Cup, it looked ridiculous. At last all the exquisite individual skills had been molded into a team.

The essence of Brazilian soccer has always been attacking inventiveness. Their greatest teams, the World Cup winners in 1958 and 1970, were goal-scoring teams with questionable, even weak, defenses.

Nowhere is this attacking ingenuity more apparent than in the assortment of original plays the Brazilians have worked out for free kicks near the penalty area, and the frequency with which they score from them. As the Uruguayan national team goalkeeper said recently: "Giving up a free kick to Brazil anywhere near the penalty area is as dangerous as giving up a penalty kick."

The Brazilians, by and large, like the ball on the ground. Where an English defender will head the ball away, a Brazilian will frequently use a chest trap to bring the ball down to his feet. Heading is not one of the strengths of the Brazilian game.

But that is a generalization . . . and it is never safe to generalize about the unpredictable, infinitely varied game of *futebol*.

End of a Dream in Haiti

PORT-AU-PRINCE, Haiti—Four nights in a row the stumpy little bus took the players of the U.S. national soccer team back to their hotel after the training sessions. Each night, as the bus pulled away from the stadium in downtown Port-au-Prince, hundreds of yelling and cheering young boys ran along behind for the first hundred yards or so. Then they fell back and the little bus sped off through the dappled nighttime of the erratically lit streets, clattering and snorting and leaving behind in the heavy warm air the raucous strains of "Yankee Doodle Dandy" or "I Ain't Gonna Grieve No More."

All along the route, the Haitians in the crowded streets stopped to turn and stare after this extraordinary parcel of foreign noise passing through their city. Some smiled, some waved, and some shouted, but they all noticed.

Not so noticeable, because a good deal quieter, was a similar bus that left the stadium earlier each evening carrying the Canadian national team.

For the moment Canada and the U.S. were just two of more than 100 national teams involved in the qualifying rounds of the World Cup, soccer's quadrennial Holy Grail, to be held in Argentina in the summer of 1978 for the 16 finalists. The two countries had started their quest, along with Mexico, in a three-nation subgroup from which two of them would go on to the next round. Mexico had won the round-robin series, but the U.S. and Canada had ended up with identical 1–2–1 records. To decide which would advance, a single playoff game at a neutral site was necessary. When the U.S. and Canada could not agree on where and when the game should be played, the World Cup organizers told them: Port-au-Prince, Haiti, three days before Christmas.

The Americans approved. They had played four games in Haiti in November, and felt at home in Port-au-Prince. The Canadians, suffering financial problems, had favored Mexico or Bermuda to keep down traveling costs. But when the World Cup organizing committee decides, there is either obedience or there is a forfeit. Canada would play in Haiti.

Coach Walt Chyzowych put his U.S. squad—players of U.S. citizenship preponderantly from the North American Soccer League—through a series of preparatory games in Curaçao and Suriname. His confidence before meeting Canada was total. "We are ready," he said. "I think the score could be 3–0 to us."

Within a minute of the start, the U.S. had its chance—two chances, in fact—to score the vital first goal. A hectic scramble in the Canadian goal mouth raised a great cloud of dust on the desert-dry field and left the ball running loose to center-forward Freddy Grgurev from the German-American Soccer League. His solid eight-yard shot spun away off the body of a Canadian defender. From the subsequent corner kick, a glancing header by Minnesota's Mike Flater was a little too finely angled, sending the ball wide of the left-hand post.

Three minutes later, Seattle's powerful Boris Bandov broke through with only goalkeeper Zeljko Bilecki to beat. Bandov's shot was taken too soon and Bilecki had the split-second he needed to dive and smother the ball.

The Canadians had been lucky, but they had survived and were playing the ball forward with a methodical coolness so different from the brittle nervousness that characterized the U.S. raids. Their first threat came on a diving header that seemed almost in the net until goalkeeper Arnie Mausser of Tampa Bay threw himself across the goal and scooped the ball away from the foot of the post.

Twenty-two minutes into the game came the crucial play, and this time the outcome was less happy for Mausser. From out near the left touchline, Canadian left back Bruce Wilson lofted a 40-yard free kick, a ball that seemed to dip suddenly as it came into the American goal mouth. Mausser came out for it, and came up with nothing. The ball ran through to Brian Budd, who volleyed for goal from six yards out. Standing on the goal line, U.S. captain Al Trost of St. Louis tried to block the shot, only to see it spin off his thigh and into the net. Canada 1, U.S. 0.

From then on, the pattern of the game was set. The Americans, needing the equalizer, would have to abandon any thought of caution. The Canadians would defend with as many as eight men, but would always be looking for the chance to counterattack, hoping to catch the Americans with too many men upfield.

When the U.S. came out for the second half, Trost was missing: suffering from an intestinal infection, he had barely survived the first 45 minutes. Urged on by New York's vociferous and ubiquitous Bobby Smith—nominally a fullback, but now running full tilt wherever he thought he could get to the ball—the Americans battered away at the Canadian defense. For 20 minutes the ball seemed to be dancing and bouncing and bubbling around the Canadian penalty area, but the sad truth for the Americans was that all of this was getting them nowhere. As so often happens in soccer, it was the counterattacks of the defending team that looked the more dangerous.

As the clock ticked on and the equalizing goal just would not come, the U.S. play, never exactly smooth, became noticeably edgy. And that nervousness finally destroyed the American hopes.

With 20 minutes left and the Canadians still hanging on to their one-goal lead, U.S. fullback Steve Pecher of Dallas—whose crudely robust tackling in the first half had somehow escaped the referee's censure—suddenly kicked Victor Kodelja's legs out from under him. It was an absurd foul, committed at midfield in a situation that presented no threat at all to the U.S. Almost before Kodelja hit the ground, the referee was racing toward Pecher, whistle blaring, his left hand groping into his breast pocket.

The only question was which card would come out of that pocket, yellow for a caution or red for ejection. The referee's arm swept commandingly straight up in the air, and in his hand a small rectangle of red flashed in the floodlights.

Pecher trudged to the bench, and the U.S. would have to play a man short. But with all the perversity that is so typical of soccer, the 10-man team now seemed to be more organized. There was Bobby Smith, for example, his straggly hair dancing on his shoulders as he raced down the right wing, delivering a perfect cross, right to Bandov racing in at full speed and heading it powerfully—but a foot or two over the bar.

With five minutes left in the game, the inevitable second Canadian goal arrived. Budd again broke through the middle, this time laying off a perfect pass for Bob Lenarduzzi to run on to and drive underneath the diving Mausser.

Even then the American agony was not over. With 10 seconds remaining, the referee detected Smith tugging at a Canadian shirt. A yellow card for Smith, and a free kick for Canada. Bob Bolitho hooked the ball over the wall of U.S. players and into the top corner of the goal, just out of Mausser's reach. A perfect free kick, executed with almost insulting ease, demonstrating that this was unarguably Canada's night. Canada *trois*, America *zero*.

For the Canadians, one big obstacle on the road to Argentina '78 had been overcome. An even bigger one awaits. In the next qualifying round they will meet the five best teams from North and Central America and the

Caribbean: Mexico, Guatemala, El Salvador, and Suriname, plus the winner of a playoff game between Cuba and Haiti. Only one of these teams will make it to the finals.

In the American locker room the players slouched on their benches, some staring at the floor, some at the bare walls, some gazing ahead with unfocused eyes. Bobby Smith broke a bottle, and the noise was magnified a thousand times by the overpowering silence. The dreams of World Cup glory, of getting to the finals—even of getting into the next qualifying round—had been snatched away.

After 15 minutes, still in uniform, they filed out into the parking lot, past all the smiling friendly boys and the hundred little hands reaching out to touch them. And again the funny little bus, the seats with no leg room, the kids running alongside.

But on this night there was no singing, no talking, barely a human sound. Just the harsh mechanical noises of the bus, the gear changes, the revs, the creaks, and the rattles—noises that no one had noticed before. And in the streets of Port-au-Prince nobody turned to watch as the bus went by.

Too Much British Influence?

NEW YORK—Remember Paul Revere? He was the great American patriot who, in 1775, rode his horse through the Massachusetts countryside yelling "The British are coming! The British are coming!" Thus alerted, the Americans rose up and proceeded to demonstrate that they no longer wished to live under British domination.

Obviously, in those days there was a unanimous opinion that the British presence was a bad thing. Yet here we are, 200 years later, suffering—in soccer, at least—from an oppressive excess of British influence. And not a Paul Revere in sight. Far from it, most people seem anxious to lay out their welcome mat for the British.

Take a look at the North American Soccer League. We have a Welsh commissioner; we have an Englishman in charge of referees. Ten of the league's 18 coaches are British (11 if you include Eddie Firmani). On the field, the total playing strength is about 40 percent American, 40 percent British, and 20 percent others (though some of those "Americans" are naturalized Brits).

The distribution varies sharply from team to team—from Minnesota, which last season was almost exclusively British, to Toronto, which did not include any British players. As it happens, those were the two teams that met in the NASL final—but more on that shortly.

The reasons for the heavy British influence are not hard to discern. When the NASL started in 1967, England was on top of the soccer world; holders of the World Cup, with coaches from all over the world making pilgrimages to England to find the secrets of success.

Originally published in World Soccer *March 1977. Reprinted by permission.*

For that reason, it was a logical mecca for Americans seeking advice and personnel. On top of that, there was the obvious advantage of avoiding language problems (most Americans can, I find, understand English accents after only a short while; Scottish takes a little longer).

So the NASL was launched with a heavy stock of British manpower. That might not have been too bad, had we gotten the best that Britain had to offer. But we did not. There were only a few people in Britain who really took the American experiment seriously, who really saw all the possibilities.

The majority of those who turned up here fell into three categories: the opportunists, who found the whole thing hilarious but who also saw the opportunity for a trip to America and some easy dollars; the has-beens, whose careers in Britain were over but who sensed the possibility of adding a few more years among the Yanks; and the mediocrities, whose chances of making it in Britain were nil but might be considerably better across the Atlantic—those who hoped to fit the old definition of an expert: "An ordinary guy a long way from home."

Of those who arrived with serious intent, I might single out Clive Toye of the New York Cosmos and Phil Woosnam, now the NASL commissioner, who have, quite justly, risen to the top. Of the majority, most of the original opportunists, has-beens, and mediocrities are gone. But what they did was to establish a British connection that makes it easy for more British players to enter the league—too many of them, unfortunately, merely newer has-beens, etc.

Their influence has not been a good thing. I am quite certain that we do not now need—if, indeed, we ever did—third-division players and third-division mentalities. There has been evidence in the past of an American tendency to genuflect to British accents in soccer matters. It is a deeply ingrained attitude—it must be, to have survived all the rather obvious contradictions of its truth that so many British imports have evidenced. At last, I believe, the attitude is changing.

In 1967, England was the world champion. In 1977, it is . . . well, how would you classify it? *Nowhere* would not be too harsh a judgment. Why should we listen to what the British have to say? I am not saying that we have nothing to learn—we assuredly have, more than most countries. But we should be paying attention to those countries that are leading the world now. We should be finding out what the West Germans are doing, the Dutch and the Brazilians.

The British style in soccer could pass muster here when that was all that most people were aware of. But what does he of England know who only England knows? As soon as other styles begin to circulate, the English style is exposed for what it is. Crude, unimaginative . . . and ultimately rather dull.

This last point is of vital importance here. In England, Halifax vs. Grimsby may turn out to be the worst game in the history of soccer, but it will not in any way damage the structure of the Football League or the future of the sport. Indeed, it is quite likely that a majority of the fans at the game, emotionally involved with their team, will be satisfied with what they saw, judging it on considerations that have nothing to do with the absolute quality of the soccer involved.

We cannot afford that sort of game. We have to have as much attractive, exciting soccer as possible. We have to have entertainment. Hence the fringe activities such as dancing girls and marching bands, hence the tiebreakers (not, as Brian Glanville implied last month, to decide the game, but to ensure that we don't get the away team playing defensively for a tie).

Soccer is in competition with four other wealthy, well-organized major-league sports here. To have a chance of survival, it has to be quality soccer, and we have got to have it consistently. If we don't get that, the alternative may be pressure toward the sort of gimmicky rule-changing that I—every bit as much as Mr. Glanville—find so deplorable.

But the fact has to be faced that in the 1970s there is far too much bad, dull soccer around. I imagine that each country has its own tolerance level for bad soccer. Let us say that in England some 25 percent of the games can be rank bad without affecting overall attendance. The general, traditional involvement with the sport, the comparative lack of alternatives for the fans, and the expectation that the other 75 percent of the games will be worthwhile, will absorb the fan dissatisfaction. But if the bad-game percentage goes up much higher, attendance will begin to fall.

In the United States, it has to be understood that our tolerance level for dull soccer is much, much lower—because the average American is not yet in love with the sport. He is not as understanding, nor as forgiving, as he would be with a sweetheart sport. He has to be seduced with something attractive. And he has other sports, which may have a stronger emotional hold on him, to turn to if soccer fails to satisfy him.

Last season was the first year of existence for the Minnesota Kicks. They set new attendance records virtually every time they played (reaching 49,000 for the semifinal game). It was a *very* English team. In the final it ran up against the Toronto Metros-Croatia—not a British player to be seen there—and was humbled. All the British running and long balls were calmly and easily nullified by the Toronto game of possession, skill, and pace control. The good fans of Minnesota, introduced to soccer by the slam-bang British style, have now seen that there is something that not only looks better, but works better too. How long will they be satisfied with what they have?

And if there were any further doubts about the poor quality of the current English game, they are in the process of being rather neatly resolved. Every week in New York (and in some 13 other major cities throughout the country) we are getting a televised tape of an English "Game of the Week." We are seeing Liverpool and Leeds and Derby and Aston Villa regularly, and it is not a pretty sight.

One is, quite literally, shocked by the crudity of most of the games. Ironically, Phil Woosnam was known to be concerned at the televising of these games, fearing that they might present a level of soccer that would put the NASL's own games in the shade. I can't imagine that he is worried anymore.

To make matters worse, in New York we have only to switch channels as soon as the English game is over, and we get a one-hour tape of a West German Bundesliga game. The contrast between the two could hardly be more vivid. From England we get hard running, bad passing, constant long balls and high punts (both usually aimless), miserable control, and ragged midfield play with ping-pong heading duels and strings of semi-successful tackles. From Germany we have finesse, superb control, marvelous changes in pace, and generally cool, cultured play.

Strangely enough, that is one of the advantages of following soccer from the United States. On television we see English, German, and Mexican games regularly, plus highlights from the Italian league, and an occasional Greek game, or a tie from the Libertadores. Live, via satellite, we have recently seen the Haiti vs. Cuba World Cup qualifying ties, and will have Colombia vs. Brazil shortly. And we get a steady stream of touring teams—Zenit Leningrad will be here soon to play Tampa, for example.

One sees a bit of everything and—perhaps more important—one is not overwhelmed by a domestic style to which one feels obliged to be faithful. We have no domestic style. Before we develop one, let us pray for a soccer Paul Revere to warn us of the iniquities of the British.

The Agony of the Feet

BUENOS AIRES, Argentina—César Luis Menotti may just be the most popular man in Argentina right now, but let me tell you something; I knew him back when. Ten years ago he came to New York to pass a long, hot, languid summer with a soccer team called the New York Generals. They don't exist anymore; they never caught on like the Cosmos—and perhaps you can tell why when you realize that Menotti was brought in from Argentina as the star attraction—the Pelé of his day, if you like.

"Cannonball Menotti" they called him. We were all advised to watch out for his ferocious left-foot shooting. Well, we never saw anything ferocious about Menotti as he drifted ineffectually about Yankee Stadium that summer. Once he was called on to take a penalty kick—that's a free shot from 12 yards out with only the goalkeeper to beat, a 99 percent sure goal. Menotti rumbled up to the ball, swung his fearsome left, and crashed the ball so high, so wide, of the goal that it was 30 rows deep in the empty bleachers before it hit anything solid.

Then, one evening, Pelé and his Santos teammates arrived for an exhibition game and, improbably and absurdly, the Generals beat them 5–3. The star of the game? Menotti. Oh yes, he could play, this tall thin man, but he needed a challenge. Playing league games against other American teams in stadiums that looked as though they had been neutron-bombed just before kickoff meant nothing to Menotti.

His playing days so cynically over, he returned to Argentina to become a coach, and in 1974 accepted the most challenging job in soccer: coach of the

Originally published in The Village Voice *July 17, 1978. Reprinted by permission of V. V. Publishing Corporation.*

In 1968 César Luis Menotti played for the New York Generals. Here, at a game in Yankee Stadium, Menotti (left) has evidently committed some egregious foul to which the Chicago Spurs players are taking exception. *Copyright Paul Gardner*

Menotti (known as *El Flaco,* the thin man) in 1978, the year he coached Argentina to World Cup victory. *Copyright Paul Gardner*

Menotti in 1994—the glare suggests strong disagreement with the author (who is seen from his best angle).*Copyright Steve Tepperman*

Argentine national team. Madness, sheer madness, of course. With Argentina due to stage the next world championship, in 1978, the coach would be expected to win it. Failure in this soccer-mad nation was too frightful to contemplate.

Yet his chances of winning were abysmal. Argentina had never done well in the World Cup, had always had good players but had always been let down by appalling organization. Its players were also held to be too individualistic to play as a team for more than a few minutes in every game. And, on top of that, the shaky finances of Argentine soccer meant that most of the country's best players were playing in Europe. And how could you form a team if you had to fly players in from Spain and France every time you wanted to hold a practice?

A year ago I spoke with Menotti at the Jockey Club, just outside Buenos Aires, where his team was training. His face was as thin as ever, the hair somewhat longer, but there was nothing of the listlessness of the Generals days. Cigarettes were produced and smoked incessantly throughout the interview, but Menotti—*El Flaco,* the Thin Man, as the Argentines call him—spoke firmly and emphatically in a deep, ringing Spanish baritone (he had learned no English in New York). Argentina would win the World Cup. He would go with the players who had stayed in Argentina, possibly bringing one or two back from Europe. His team would play *fútbol*—a double riposte to those teams that played the dull defensive game, and to those critics who for years had been accusing the Argentines of being nothing but thugs in soccer boots. When I left Menotti I did not believe that Argentina could win the World Cup—but I was in no doubt that he believed it.

On June 25, 1978, at 5:10 P.M. Buenos Aires time, Menotti's faith caused one of the biggest outpourings of national fervor Argentina has ever seen. Indeed, many people told me that it far surpassed anything they had ever seen, even in the organized Perónist days. Argentina, with a 3–1 overtime win over Holland, had won the World Cup. As people swept into the streets all over the country, as blizzards of confetti and streamers turned whole avenues white in downtown Buenos Aires—Menotti stood on the sidelines at the River Plate Stadium, surrounded by a mob of officials, players, well-wishers, and heaven knows who else, his raincoat collar turned up, a big grin on his face. Watching him through my binoculars, I realized that I had never seen him smile before.

That smile had been earned after a lonely four years. For I am convinced that there were few Argentines who really believed Menotti could succeed. Not only in the soccer sense; for there were important critics, both inside and outside the country, who felt that Argentina should not be staging the tournament at all.

The decision to hold it was, naturally, a political one, made by the Perónists in 1973. A move to court popularity. For the same reason, when the military junta took over in 1976, it confirmed that the World Cup would be held as planned.

In Europe a campaign was mounted by sports journalists and others to take it away from Argentina on security grounds—these were days of rampant Montonero and ERP guerrilla activity.

The junta looked at the work done by the Perónists and was not impressed. Virtually all of the organizing committee was replaced with military personnel. The head of the new *Ente Autarquico Mundial* (EAM), responsible for running the tournament, was General Omar Actis. On his way to his first press conference he was assassinated in a Buenos Aires street.

A gloomy start this, but in fact it marked the end of any effective guerrilla interference. A year later the Montoneros—no longer in a position to stage their mass attacks on army barracks—issued their famous statement to the effect that they had no interest in upsetting the World Cup as they, too, were "*hombres y mujeres del pueblo.*"

For EAM, the problem now was getting everything ready for June 1, 1978. The chief organizer, navy captain Carlos Alberto Lacoste, told me a year ago: "We will be ready. I am still here, you see—when you don't see me in the country, you can start to worry. But there is much to do. For three years the Perónists did nothing. Less than nothing." A powerful man with huge hands and small, steady eyes, Lacoste brushed aside suggestions of terrorism: "We don't have guerrillas here now, they're finished. Individual acts of terrorism, perhaps, but you have those everywhere. Even in the United States, I think? Now we are working hard. Under the Perónists you had 3 days of work and 362 days of strikes a year. We work 365 days a year. There are no strikes now. We have banned them." And the powerful hands come slowly to rest, twisting a metal cigarette lighter.

The Perónists did leave behind one rather embarrassing legacy: the official symbol for the tournament. Embarrassing because it so obviously was a stylized version of General Perón's crowd-saluting stance, arms upraised, hands open. Isabelita Perón's private secretary, Pedro Eladio Vasquez, had publicly proclaimed that the symbol represented "the stylized arms of General Perón, symbolizing the open arms of all Argentina."

The symbol was already, in 1976, too widely known to withdraw it. The military men at EAM simply had to put up with it—until last year, when they came out with the official World Cup poster . . . which showed two soccer players embracing each other, presumably after one of them had scored a goal. The official English version described it as showing "the happy instant lived by the protagonists of the spectacle when the magic taking place on the field culminates in the symbolic and fraternal evidence of a task well done." Whatever that may mean, the poster clearly showed one of the players with both his arms upraised, hands open. So much for the stylized arms of General Perón.

Come June 1, Captain Lacoste was still around in Argentina, and by and large things were ready. Certainly, the new terminal at Buenos Aires's Ezeiza Airport showed a lot of gaps in the ceilings, and some doors without handles, and a lot of workmen scurrying about. But it worked. So, too, did the three new stadiums built in Mendoza, Córdoba, and Mar del Plata, and the renovated 80,000-seat River Plate Stadium in Buenos Aires itself.

Argentina was ready to receive the 15 other national teams that were after the championship—teams like Tunisia, Iran, and Mexico, all of them without much hope—and teams like West Germany, and much-fancied Holland and Brazil. The Scots were also much-fancied, mainly by the Scots.

A first round of 24 games, after which eight teams were eliminated. Among those to go were the French—unluckily, for they had played good soccer but had been plagued by money problems among the players, some of whom thought they should have been getting more for wearing brand-name equipment. Disgusted with the scene, their coach, Michel Hidalgo, resigned, was persuaded to stay, only to see his team go out on a farcical note. For their final game, the French turned up at the stadium wearing the same color shirts as their opponents, Hungary. It was 40 minutes before alternative shirts were found. The French have since been ordered to pay any expenses incurred to worldwide television by the delayed kickoff. One hopes they will have the good sense not to do anything of the sort.

The Tunisians surprised everyone by beating Mexico—the first time a team from Africa has *ever* won a game in the final rounds—then went on to lose unluckily to Poland, 0–1, and tie West Germany 0–0. It wasn't just that the results were good: it was the *manner* of them. For here was a sophisticated-looking team that would surely have done better had they not underrated themselves. Perhaps, at long last, the long-awaited African soccer explosion is on the way.

The only team to come badly unstuck in the first round was Scotland. Sent off from Glasgow by delirious crowds lining the route to the airport (this, mind you, after a 0–1 loss to England!), the Scots had arrived full of confidence and, as it turned out later, full of shit.

I suppose when you are convinced you're the best, you don't have to look at the opposition. So coach Ally MacLeod didn't bother to scout Peru. So Peru beat the Scots 3–1, and MacLeod said he was surprised at the speed of Peru's wingers. A day later the roof came crashing down in earnest. Willie Johnston, urine-tested after the Peru game, was found to have taken a stimulant. "A stimulant?" remarked one of many shocked Scot fans, "I thought they were all on tranquilizers." "That," added a former player, "was the sort of performance that will get pep pills a bad name."

Sympathy for Willie Johnston, sent home in disgrace, was immediately dispelled when he started negotiations to sell his story to the highest bidder. The Scots did even worse in their next game, only managing to tie a weak Iran team, then played splendidly to beat Holland 3–2. Too late, alas, and the Scots fans, with their bagpipes and their kilts, were a forlorn lot in Cordoba, parading the streets and shouting insults about the Scottish Football Association. Thirteen of them were arrested amid rumors of drunkenness, smashed windows, and punchups. They were released two hours later by the police, who said all the rumors were totally false but failed to explain why the arrests were made in the first place.

The Scots went home, where coach Ally MacLeod blamed the fiasco on the press for writing nasty things about the team.

Drama and chaos seemed to stalk the Brazilian camp down in the little seaside town of Mar del Plata. An opening tie against Sweden was followed by another tie against Spain, a dreadful performance by the Brazilians. The thousands of Brazilians who had come to follow their team to victory marched through Mar del Plata and burned an effigy of the coach, Cláudio Coutinho.

Coutinho himself announced that he would no longer speak to the foreign press because an Italian journalist had written that one of his star players, Rivelino, was a homosexual, and that Coutinho (an army captain) was actually a member of the Death Squad.

By this time, Coutinho's authority was in much doubt. It was rumored that he had been fired and that Pelé was about to take over the team. Pelé, in Argentina to cover the game for Venezuelan television (his comments were later to be called "the most boring ever heard on Venezuelan TV"), was not around. He had raced back to New York, where his wife was about to give birth to a daughter—who, the local press insisted, would be called Argentina.

Pelé was not the new coach of Brazil. But the president of the Brazilian Sports Confederation, Admiral Heleno Nunes, moved in alongside Coutinho, and left no doubt that he would have a hand in the team selection from now on. Needing to win their final game of the first round, Brazil squeaked to a 1–0 victory over Austria, and looked totally unconvincing doing it. For the first time in my life, I was actually bored by a Brazilian team. Mar del Plata that evening staged a Brazilian mini-festival as the fans paraded around the streets celebrating, I suspect, as much their survival as their passage to the next round.

Up in Buenos Aires the following day, the celebrations were on a much grander scale as the Argentines, despite a loss to Italy, went into the second round. Menotti's team had beaten Hungary and France by 2–1 (helped, said the cynics, by biased refereeing—an accusation I do not agree with) and, if nothing else, had shown that they were a team committed to attacking soccer—certainly more than one could say about the ponderous West Germans (holders of the trophy, won in 1974), the unimaginative Poles, and the enigmatic Dutch, all of them also qualifiers.

Six floors above the Calle Maipu (or was it Avenida? I never found out) in downtown Buenos Aires, the sign on the apartment door says simply BORGES.

The housemaid answers my ring and shows me into a room lined with bookcases, the winter sun drifting in through the blinds. A lovely white cat is washing himself in an armchair.

"Good morning, sir." Jorge Luis Borges, blind, nearly 80 years old now, the grand old man of Latin American literature, stands in the doorway and waits for me to lead him across the room.

"You are here for this international tomfoolery, this football cup. I don't like it. I like football, but not all this winning and losing. And besides, it goes on too long."

Well, I venture, maybe a two-week championship would be better.

"That would still be two weeks too long for me."

The English is perfect, the good humor unmistakable.

"And another reason I dislike it, it encourages nationalism. I hate nationalism."

But it doesn't *really* bother him, I protest.

"It does, I hear it, you know, in the streets. And the cost. There are two hospitals closed down right now, and people without places to live. We are spending all the money on football."

The talk turns abruptly to Robert Frost and why he is the most important American poet of this century, of why New England is so important to American literature, of why Borges likes Texas and Arizona.

"Come with me." Arm in arm we go across the room, where Borges feels along a bookshelf. The volume he selects is of Kipling poems, not my favorite by any means, but I do a reasonable job of reading some of them.

"You hear that?" asks Borges. "That phrase 'drumming up the night,' you can't say things like that in Spanish. Only in English."

We sit for another ten minutes, discussing Chesterton and Shakespeare, and Borges—this frail old man, living alone in a world of darkness and penetrating vision, who knows so much more about English literature than I will ever know—recites a poem in Icelandic.

As I leave, I pat the white cat.

"His name is Beppo. Byron, you know. Come again. Let us hope Argentina doesn't win tomorrow, then we can get some sleep."

Borges is no doubt right about the cost of the World Cup. Surely other, more important matters have been neglected to stage it.

How much money has been spent? Officially, it is supposed to be $700,000 for the stadiums and airports and communications system. The figure seems absurdly low. Last year Captain Lacoste told me that some $200,000,000 would be spent on permanent improvements, so someone is doing some wool-pulling somewhere.

Not that Argentina is the only country spending freely on soccer matters. Brazil is estimated to have spent $4 million in preparing its team.

On the whole, for journalists the organization of the tournament went smoothly. There were some initial screw-ups over game tickets—one English journalist was handed a wallet containing no tickets at all, but two parking passes for a car that he did not have, while others without tickets were asked to sign an official receipt saying they had received no tickets.

The press center at Cordoba acquired a saucy reputation because of the sauna bath there and the "mad masseuse"—a woman of about 50 (I was told; I had no personal experience in this, you understand) who, the minute her much younger assistant left the room, indulged in a fellatious rape of whoever happened to be around. On the assistant's return, the fellatee, finished or not, would be unceremoniously pushed onto his stomach for a more conventional massage.

Hotels seemed to be the only places where overcharging was rife—anything from $50 to $120 a night for rather ordinary rooms—but, as we all knew the prices in advance, there wasn't much room for complaint there. At least my hotel had an all-night snack bar, complete with a 24-hour security guard outside the hotel and in the men's room.

In some hotels there were problems getting food late at night. Returning from an outing on the river, tired and starved, an English colleague had to bribe a member of the hotel staff to go into the kitchen and scrape up some food. The food was produced, and left on the table while the journalist went to the bathroom. When he returned, it was gone. In another corner of the dining room sat an East German journalist, wiping his lips over an empty plate. The irate Englishman rushed into the kitchen, gathered up every unappetizing piece of stale food he could find, and returned to the dining room to push it under the German's nose.

"*Essen?*" he asked in lousy German.

"You," came the answer with heavily accented Teutonic precision, "can go and fuck myself."

Eight teams were left in the second round, divided into two groups of four: an all-European group of West Germany, Italy, Holland, and Austria; and a nearly all–South American group of Argentina, Brazil, Peru, and Poland. The winner of Group A to play the winner of Group B in the final.

In Group A it looked like the Italians, playing so well and so attractively. But in their first game against West Germany, on a gray, misty afternoon in River Plate Stadium, the Italians lost their nerve. A game that, with a little more will to attack, they would certainly have won, ended in a 0–0 tie. While, at the same time, the Dutch were clobbering the Austrians 5–1. After Holland then tied the West Germans, all it needed against Italy was a tie; it did better, beating the suddenly shaky Italians 2–1. Holland would be in the final for the second World Cup running—in 1974, they had lost 1–2 to West Germany.

A sad note here. West Germany's long-serving and much-respected coach, Helmut Schoen, went home with a defeated team. He had announced before the competition that he would retire as soon as the tournament was over, and one felt this would make the German players more eager to play for him. There is a revolting European "tradition" that has grown up in recent years—members of a soccer team that has won something big, or looks as though it might win something, get together in a studio and record some silly soccer-related song. The resulting disc, being raucous, strident, and utterly tuneless, is indistinguishable from your average rock hit, and climbs straight to the top of the hit parade. The German team recorded a song called *The Man in the Cap*—for Schoen, who always wears a cap. Many of the players were in tears, it seems—yet this affection was not strong enough to stave off a humiliating defeat by Austria in West Germany's last game. Schoen went home a bitter man: "I was let down by the younger players."

Events in Group B turned positively Byzantine in no time at all. Brazil beat Peru 3–0, and the same evening Argentina beat Poland 2–0 in Rosario. I saw this game in a theater in Buenos Aires, on a large screen, surrounded by thousands of Argentines every bit as noisy as they would have been at any stadium. Occasional bench shots of Menotti, puffing away at the inevitable cigarette, produced roars of approval. The roar was, if anything, even bigger for the single cutaway to the president—army general Jorge Videla, a regular at all the Argentina games, in his civilian clothes.

Argentina took the game on two superb goals by Mario Kempes, the only player Menotti had brought back from Europe and fast emerging as the tournament's only real individual star. And, once again, the streets of Buenos Aires were jammed with people and cars and trucks, flags waving, noisemak-

World Cup 1978: Argentina take the field—and suddenly the stadium erupts in a vast, swelling roar of acclaim and a blizzard of white confetti. The most exciting moments of pure, raw, sports theater that I have ever experienced. *Copyright Paul Gardner*

ers shrieking, horns burping long-long-short-short, AR-HEN-TEEN-A. Every few minutes, the procession of people would break into the song *Vamos, vamos, Argentina! Vamos, vamos a ganar!* as everyone jumped up and down as though on pogo sticks. I went to bed at midnight; the noise and the number of people seemed as great as ever. And once again I was struck with the impression that *still* these people didn't really believe that Argentina could win anything, that they were all out here because they were afraid this might be the last time they would have anything to celebrate.

It looked, then, as though the final positions would depend on the game between Argentina and Brazil in Rosario. The atmosphere there, already tense, was further tightened by accusations from the Brazilian press that Kempes had taken drugs before the game against Poland, rumors that were quickly and officially quashed.

The stadium at Rosario is an old one, renovated, but with the crowd much closer to the field than modern architecture allows. Before the game the atmosphere was as electrifying as any I've experienced anywhere in the world—the singing, the chanting, the overall feeling that this was likely to be the biggest game of the tournament so far. Expectations that were to be shattered very quickly by a curiously half-hearted game, full of rough play from both sides, with Brazil unquestionably the stronger and better team, yet with neither able to score. Speaking to fans after the game, I found them suddenly very pessimistic, as though they were saying that the team's magic streak had ended, that this was the real Argentina, disorganized and without scoring punch.

The game, of course, with neither side able to score, decided nothing. In the final two games, it was assumed by everyone that Brazil would beat Poland and that Argentina would beat Peru. What would make the difference would be the number of goals scored. And here Argentina appeared to have something in its favor. For it would play its game at night, an hour after the Brazil game was over, thus knowing exactly how many goals it would have to score. The Brazilians demanded that both games be played at the same time, a request that was firmly rejected by the organizers.

And then the rumors really started to fly. The crux of the matter was that Peru, having lost to Poland, was, in effect, out of the competition. What possible incentive could they have to put up any sort of a showing against Argentina? The Argentine press soon found one. They reported that official Brazilian representatives had been seen at the Peruvian camp, bearing suitcases full of dollars. They also discovered that a Brazilian businessman was offering the Peruvian players plots of land if they held off Argentina.

The Brazilians were spreading their own rumors. They pointed out that the Peruvian goalkeeper Ramon Quiroga, surely a key man in keeping out the Argentine attack, was actually an Argentine, now naturalized Peruvian. In fact, he came from Rosario, where the Argentina-Peru game would be played. Would *he* want to go down in history as the man who kept Argentina out of the final? Having seen the erratic Quiroga play on a number of occasions— so impossibly brilliant one minute, so banally inept the next—I confess I would have found it very difficult to decide whether he was throwing a game or not.

On the afternoon of June 21, Brazil duly dispatched Poland by a score of 3–1, beginning to look at last like a real Brazilian team instead of the tawdry imitation they had presented up until then. A good win, one that was big enough to send the Brazilians back to their camp to watch Argentina-Peru on television with high hopes.

Argentina now knew that it had to win by at least 4–0 to get to the final, and for the first 20 minutes of the game the weight of that knowledge seemed to paralyze the players. The Rosario crowd, as noisy and as physically present as ever, added to the team's nervousness. At last, it was the ubiquitous Kempes who, like an ice cube in the boiling cauldron of the stadium, coolly took his first chance to put Argentina one up. By halftime it was 2–0. Early in the second half, the Argentines scored twice within minutes, and the Peruvians simply faded away. The final score of 6–0 could have been 10–0. *Llora Brasil, llora Brasil—weep Brazil, weep Brazil,* chanted the crowd.

So it would be Argentina vs. Holland in the final, with Brazil left to play for third place against Italy. Brazilian coach Coutinho recalled the words of the Peruvian captain, Héctor Chumpitaz, before the Argentina game—"We are conscious of our responsibility to defend the decency of soccer"—and commented sourly, "This game will go down in soccer history as the Game of Shame." In Rio de Janeiro, the Peruvian consulate was attacked by furious Brazilian fans, who also threatened to blow the place up.

A fixed game? No, I think not. Simply a game that meant everything to Argentina and nothing to Peru. The fault for that, if there is one, lies with the organization of the tournament.

The day of the Great Triumph (which is Argentine for Game of Shame), I went to the Plaza de Mayo in Buenos Aires with many other journalists, to see the Plaza Mums. That is the name the English-language *B. A. Herald* uses to describe the mothers who gather every Thursday in the Plaza to protest the disappearance of their children. Some 200 women and one man were walking in a slow, orderly circle, blank, expressionless faces, silent mouths. A funeral procession, yes, kept from being funereal only by the noise all around. As everywhere in Buenos Aires on that day, there were groups of kids waving Argentine flags, chanting AR-HEN-TEEN-A! AR-HEN-TEEN-A! And there were largish groups of onlookers. A woman passing held up a small card, with the handwritten question: *Dónde está mi hijo Alfredo Gonzalez?* A Danish photographer moved in for a better picture and was suddenly pummeled and punched from behind by two or three men. One did not have to be too clever to spot the plainclothesmen in the crowd. Within minutes another had encouraged the boys to run with their flags through the procession, breaking it up into little groups.

I found myself at the center of a group, listening to a mother protesting that she was totally nonpolitical, she was just a mother. Where was her son? Confronting her, mocking, not listening, a man wanted to know why she wasn't working, and what kind of a mother was she who didn't know what her son's politics were? I had seen this man before—well, not him, his brother, his blood brother, the essence of the plainclothesman, in Rome in 1966. There was some sort of student demonstration going on, when the *Celere* arrived; one of them, stocky, balding, pounced on a teenage boy, roughed him up, spat at him, screamed in his face, then kicked him into a waiting car. Mission accomplished, he turned around and caught me staring: "You want something?" he asked derisively. "No," was my useless reply.

This was that same face—those same restless, unseeing eyes, the trim little mustache, the half-grin, half-leer, the film of sweat. I moved to another group where the lone man among the protesters was claiming that his daughter had nothing to do with politics: "She disappeared because they fancied her." Among the listeners, more restless eyes in sweaty faces.

The following morning, the *Herald* published a report of the scenes, mentioning that ". . . three of the middle-aged men who had begun the chants of Argentina! Argentina! drove off in a Ford Falcon which was waiting in a no-parking zone next to the Banco Nación."

The *Herald* is the only Buenos Aires newspaper that has regularly covered the Plaza Mums. Its editor, Robert Cox, is worried that a campaign may be under way to discredit the Mums, to paint them as unpatriotic or as publicity seekers. The *Herald* lives precariously, daring more than the Spanish-language papers, but always in danger of offending someone, the government or the right or the left.

"There was a time," says Cox, "when we simply didn't know who might be coming to get us. We published a story once by V. S. Naipaul in which he mentioned that Eva Perón was supposed to be good at fellatio; the Montoneros called a meeting and took a vote on whether to bomb our offices. They decided we weren't important enough."

The plainclothesmen in the Plaza de Mayo remind me of the matter of security in general. Well, we heard a rumor or two of bombs going off; nothing was ever confirmed, the police never admitted anything, nobody had ever actually seen anything happen. No tanks, no armored cars, no barbed wire, no massive police presence anywhere did I see—though others told me that Mendoza was alive with cops. Walking for an hour through the center of downtown Buenos Aires one Saturday night, I tried to count uniforms. The total was three.

Another rumor that took wing one day was that 13 members of the Red Brigades had arrived from Italy. Ten had been arrested, three were being sought. Never confirmed or denied. Not an unhelpful rumor, that, for a government that believes that the real terrorist problems are in Europe these days.

So to the final act of Menotti's Miracle. The afternoon of Sunday, June 25, when Argentina took the lead against Holland on a wonderful goal from Kempes, then gave their supporters a second half of almost uninterrupted agony. The Dutch pressure grew and grew, the Argentines became more and more desperate. They held out until nine minutes from the end of regular time, when the big Dutch striker Dirk Nanninga headed home the equalizer.

The game went to extra time, and I would have put money on Holland. Argentina looked an exhausted and a ragged team. As the two teams prepared for the restart, I watched the Dutch coach Ernst Happel, on the field, nervously moving from player to player. Menotti was not on the field; he stood commandingly tall by his bench, talking constantly as his players swigged from bottles and twisted their bodies and massaged their legs. I was sure they could not last those 30 awful minutes that were coming up.

I was wrong, completely wrong. I had underestimated them, but above all I must have underestimated Menotti. I still don't know what he said to them (we'll have to wait for his book, due shortly, to find out), but it can only have been his words, some simple basic appeal, that, for the second time, turned the game around.

It was Argentina that made the running, and the brilliant Kempes who scored the goal, beating two defenders, seeing his shot blocked by the goalkeeper, then beating two more defenders to put the rebound into the net. A third goal, from winger Daniel Bertoni, emphasized Argentina's superiority.

A wretchedly tough defeat for the Dutch, who had once again reached a World Cup final only to be beaten by the host team. For César Menotti, the challenge was over. He had taken a rather ordinary team, added one soccer genius in Mario Kempes, and with a strategy of attacking soccer had done what so very few people really thought was possible.

For Argentina, too, the tournament had brought success that had once seemed so unlikely. A total lack of incidents, an organization that had worked smoothly, and stadium crowds that had behaved impeccably.

Living within me is an image of those hundreds of thousands of Argentines, men, women, boys, girls, little children, who crowded into the Buenos Aires streets to celebrate their team's victory. Behind them, the smiling face of *El Flaco* . . . and the mute, expressionless faces of the Plaza Mums on their silent despairing march.

U.S. Is Seeing the Light on Olympic Soccer Amateurism

NEW YORK—It is Mexico City, 1968, and the Olympics are in full swing. At the vast Aztec Stadium, the press interview room is hot, noisy, and crowded. Most of the newsmen are Mexican, and they are in an indignant mood. Their soccer team has just been beaten by the French. When the French coach André Grillon says it feels good "to beat the host . . . and their professionals," there are shouts of protest.

These are the Olympic Games, the protesters say loudly, "We don't use professionals." The coach smiles and says, "Come, my friends, everyone knows . . ." End of protests. Everyone *did* know.

And everyone still knows. Soccer at the Olympics, the bastion of amateurism, is not for amateurs. Since 1948 the tournament has been dominated by the Eastern European Communist countries, with victories for Hungary (three times), Yugoslavia, the Soviet Union, Poland, and East Germany. In an attempt to stay competitive, other countries, particularly the South Americans, have fielded teams composed of young pros. Still others, notably Britain, have simply given up and do not enter a team.

Now it seems that the United States has awakened. Having failed to achieve much in 1972 and 1976 with teams composed of college players (though the 1972 team did qualify for the tournament), the United States team now has a much more worldly look. All the key players are already under contract to pro clubs of the North American Soccer League.

Compared with players on previous teams, these are older, more skilled, and more experienced. But are they amateurs? How can someone who trains and plays on a full-time basis with a pro club remain an amateur?

The problem peaked in early 1977 when the Cosmos announced that they were signing Gary Etherington straight from high school. Here was a promising young player whom Walt Chyzowych, coach of the Olympic team, did not want to lose to a pro club.

The Cosmos were asked if they would agree to sign him to an amateur contract. They replied, in effect, are you kidding? A player signed to the standard amateur forms of the United States Soccer Federation (USSF) belongs to his club only for a season; in some cases he can simply give two weeks' notice and switch clubs, and in all cases he is a free agent once his contract expires.

So Etherington became a pro, was lost to the Olympic team, and the USSF set about devising a plan that would enable an amateur to sign with a pro club and still retain his amateur status.

They came up with the so-called Olympic registration form, a three-way agreement between federation, club, and player. Under it, the club retains the player until the end of the Olympics (or until the United States is eliminated), the player remains an amateur and agrees to train and play for the Olympic team if requested to do so. The contract was first used in July 1977, for the signing of Bernie James by the Seattle Sounders. Nearly 50 players are now registered on Olympic forms.

So far so good. The gray areas start to appear, inevitably, when one looks at the money side of the contract. As the players are supposed to be amateurs, the pro clubs cannot pay them for playing; they can only pay them expenses. Nobody is certain how much that may be.

"Under USSF regulations," said a North American Soccer League spokesman, "our clubs can pay up to $50 a week to a player for expenses."

"No, no, that's not so," said a federation vice president. "We did away with that figure two years ago. We don't state any amount now."

The argument becomes academic when one considers the lives of some Olympic players. Rick Davis of the Cosmos, for instance, is given an apartment, use of a car, and $100 a week in expenses by the team. But his total earnings are brought up to about $20,000 by a separate contract he has with the Cosmos owner, Warner Communications. Under that contract, Davis is paid for doing clinics, making dinner appearances, and the like. Ty Keough is paid about $30,000 by the Cincinnati Kids of the Major Indoor Soccer League (MISL) for the same sort of work.

Most of the Olympic players' salaries are in the $10,000–15,000 range, but the money is always supposed to be for off-the-field work. Some clubs give those players titles: Greg Makowski, the Olympic team captain, is assistant director of clinics for the Atlanta Chiefs; Curtis Leeper is assistant instructor in clinics for the Fort Lauderdale Strikers. Whether such players actually do the work to justify their salaries is moot. Rick Davis reckoned he had participated in 20 to 25 clinics last year; Keough is averaging four a week (though the MISL season lasts only three months).

What is clear is that the day-to-day life of the Olympic players varies hardly at all from that of their pro colleagues. And all the clubs questioned insisted that the players were not suffering financially because of their amateur status. Most of the players agreed.

Nonetheless, the arrangement leaves many people with a feeling that all is not right. Keough admits to "feeling uncomfortable" when asked about the sacrifice he was making by remaining an amateur. Greg Makowski says, "I think my clinic work justifies my salary; I put a bit more into them than the others do."

For the Atlanta Chiefs coach, Dan Wood, the arrangement is OK, "provided people realize it's a device to strengthen our Olympic team." Jack Daley, the Seattle Sounders general manager, is less happy about it: "In Seattle we pay our Olympic players only expenses. I just don't believe in creating fake jobs. I know other clubs do it, but we don't."

For the pro clubs, there may also be a legal problem with the Olympic contract. It is unclear whether, at the contract's termination, a club has any rights over the player. The thought that their Olympic players could suddenly become free agents has induced several clubs to have players sign letters of intent that they will negotiate a pro contract only with their original club.

John Kerr of the NASL Players Association (which claims an 80 percent membership of league players but is not yet recognized by the league) is also unsure if Olympic players whose contracts are up are free agents or not. "In any case," he said, "we're dead against Olympic contracts. The players can't be members of the union. They lose benefits, such as legal advice. In my estimation, it's a total farce. It'll have to stop eventually, because the pro players won't allow amateurs to play in the league."

Gene Edwards, USSF president who is also a member of the United States Olympic Committee (USOC) executive committee, said: "Our players are all amateurs, compared with other countries."

The big test for the United States Olympic amateurs comes later this year in the first qualifying games. Their opponents will be Mexico, where not much has changed since 1968. Mexico will be using young pros, and no doubt they, too, will be on amateur forms.

Note:

These events grew increasingly distasteful before the fates intervened to set things right. The U.S. lost both its qualifying games against Mexico and was therefore eliminated. But then USSF secretary Kurt Lamm claimed that he had seen the Mexican players' passports, in which they were identified as professional players. A protest was lodged with the International Olympic Committee. The Mexicans withdrew, and the U.S.—fielding players who were almost certainly earning much more money than the Mexican "professionals"—advanced to the finals in Moscow. But the Soviet invasion of Afghanistan led President Jimmy Carter to pressure the U.S. Olympic Committee into boycotting the games. The American "amateurs" stayed home. They were replaced by Cuba.

Cosmos Cheerleaders

NEW YORK—Not wishing to find myself at odds with Emerson, who once said "Always do what you are afraid to do," I went along to the finals of the great Cosmos cheerleader competition.

Things did not get off to a good start. I drove past the motel where the event was being held, in wildest New Jersey, under the impression that the place was still under construction or perhaps simply falling down. Too late, I saw the billboard announcing COSMOS CHEERLEADERS. Highways being built on the "no returns" principle, it took me nearly 10 minutes to find my way back again. Inside there were one or two journalists, some dubious-looking onlookers, refreshments (mostly gone by the time I arrived), and what seemed like hundreds of girls. A huge television cameraman was barging about, crashing into people and knocking things over. Various celebrities were scattered about the room, defying my attempts to identify them. I was saved the bother when they assembled at the top table, each with a little notice on the table spelling out who was who.

A ponderous English voice opened the proceedings, introducing Sylvia Miles as "an actress." "Well," interrupted Ms. Miles, bristling, "I *have* been nominated for two Academy Awards, you know." People shuffled their feet and giggled. The girls, all 32 of them, sat nervously through further introductions—Pelé, the Smothers brothers, Ahmet Ertegun. These were the judges, sitting facing a small area of cleared floor.

The girls were given leave to go and change into their dancing or cheering or high-kicking clothes. I expected them all to return wearing Cosmos T-

Orignally published in Soccer Express *March, 1979.*

shirts, at least. Not a bit of it. Back they came in a vast variety of attire—covered legs, bare legs, shoes, no shoes . . . whatever clothing there was seemed to be pretty tight. But no Cosmos propaganda—it seemed a strange oversight.

One by one, the girls stepped up to the judges and delivered a short talk on why they wanted to be a Cosmos Cheer. Nothing very original here: "I have radiation and excess energy to get the whole stadium cheering"; "I want to cheer for the number-one soccer team in the world"; "I just wanna be part of the fastest-growing sport in America"; "I just love them, I'd audition for the team if I could"; "I scream when we get goals, soccer's going to bowl all the other sports out of the way"; and so on, all delivered with that perky, bouncy, perma-grin look.

The judges scribbled various things on their notepads. One girl said she'd been sent on assignment for her paper, but was now so caught up in the whole business that she genuinely wanted to be a Cosmos Cheer. Another seemed to me to be considerably more honest than all the rest: "I sit down among the fans for the games, fans from all different countries; but whatever language they speak, you know what they're looking for in a cheerleader . . . and I can project it."

Then we had the girls coming up in lines of eight and performing a sort of chorus-line dance (while the phonograph blasted out a disco version, barely recognizable, of "Somewhere Over the Rainbow"), the climax of which was a menacing mass surge toward the judges, ending with a shout of *Cosmos!*

Four times that rather silly exercise was performed while the hideous music screeched and scratched at our ears. Then all 32 girls were lined up in front of the judges and asked if they would present their rear views for five seconds. More scribbling and shuffling of papers from the judges.

Then a long pause while the votes were counted, during which the ghastly music continued and the press were invited to dance with the girls, which they did not do, preferring to help themselves to the replenished food and drink supplies.

After 10 minutes of suspense, the choices were made: 16 girls were now officially Cosmos Cheers. As the names were read out, there came shrieks of delight and wild embraces as the successful girls sprang forward. Left sitting on the chairs, softer faces, quiet, feeble grins, were those who didn't make it. The television cameraman was busy sweeping all before him again; some of the girls were being interviewed, others were posing for photographers. One, so conscious of the cameras, was leaning over to kiss Ahmet Ertegun's shining bald head.

Enough is enough. It could have been worse—certainly this year's girls are younger than last year's, and seem *not* to have the rather jaded professional look that so many had in 1978. Still, their main function is to be prurient—even though the one girl who drew attention to this didn't make it (so that'll show *her* whether it pays to be honest). Also, the Cosmos have said that this year the Cheers will perform only before and after the games, and at halftime, not during the game—a sensible step, as there is no logical time to go through their silly routines during a soccer game.

I don't begrudge the girls their success. "I don't believe it, I don't *believe* it!" one was crying rapturously as I left; outside in the lobby, a mother was grinning into a phone, "Yes, Morris, she made it." But I am glad that the game itself can go on without those meaningless pom-poms waving about in the background.

Carlos the Great

NEW YORK—Sometimes he took the train, sometimes the bus, sometimes he pocketed the fare and just walked. At age 15, office boy Carlos Alberto worked his way around Rio de Janeiro collecting rents from his boss's properties. He got to see a lot of the city, but not nearly enough of the one place where he wanted to be: the Fluminense Soccer Club. That also happened to be the one place where he was forbidden to go by his father, who did not want a pro soccer player for a son.

So Carlos Alberto told a few little lies. With the hopelessly transparent cunning of the young, he fed the traditional office boy excuses to his boss— he felt sick, there was an illness in the family—and he began to spend an evening a week training with the Fluminense juniors. Looking back at those evenings of 23 years ago when the shouts and laughter of a score of happy young boys echoed thinly in the empty stands, Carlos grins and shakes his head at the innocence of it all. An innocence that didn't last too long.

One evening it seemed to Carlos that the stand was suddenly crowded. With one man. "I looked up and I saw my father, just standing there, all alone. I looked away quickly. I didn't want to see him, didn't want him to be there. For a few minutes I kept looking, secretly. Then he was gone."

It was a puzzled and slightly worried Carlos who went on to night school and then home late to an already sleeping family. Quietly, more quietly than usual, Carlos went to bed, to dream his dreams of soccer glory, to be surrounded by backslapping and cheering teammates . . . until the backslapping

Originally published in New York Sunday News Magazine *June 27, 1982. Copyright 1982 by Paul Gardner.*

grew too rough to bear and the cheering became a single angry shout of *Vagabundo! Vagabundo!*

Suddenly, violently, awake, Carlos scrambled out of bed to stand facing his furious father, who, belt in hand, was yelling that Carlos was not going to waste his life playing soccer: *Vagabundo!*

"My father was an auto mechanic, we were a poor family, and they wanted me to study, maybe I would become a lawyer or a doctor. But I *knew* what I wanted. It was very early in the morning, but I got the whole family up, my mother, my sister and my brother, all round the table, and I told them that I was going to be a soccer player. We argued and shouted, my mother cried, but my father at last said OK. But I had to agree to keep going to night school."

In the end, the night school didn't matter too much. If Hollywood ever feels like making a soccer movie, it has in Carlos Alberto's career a script that would surely inspire a mountain of guck-filled platitudes from the publicity types. Rags to riches, brilliant, distinguished, stellar, trophy-laden, horror-filled, Carlos's career has been all of them. But not one of those terms, nor even all of them together, conveys the excitement Carlos brought to the normally unspectacular position of right fullback, the sheer *quality* of his career.

It included 10 years as a teammate of Pelé on the great Santos club of the 1960s, and reached its climax with the captaincy of the Brazilian national team that won the World Cup in 1970. Seven years after that famous final, as his playing days were fading uneventfully away with the Flamengo club in Rio, Carlos Alberto got a call from the Cosmos. And at age 33, he came to New York to play once again with Pelé, then in his final year with the Cosmos. It was sassy enough that Carlos should be prepared to start a new career at an age when most soccer players' legs are beginning to wobble a bit. It was astonishing too, because Carlos was to play a position he had never played before—sweeper. And it was downright preposterous because the Cosmos already had a sweeper, none other than the great Franz Beckenbauer, who had singlehandedly created the role of the attacking sweeper in modern soccer.

But the Cosmos have never quite managed to do things the way everyone else does. In 1977 coach Eddie Firmani wanted Beckenbauer to play in midfield, where he would get more of the ball. The sweeper would be the 33-year-old Brazilian novice, who immediately looked as though he'd been playing there all his life. If brushes are the tools of a sweeper's trade, then this was no clumsy broom that Carlos wielded. This was rather the artist's brush—at one moment subtle, teasing, and playful, and the next bold, decisive, and arrogant.

He was at his best in the penalty area, where defenders and opposing forwards converge around the ball in straining muscular confusion, where all is tangled high-speed desperation. It is the Gordian knot of soccer, and its

Alexander is Carlos the Great, who seems to possess some secret, shatteringly simple way of unraveling it. The sight of Carlos Alberto trotting into the melee and swiftly emerging with ball under control—without seeming to have made any particular effort to get it—is one that continues to delight Cosmos fans. It is all made to look so ridiculously easy, so laughably easy, that as often as not the response from the crowd is just that—delighted laughter.

How does he do it? There seems to be nothing exceptional about the body, a slender un–muscular-looking body that bends and twists in a not-quite-elegant way. The movement is sort of feline, not quite pantherine, but quite unmistakably Carlos Albertine. The arms seem a fraction too long, hanging and swinging a bit too loosely. The legs are just ordinary legs—legs that lope, legs that stroll, but never legs that race. Above them the slim body leans forward, bobbing springily up and down with each step. The stoop means that Carlos Alberto's face always appears to be tilted upward, the large knowing eyes pushing hungrily forward, catching every move, every nuance of the game.

When you run down Carlos's basic soccer skills, they don't exactly dazzle, either. The enigma was set out by another of soccer's all-time greats, George Best of the San Jose Earthquakes: "You know, Alberto is not a good tackler, he can't head the ball properly, he's not fast, he's not rugged, and he can't mark man-to-man, so I keep asking myself—why does he always end up with the bloody ball?"

Does Carlos himself know? He claims to: "I *feel* the play before the ball comes. I know when a player is going to make a long pass or a short pass by looking at him in his eyes. To look at the ball, that is no good, the ball can't tell you where it is going to go. I see from his eyes, that is why so often when the pass is made, I put up my foot, and the ball comes to it."

If there is a clue to the mystery of Carlos's mastery, then it has to be what the English would call his unflappability. We know it as cool. His Cosmos teammates see it in every game, but it still leaves them gaping. Says Jeff Durgan, the young American stopper on the Cosmos, "I suppose he does push himself sometimes, but I've never seen him huffing and puffing. He's a very calm player. He's always two steps ahead of everyone else."

Defender Bob Iarusci remembers a game where "the ball got played over my head into the penalty area. It was dropping near goal, and one of their forwards was racing in for the head shot. Carlos was there, but he didn't go for the ball, he just waited. The guy jumped for the header, and the ball went inches over his head, just as Carlos knew it would. With another opponent racing in to challenge him, Carlos took the ball on his chest and, before it fell to the ground, got his foot under it and lifted it gently over the guy's head, and then made a perfect pass to our left back. What can you say?"

August 16, 1978: Giants Stadium, New York Cosmos versus Minnesota Kicks—Carlos Alberto's famous shootout triumph. Said Giorgio Chinaglia: "If he misses, we're finished. The whistle goes, and we see him scoop the ball up with his foot and run forward bouncing it off his thigh. We couldn't believe it, we all thought he was crazy. . . ." *Copyright Richard M. Casanas*

Giorgio Chinaglia remembers the time in 1978 when the entire Cosmos season was riding on Carlos's shootout attempt at the end of a playoff game against the Minnesota Kicks: "If he misses, we're finished. The whistle goes, and we see him scoop the ball up with his foot and run forward bouncing it off his thigh. We couldn't believe it, we all thought he was crazy. And he scored so easily, just lifted the ball over the goalkeeper like it was a little kids' game. I swear he'd never even practiced that move before."

For three years sweeper Carlos majestically swept all before him, and all behind him, and all to both sides of him. Until a new coach arrived at the Cosmos in 1980, the internationally famous but dourly disposed West German Hennes Weisweiler. "He didn't seem a happy man," says Carlos, "He never *looked* happy, and all he thought about was defense. Every game, all he said to me and Beckenbauer was 'Carlos and Franz, you must stay on defense.'"

Weisweiler's obsession with defense flowered into patent absurdity at the end of the season when the championship game, Soccer Bowl '80, saw Beckenbauer playing at sweeper and Carlos Alberto on the bench. "He told me I would play in the second half," says Carlos, "but he waited till 10 minutes from the end before he asked me to go in." Carlos refused.

The Cosmos won the title 2–0, but there was consternation among the Cosmos brass because Carlos had told reporters, "I will never play for that man again." Warner Communications chief Steve Ross (Warner owns the team) and Cosmos chairman Nesuhi Ertegun pleaded with Alberto to stay. He yielded and went off with the team on a postseason tour of Europe.

The inevitable clash came in Rome during a game against Chinaglia's former team, Lazio. At halftime, the Cosmos were losing 3–0 and stinking the place out. Carlos remembers:

"As I walked to the locker room, I could hear Giorgio already shouting at the players. When I got there, they were all quiet, waiting for the coach. So Hennes starts talking, and it's the same thing—'Carlos and Franz stay on defense'—I tried counting, one, two, three, four, but it was no good. I started screaming at him, telling him that it was his fault that we were playing badly, that I knew more soccer than he did, that he didn't know what he was doing, and a lot more stuff I don't remember. At first he shouted back. Then he went very quiet."

Quiet but smoldering. Weisweiler took his revenge early in 1981 during a Cosmos tour of South America. Carlos Alberto left the team and flew to Rio for the *carnaval*—with permission, he claimed. Without permission, said Weisweiler, who banished Carlos from the team. "There was talk of a reconciliation, of bringing Carlos back," says Cosmos executive vice president Rafael de la Sierra, "but Hennes wouldn't hear of it. He was adamant, it was him or Carlos." Alberto left New York to join the California Surf, while the crowds at Giants Stadium grew smaller and the boos for Weisweiler grew louder. The Cosmos had made a huge error, but far from admitting it, they tried to justify it with a publicity campaign stressing how young and how fast the new Cosmos team was—the implication being that this was no place for geriatric cases like the 37-year-old Alberto. The Alberto-less Cosmos reached Soccer Bowl '81, where they played a typically cautious Weisweilerian game and lost to the Chicago Sting. Within two months Carlos Alberto had rejoined the Cosmos for the indoor season. Three months later, Weisweiler and the Cosmos announced that they were parting company. Nesuhi Ertegun explained: "Why did we take Carlos back? Two words—public demand."

The date is wrong, and the place is wrong, but there is a *carnaval* going on—frenetic samba music, singing, dancing, laughing, cheering. A little golf cart is stuttering its way through the crowd. On the front a notice reads "Carlos Alberto—King of the Carnival." It is May 1982, in parking lot number 11 at Giants Stadium. Standing on the hood of the golf cart, Carlos's

May 1982: Frenetic samba music, singing, dancing, laughing, cheering—there's a Brazilian *carnaval* going on in parking lot No. 11 at Giants Stadium. And the King of the Carnival, with his cardboard and velvet crown, is . . . Carlos Alberto. *Copyright Richard M. Casanas*

actress wife Teresa sings and sways to the music. In the back, Carlos—a gaudy crown of gold cardboard and red velvet perched on his head—struggles to sign autographs as the cart jumps excitedly up and down. The cart moves slowly forward, then jerks to a sudden stop. The crown slips off but—easily and smoothly, almost without looking—Carlos moves his right arm and catches it.

The image of Carlos's slipping crown, gracefully retrieved before it is damaged, has a more sinister application. For there have been times in his career when Carlos the Great has behaved more like Carlos the Terrible. Like the crucial 1979 playoff game that the Cosmos lost in Vancouver. Carlos was convinced that a linesman had made a bad offside call that allowed the Vancouver Whitecaps to score. In the tunnel after the game, Carlos assaulted the linesman . . . or did he? "No, I just tossed my shirt to him," says Carlos. But linesman George Lingard says Carlos threw the shirt and then spat on him.

Earlier this year, again in Vancouver, Carlos was fouled by Chicago's Rudy Glenn. He spun around and punched and kicked Glenn to the ground. Cosmos coach Julio Mazzei raced onto the field to wrestle Carlos away, but not before a shouting match had developed with another Chicago player, Pato Margetic, whom Carlos was threatening to "get in the hotel later." A few minutes later, at halftime, Carlos was sitting in the Cosmos locker room when the Chicago players walked past the door. Spotting Margetic, Carlos sprang up and raced across the room. In the doorway, he collided heavily with Jeff Durgan, smashed his head against the doorpost, and fell to the floor where players and trainers had to hold him down. "When Carlos is like that, he looks like he's gonna kill somebody," says Mazzei. "But then in five minutes he is muttering, 'What stupidity.' You know he's embarrassed, but he doesn't apologize. No, not that. He just sits smiling like a little boy who knows he's done something wrong."

I know that smile. I saw it in 1980, after a narrow Cosmos victory over the Dallas Tornado. A victory that Carlos had ensured by brutally and quite deliberately kicking Dallas's key player, Omar Gomez, on the back of the knee, and out of the game. I had spoken to Gomez in the Dallas locker room, a forlorn figure with ice on his knee, genuinely disturbed that Carlos would do such a thing. I put the question to Carlos—how could he do that? I got the smile, then "Well, you saw . . . he was their best player." The smile again, and an untroubled exit to the showers.

Now I am sitting in Carlos's midtown Manhattan apartment, waiting to ask the same question. Well, the apartment belongs to the Cosmos; there's not much of Carlos in it, except perhaps that battered gold and red-velvet *carnaval* crown on top of the bookcase. Carlos relaxes on the sofa and leans forward slowly to catch the question. I want to know why we get these violent outbursts, what goes on inside him, what happens when cool turns to cruel? And all I get is the smile and the rich voice, English words bathed in beautiful Brazilian vowel sounds: "I can't explain it . . . sometimes you get mad . . . I get mad if I think someone is damaging my team . . . I've promised myself: no more, I don't want any more of that, not now . . ."

Above all, not now, because that would be no way for one of the game's legends to end his career. This is the last season for Carlos Alberto, his 20th year as a pro. He will stick with soccer: "Everything I know is soccer—that is always my first thought. Fluminense wants me as their coach in Rio, but I would like to stay in New York. Sure, I would like to coach the Cosmos—but they didn't ask me! No, I can stay here with other work. I can have a soccer camp for kids; that is a soccer job, no?"

Carlos has a couple of other options. For years he has written a soccer column for the Brazilian newspaper *O Globo,* something that has earned him membership in the sportswriters' union. With his union card, he can become a television commentator. (Pelé, not a member of the union, is not permitted to broadcast soccer in Brazil—he is working for Mexican television during the current World Cup tournament.)

Or Carlos might want to cash in on his surprising 10-year hobby as an artist. He paints only clowns' heads, in oil. Seven years ago he had a show in São Paulo: out of 30 clowns' heads, 20 were sold on the first day. "I have more paintings, but they're all in Rio," says Carlos. "Maybe I bring them here for a show. In September. The week before my retirement game."

The end of a career in New York . . . but a new beginning in Rio de Janeiro. Training with Fluminense juniors, just as Carlos Alberto did 20 years ago, is a promising 16-year-old boy, Carlos Alexandro. Son of Carlos Alberto.

On the Decline and Demise
of Professional Soccer

NEW YORK—It hurts to say it, but the North American Soccer League is dead. Not, perhaps, quite as dead as the proverbial doornail. But dead enough. Dead in the sense that it has lost its spirit, its vigor, and its promise; dead in the sense that it can continue existing only as a faint shadow of what it once was.

At the NASL's New York headquarters on the Avenue of the Americas, once a warren of bustling offices that spread over two floors, the staff is down to a paltry six. In the largest of the few remaining offices, enveloped in a dense cloud of cigar smoke, sits—or more likely, paces—the interim president, Clive Toye.

He is trying to conjure up enough clubs to put together a 1985 season. In the unlikely event that he can succeed, it is clear that such a season would be a short, low-budget affair that would entail a dramatic drop in the caliber of operations and level of play that the NASL established in its halcyon days of the late 1970s.

Almost certainly, it would be a season without the Cosmos. For so long the very symbol of glamour and quality in the NASL, the Cosmos are now in deep financial trouble, searching frantically for investors to prevent an imminent collapse.

Yet it was only 10 years ago that the same Cosmos—then managed by Clive Toye—sparked off the soccer boom of the 1970s by signing Pelé. The dramatic coup shoved the sport of soccer firmly under the nose of the American public. It worked, no doubt about that. Within two years, the Cosmos were drawing crowds of more than 70,000 at Giants Stadium, and the NASL grew to 24 clubs.

It was an undeniably feverish growth as the NASL tried to do in the space of a few seasons what had taken the National Football League 40 years. The rat race was on within the NASL, and the name of the game was keeping up with the Cosmos. Other clubs began spending lavishly—and usually not too wisely—on imported foreign stars.

To cope with skyrocketing player-salary budgets, the NASL had to get a national television contract. That came in 1979, with ABC. It really did look as though the final piece was in place for the triumph of soccer.

The turning point came quickly, just one year later. After the 1980 season, ABC—discouraged by poor ratings—did not renew its contract. The number of NASL clubs dropped to 21, and the slide to oblivion was on. The owners had had a glimpse of the promised land, and it didn't look that good after all. Profitability was still a distant prospect, national television had come and gone, attendance was stagnating, expenses were getting higher.

By then, the NASL was finding out that its tentative efforts to encourage the development of American players were backfiring. A new generation of young Americans was with the clubs, vociferously opposed to the very idea of expensive foreign imports. This new breed of home-grown players came with agents, and they were backed by a flagrantly partisan players' union. They demanded, and they got, high salaries. The expense spiral corkscrewed its merry way upward and onward.

When Howard Samuels was brought in as the NASL president in 1982, he had but one task: to bring financial sanity to the league. He was horrified by what he found—a lack of fiscal responsibility, owners who would not implement his budget-control ideas. "They're crazy," he said, "and then they complain about the huge losses and threaten to get out of the sport." The NASL was a league that had dangerously overreached itself and its problems could be—indeed, had to be—defined solely in financial terms.

But the NASL had always had other problems, unique to soccer, that it had never solved, and in some cases had never really faced up to. A basic difficulty was that of introducing a new sport to Americans—with the selling to be done by people who, by and large, had very little intimate knowledge of that sport.

Pitifully few of the NASL's owners ever displayed more than a superficial grasp of the essential nature of soccer. They saw it first and foremost as something that was widely popular everywhere else in the world, a commodity that could be marketed for the American audience.

Soccer is not a commodity. It comes with a 100-year history of intense human involvement. It is a sport that seems to call for a peculiarly intimate and passionate involvement with its fans. But there is no such thing as instant intimacy. It takes time to develop, it needs a history. And that was something that the American public could not bring to soccer. It is just that intimacy that allows the world's soccer fans to forgive their sport its excesses and its aberrations, to overlook its shortcomings. The aberration that American owners could not forgive was that soccer was too *inconsistent* a game. When it was good it was very good, but when it was bad it could be deadly dull.

The boring games were—quite rightly—a source of much perturbation to the NASL owners. Searching for a solution, they focused on goal-scoring, and all manner of largely silly ideas were advanced to increase the number of goals. But here the owners ran into another obstacle that infuriated them. The ultimate control of soccer's rules lies with the Fédération Internationale de Football Association (FIFA). And this group—a *foreign* body, if you please—refused to allow the Americans to play fast and loose with the sport's rules.

The only other method, it seemed, to guarantee top-class, exciting soccer was to keep on signing up the world's top players. But the frequently poor judgment by club managers in deciding just who was and who was not a top player added to the mercurial nature of soccer itself, rendering this a totally unreliable answer.

Frustration, boiling over into apoplexy, was a common condition among NASL owners. It is not a condition that can be sustained for too long, and the NASL has inevitably had a high level of transient owners. Only once in its 18-year history has the league fielded the same lineup of clubs in consecutive seasons. Without club stability, there was never any league identity, and the rivalries—so essential for this sport, wandering traditionless in a foreign land—never developed.

Despite repeated assurances from owners that "we're in this for the long haul, we're going to stick it out," not more than half a dozen have shown any long-term persistence. Most simply folded their tents and crept away.

Others, frustrated in what they saw as their attempts to Americanize soccer, turned to indoor soccer, where FIFA's control is much less well-defined, and where rules can be changed to suit what is seen as "the American way."

The rise of the indoor game, represented by the Major Indoor Soccer League (MISL), was the final blow. As the NASL tried to cut its player salary budgets, the MISL began outbidding it for players. The result has been the loss of many of the NASL's top players to the MISL.

Undeniably, the attempt to impose a new sport, soccer, at the pro level has failed. For now. What the NASL *has* accomplished is to spread the sport throughout the United States, to plant the roots that were so lacking when it started in 1967. All over the country—in Florida, in Texas, in California, in

Oregon, in New York—the anomaly is that youth soccer is flourishing as never before. Add to that the evidence of last year's Olympic Games when crowds of more than 100,000 turned out to watch the soccer tournament, and it really does appear that there is strong hope for a future pro soccer league in the United States.

But not right now. The only hope for the NASL is to keep the flame of the pro sport burning until the current soccer-playing youth, both boys and girls, become parents. At that point, soccer will begin to have the tradition that it lacks in this country. With that growth, too, will come the all-important intimacy between fan and sport.

For the moment, the fans are not there in sufficient numbers, and the NASL has learned that Sam Goldwyn was right—"If they don't wanna come, you can't stop them."

"Look Southward, Gentlemen. Look to Brazil."

NEW YORK—As last week's *Soccer America* survey* made clear, the United States Soccer Federation has decidedly European-oriented thoughts about the future of American soccer. Logically enough, I suppose, because 8 out of the 10 USSF high-ups interviewed are of European origin.

So this narrow-based group—incredibly, it includes no Latins at all—is pushing us toward a European-style future. The tilt is toward West Germany. Fine, as far as organization is concerned. But should we play like West Germany, too?

No, we should not. If we take that route we shall be making a serious error. Worse, we shall be *repeating* a serious error.

Our soccer, since its distant beginnings, has been heavily European-oriented. When the NASL arrived, it immediately fell heavily under British influence. The Anglo-German North-European concept of soccer has had a long run in this country, and it has not triumphed, it has never captured the imagination of the American public.

It has failed, I think, because it is too restricted a version of soccer, one that does not allow the full richness of the sport to flower. More specifically, it does not provide the framework to incorporate the enormously varied talents that U.S. soccer could, and should, feature.

Of all sports, soccer is the least rigid. It has achieved vast worldwide popularity because of its ability to assume so many different guises, to absorb all sorts of subtle national characteristics and yet remain recognizably soccer.

Originally published in Soccer America *January 21, 1988. Reprinted with permission of* Soccer America *magazine.*

This wonderful flexibility will work to our advantage—if we wish it to. It will allow us to build a style that will reflect our diversity.

If soccer is to be successful here—if it is to become a truly *national* sport—then it must be played in a way that allows all of our ethnic groups to participate. To base the future on the ugly misconception that all of our players are European-style is to invite failure. Indeed, such a decision deserves to fail.

The number-one reality that must be incorporated right from the start is that we have a multiracial society. Why on earth should we be looking for guidance from England and West Germany, two countries that until very recently have had virtually no racial mix at all?

We should be seeking not the rigid framework of an established British or West German mode of play, but rather a flexible basis that we can fashion to fit our talents. We should be looking not at a foundation of discipline and power and strength, but at a starting point of infinitely varied ball skills.

Only in this way can we realize the enormous potential of American soccer. The first step in that direction is to turn away from Europe . . . toward South America.

The good gentlemen at the USSF should listen to their colleagues Art Walls and Sunil Gulati, both of whom—without any shilly-shallying—opt for Brazil as the model for what we should be doing.

And why not? Americans like to aim high, to be the best. Why should we not aim to produce the attractive, successful soccer that has become Brazil's trademark?

Brazil, like the United States, is a huge New World country, and it is peopled by a bewildering array of racially diverse immigrants. From that background, Brazil has become the leader in the soccer world. Why can we not do the same?

There are so many lessons to be learned from Brazil. To take just one example: the matter of black players. Brazil is the only major soccer power that features a high proportion of black players. Their influence on the Brazilian game is undeniable—and exciting. The United States has a large reservoir of potential black soccer talent, almost totally unexplored. That is a shameful blot on the U.S. soccer landscape, one that we should be actively seeking to correct. Are we?

While the black player is ignored by American soccer, the Latin player is viewed with suspicion as someone who "doesn't fit in" with the American way. Given the European bias of the American way, that is probably a fair judgment—but it is the system that needs to change, not the Latin player.

I cannot believe that we have a deliberate policy to exclude blacks and Latins, but I must say that I do not see much feverish activity to get them involved in U.S. soccer.

It is not pleasant to realize that our sport, as presently structured, has a detectably racist aspect to it. I am not saying that the people who run American soccer are racists—they clearly are not. But they function within a system that, whatever may be its intentions, sharply discriminates against minority groups. The "country club" background (to use one of under-17 national team coach Roy Rees's favorite phrases) of most of our youth programs means that our players are overwhelmingly white and middle class—a bias that is perpetuated by the colleges at the next stage of development.

I don't see much hope of correcting this situation if our future is to be along British or West German lines. We have already traveled perilously far along the exclusionist road.

We must turn back and embrace instead a future that can find a place for *all* forms of talent.

A newer and fresher vision of soccer is needed. That vision is Brazil and the glittering, sparkling soccer that it plays.

Can we play like Brazil? I think we can. One of the first factors to be considered is that of weather. This has been such an important factor in the development of national styles over the years. The British style is suited to cold and muddy winters. The Germans have managed to get away from that to some extent, but they are not going to produce the same style as a country that enjoys year-round sunshine like Brazil, and the south of our country.

To adopt a Brazilian style, we shall have to make use of our good-weather areas—Florida and Southern California in particular. This will mean shifting the center of gravity of American soccer from the inhospitable north to the sunny south. Perhaps we can even lure the USSF out of its mountain retreat in Colorado?

With the geography settled, there looms the problem of mentality. Obviously, we shall not be able to play like Brazil if, right from the start, we listen to those who say "Of course, we can't match 'em for skill, but we can out-hustle 'em." I have been hearing that thought, in various forms, for nearly 30 years. It is utterly defeatist, and it gets us nowhere. In the future, anyone uttering it should be instantly banished from American soccer.

We *can* "match 'em for skill"—if we choose to; if we choose to adopt, wholeheartedly, a Brazilian approach to the game.

We have all the players we need. Our problem now, as Bob Gansler pointed out in the survey, is not quantity but quality. In this connection, there is another frequently heard phrase that should also bring with it instant excommunication from American soccer. That one goes "we won't be successful until we get the best athletes playing soccer." Humbug. These "best athletes" are presumably the ones who now choose to play football or basketball or baseball. Very few of them would have made good soccer players. Turn it around and ask yourself if Maradona or Pelé or Beckenbauer or Cruyff would have made their high school basketball or football teams. Too small, all of them. Not among the "best athletes."

We don't need the big guys. There is a wealth of average-sized players in this country who are potentially top soccer players. The strength of these players would be precisely that they are *not* oversized. They would be good players not because of their size, but because they have learned to base their game on ball skills.

Or, perhaps, they have been *taught* the fundamental importance of ball skills. The question of teaching boys how to play soccer is one that I have touched on many times. Suffice to say that in this country, at this moment, it is a vital element, one that we have managed to get deplorably wrong in the past, thanks largely to our European-dominated coaching schools.

If we must have coaching schools—and, with the utmost reluctance, I am forced to admit that in this country, we probably can't do without them—then for heaven's sake let's make sure that they are teaching the right things. Things that will release the variety of American soccer, rather than imprison it in the rigidity of drills and discipline.

And here we come to the major stumbling block. Our coaching schools would have to be thoroughly reformed—not to banish the dominant European influence, but to substantially reduce it. And to introduce Brazilian coaches.

When asked which country has the most to teach us right now, Roy Rees was the only one of the USSF biggies who thought we should take a look at the successful programs of the Middle Eastern Arab countries. Countries where they have openly opted for Brazilian coaches. Countries, like Qatar and Saudi Arabia, which have learned in a short time to play Brazilian-style soccer.

Of course, I am not sanguine about the possibility of change in the orthodox doctrine of our coaching schools. Those schools, by their very nature, are bound to be depositories of the most rigid, unthinking dogma. Once a small group has decided that it, and it alone, holds "the truth," genuine dialogue disappears.

The whole thing becomes deadly serious, there is no room for individuality or personality. Walt Chyzowych, the National Coaching School program director, takes himself so seriously that he can even send around a letter to his staff saying "it is imperative that the teaching does not deviate from the prepared curriculum . . . instructors cannot go off on a tangent which is unrelated to a specific topic . . . It is important that the staff follow the syllabus religiously."

Religiously? As I said, it won't be easy introducing fresh air into that sort of atmosphere, but someone has to make the effort. The future of soccer in this country is too important to be left in the hands of the coaching schools.

Messrs Fricker, Walker, Miller, Gulati, Walls, Woosnam, Osiander, Gansler, Rees, and Chyzowych: you are the ones making the important decisions. Rise above your own predilections, your own backgrounds, and give us a soccer future that can involve all Americans. A soccer future that will give us the sport at its most glorious—with artistry and skill alongside physical commitment, with individual inventiveness wedded to teamwork. Turn your backs on the "can't match 'em for skill" crowd—not just by repudiating the words, but by taking the necessary steps to ensure that we do develop skilled players.

And give us a style that will allow a place for the variety of styles that we already possess in this country.

Look southward, gentlemen. Look to Brazil.

Note:

* In its January 14, 1988, issue, *Soccer America* put a series of questions about their soccer backgrounds and preferences to 10 leaders of American soccer. They were, with the positions they then held: Werner Fricker (USSF president), Sunil Gulati (chair of the USSF's International Games Committee), Lothar Osiander (national team coach), Art Walls (chairman of USSF Coaching Committee), Roy Rees (under-17 national team coach), Keith Walker (USSF national administrator), Al Miller (general manager USSF national teams), Phil Woosnam (member of the USSF National Team Management Group), Bob Gansler (under-20 national team coach), Walt Chyzowych (USSF director of coaching).

Urgent Memo to the USSF: Bring on Tahuichi

NEW YORK—Should the unthinkable happen—should FIFA nix the United States Soccer Federation's bid to stage the 1994 World Cup—I have a vision of quite dreadful things happening. A mass suicide by the USSF leadership, bodies cascading out of windows in Colorado Springs—or at the very least, formerly well-behaved soccer luminaries found muttering to themselves as they wander naked through the Rockies.

If FIFA does the dastardly thing, does snatch the Cup away from our panting lips, then this is what they must do to soften the blow. Immediately create a new World Cup—and give it to us. This new World Cup would be to decide the champion nation in soccer clinic–giving.

We'd win that one without even raising a sweat. When it comes to clinic-giving, this is the place to be. The idea started, I gather, in Greece of ancient times. The word *clinic* comes from the Greek word for *bed,* and originally meant a teaching session at which students watched a physician at work on a real, live patient. At the patient's bedside, that is.

Soccer clinics are not given by physicians, but by coaches. Not any old coach, but by a special breed known as *clinicians.* Clinicians are rated very highly in this country. "He's a good clinician," we say, and that settles it—he is immediately in line for a national team post. Or we hiss, "He's not a good clinician," and he'll be lucky if he can find anyone who'll want to be seen talking to him.

Originally published in Soccer America *April 21, 1988. Reprinted with permission of* Soccer America *magazine.*

Sad to say, our worthy clinicians have rather lost sight of the crucial element in the original clinic idea: the fact that it was based on a real, live patient in a genuine setting. It was, I should imagine, an attempt to get away from the inevitable artificiality of the classroom. But our soccer clinics have taken us slapbang *into* the classroom.

The soccer clinician lectures, he will probably draw a few mysterious charts on a blackboard, and the students sit around and take notes. On the field, a highly stage-managed and totally synthetic version of soccer will be acted out. The clinician will strike some impressive poses, may even join in the action occasionally to show that he "still has it." More notes will be taken, silly questions will be asked and will receive even sillier answers, and then it's time to go home or to the bar.

And the whole exercise bears the same relationship to real soccer as a Meccano set does to the Golden Gate Bridge.

A pity—because a clinic sounds like such a good idea. Of course, it *is* a good idea in its original sense of learning by intelligent observation of the real thing.

This is the sort of thing that I mean. In 1910, the famous English amateur club Corinthians made a tour of Brazil. The Brazilians were impressed with the game they played, and wanted to play like that. One of the clubs that was founded that year in São Paulo was called Corinthians. It still exists, much, much more famous than the original inspiration. I don't know whether they talked about "giving a clinic" in Brazil in those days, but that is what the English Corinthians obviously did. Just as Real Madrid gave a clinic in the 1960 European Cup final. And Brazil did during the 1970 World Cup.

OK, OK, but this is 1988. Where are we going to find a team like those *now*—one that can come and give us a real, live demonstration of superior soccer?

Miraculously, there is such a team. Even more miraculously, it is a youth team. I am talking about the extraordinary Tahuichi team from Bolivia.* They were here again recently, winning the under-19 bracket at the Dallas Cup. They are not merely an excellent team—they are a soccer phenomenon.

They generate—in a way that, perhaps, only the Brazilians at their best can—enormous excitement. I quizzed dozens of people—fans, players, coaches, Americans, foreigners—about their reaction to Tahuichi. Without exception, all were tremendously impressed. A few examples:

- Roy Rees (U.S. under-17 national team coach): "I heard a lot of comments, people saying 'Have you seen the Bolivians? They're great.' Certainly, they excite me. They play a game of beauty. As a fan, I'd pay to go and watch them."

- Al Miller (former manager of the USSF's national programs): "Tahuichi made a very positive impression on me. It's next to a goddamn miracle what they've done. Everyone who saw them was enthralled by their ability."
- David Miller (columnist for *The Times* of London) wrote: "Head and shoulders shorter than almost every team they meet here, vulnerable to being physically overwhelmed, Tahuichi are nevertheless in a class of their own. They enchant everyone who sees them with their persistence in relying on skill."
- And so to SMU coach Schellas Hyndman, who said: "Tahuichi have given us a clinic."

Exactly. Tahuichi showed everyone—under real, competitive playing conditions—how to win with stylish, skillful, joyful, attacking soccer. And Americans responded to Tahuichi exactly as soccer people in places as diverse as Sweden, Spain, China, and Argentina have been responding for the past eight years: with exhilaration and admiration.

During the past four and a half years, I have seen various Tahuichi teams play some 20 games. Every one of those games has featured memorable soccer—not only from Tahuichi, but frequently from their opponents because Tahuichi play their game, and they let the opponents play as well. Their challenge is simply that they will play better. It is a challenge that makes for great games.

In this modern age of negative, defensive, overcoached, highly organized soccer, you are not supposed to succeed doing what Tahuichi do. But Tahuichi have an incredible record of success, stretching back to their first international title, won in 1980.

I repeat—they are a phenomenon. A real, live demonstration of how the sport of soccer should be played. They should be seen by everyone involved in the sport.

So I have a suggestion for the USSF: bring Tahuichi to the United States, with an under-16 or under-19 team. Or both. Send them on a nationwide tour. Have them play the regional teams, and as many state teams as possible. Tahuichi will win most, possibly all, of those games. But that is not the point. The main idea is to make sure that as many people as possible who are involved in youth soccer see Tahuichi.

I guarantee that a large majority of the spectators will be impressed. For many it will be a revelation. It will be a clinic that, so to speak, deals with the whole, live patient. Here is soccer in its entirety, not broken down into easy-to-digest fragments. Fragments that have a tiresome trend to become unrecognizable and unworkable once the real game starts.

Once the clinic has been given, that is the time for the explanations. After each game, a Q & A session should be arranged with the Tahuichi staff and players, to be conducted by a competent bilingual soccer person. Those who want to see Tahuichi practice, to find out if they have any secret drills (they don't) would be welcome at their training sessions.

How much effect would all this have on American coaches? Who can tell? But if only 20 percent are inspired to fashion a style on Tahuichi's, then we're off to a good start. Maybe 10 percent is enough. Because if they make it work, others will follow.

Another important point: what Tahuichi have done, the way that they play, cannot be peremptorily dismissed as beyond our reach. We are not dealing here with young professional players belonging to top pro clubs in a top soccer country like Italy or West Germany or Brazil. We are talking about Bolivia—one of the least successful soccer countries in South America. We are not dealing with vast numbers. Tahuichi's players, with few exceptions, come from the city of Santa Cruz. The total population of Santa Cruz is around 700,000. Compare that with our much-touted figure of 1.2 million registered youth players. Most of the boys who arrive at Tahuichi (they start at age five) are not in particularly good physical condition. Medical and nutritional problems are frequent.

So we are not talking about supermen from a world-class soccer power. They're ordinary boys who've been given some rather extraordinary training. It would help the development of soccer in this country for us to know a lot more about how Tahuichi operates. I am not saying that we can then mobilize all the fabled American resources and quickly duplicate Tahuichi's success. It won't happen that way.

What I would hope for is the beginning of a new mentality among youth soccer coaches. Yes, I realize that, to a very real degree, I am asking the USSF to sponsor a tour that would undermine much of what its benighted coaching schools preach. If that is the price to be paid for getting the philosophy of youth soccer on the right track, it seems eminently worth it to me.

Note:

* In 1978 Bolivian engineer Roly Aguilera hired a private coach—a Brazilian—to teach his two young sons soccer at his Santa Cruz home. Soon other relatives, then friends, then total strangers turned up for the lessons. From this beginning, Aguilera built the Academia de Fútbol Tahuichi Aguilera, now recognized worldwide as of the most remarkable youth clubs in soccer. In 1996 Tahuichi had a direct effect on U.S. soccer, when D.C. United won the MLS championship. Two of its top players—Marco Etcheverry and Jaime Moreno—were ex-Tahuichis. See also 210.

Performing Cats
and Tin-Eared Coaches

NEW YORK—One of the things that I find most intriguing about the sport of soccer is its sheer unpredictability, its persistent refusal to behave as expected, its almost mocking delight in doing the very thing that it's not supposed to do.

It reminds me of cats—another mysterious realm that I love dearly. All cat fanciers know the routine: you have an admiring audience, you encourage the cat to perform its special, unique, unbelievably clever trick . . . and the cat turns its back and settles down to wash itself.

You can see soccer in that behavior—organize an all-star game or a grand final, and you can be guaranteed a good game? Not a bit of it. Soccer has, like cats, a record of turning its back when it's asked to follow instructions.

This perversity is understood by cat lovers. The cat is allowed to do its own thing, to develop its own personality. It's allowed to be a cat. Sure, it can be infuriating and frustrating, it can conjure up thoughts of felicide or even suicide. But if you want a *cat*—as distinct from some supine extension of your own personality, or a show-off automaton or a posing toy—you leave the animal alone.

If only our soccer experts showed the same sort of wisdom. The fact is that, to an alarmingly large degree, they don't. Worse, they persist in flying in the face of such wisdom.

I'm talking, of course, about the coaches who insist on trying to devise intricate plans for the playing of soccer. The planners, the diagrammers, the charters, the programmers.

Originally published in Soccer America *October 13, 1988. Reprinted with permission of* Soccer America *magazine.*

If you succeed in programming a cat (and I'm not aware that anyone *has*), whatever you end up with won't be a cat. Yes, yes—it may well *look* like a cat, it'll have four legs (one at each corner), whiskers and fur, and it'll have a tail. But it won't *behave* like a cat. And no true cat lover could ever be deceived.

So with soccer. The programmers can twist, bend, corrupt, and distort the sport beyond all recognition. Frankly, it's not that difficult to do. It can't be, or one wouldn't see so many pitifully poor teams in action. And like the cat with four legs (one at each corner) that looks like a cat, these nightmare versions of soccer can, superficially, *look* like soccer.

To take the obvious example, the ultimate extreme in disfiguration: indoor soccer. I shall quote the U.S. Olympic captain Rick Davis on the matter: "You still kick the ball with your feet, you still can't touch it with your hands, you're still trying to score goals by shooting the ball and heading the ball, you still have defenders, midfielders, and forwards . . . and unless they've changed something, to me that's soccer."

Really, now? Using that sort of reasoning, I cannot understand why I am not making millions of dollars as a concert violinist. After all, I *look* like Itzhak Perlman, I have two legs and two arms (approximately at the corners), I can wear the same clothes, I can hold a violin properly, I can stand in front of a symphony orchestra, and I can draw a bow nicely across the strings.

The only difference between me and Mr. Perlman starts at that point—he will produce the most heavenly music and I shall produce nothing but screeches, screams, squawks, and squeals.

I may look like a violinist, and I may fulfill all the superficial criteria for being a violinist. But I am not, and never shall be. Anyone who thinks I am a violinist—well, what can one say about such people? They must have the thickest of tin ears.

And if Rick Davis really does believe that indoor soccer is the same thing as soccer, then in soccer terms, he is decidedly tin-eared. It is the same thing with the coaches who inflict upon us their threadbare versions of the outdoor game—because I have no reason to doubt that they really do believe, genuinely believe, that what they are giving us is soccer.

In the furtherance of this delusion, they have managed to convince a large number—probably a majority—of American boys that they are playing soccer, when in fact they are doing no such thing.

It is the same sort of thinking that Rick Davis has applied to the indoor game: as long as you have a soccer field, with 22 appropriately uniformed players, and they kick the ball and don't use their hands, etc., etc.—then it must be soccer.

So you can put 22 boys on the field and have them charging aimlessly about all over the place, merrily whacking the ball as far as their toes will propel it, knocking each other down with a consistency worthy of better ends. And it must be soccer?

Well, I suppose it might have been, but in the sport's Stone Age. Things are supposed to be a little more sophisticated now. The problem is that so much of the sophistication is of the superficial variety. We do now have young players who know what a bent run is (I don't, if you were about to ask), can spin-turn and do double-reverse check-off, stop-go interchanges, who can shout clever things like "Man on!" (do they really shout that in women's soccer?), and who—if they are goalkeepers—can spend the entire game bawling "Out! Out!" We have all that, and much, much more. We have coaches with lovely badges, too.

And we still get Stone-Age soccer. We still—far too often—get aimless charging about. Because the cat has not been allowed to be a cat. Because the soccer player has not been allowed to be a soccer player. He has not been allowed to understand the game on its own terms; he has not been allowed to develop a *feel* for the game, an instinctive understanding of the game. Or, conversely, he has not been allowed the freedom to show, quite clearly, that he will never understand these things, that he will never be a soccer player.

So we end up with far too many potentially good players who are stifled because the fatuous rigidities that are imposed upon them prevent their development; and with far too many players who are simply not good enough but who are encouraged to remain in the game merely because they can perform some narrow, sterile role on the field.

Of course, to suggest that young players be allowed the freedom to play things the way they see it is to invite derision. "What am I supposed to do?" asks the coach. "Just send them out there and turn my back on them?" One is greatly tempted to say "Yes" to that—for while there may be an initial anarchy, could not the players themselves fashion some order? And having done so, would they not have learned something? In any case, one can make out a pretty substantial case for the anarchy, even if it persisted, being more interesting than what the coaches' schemes so often give us.

But that's not the way it should be. The coach should be there, encouraging his players . . . to be players. Not automatons, not role players. Not performing cats.

In a recent conversation, Columbia University coach Dieter Ficken put it beautifully: "The moment you have a plan that the players *must* follow, you're immediately playing non-soccer. In a game, players under pressure will play to their strengths. The moment you start giving them roles, then the players are not playing *their* game, but a game that the coach perceives as soccer."

So far this college season, I have seen 12 different teams. In my judgment, only one of them—Long Island University—plays with a consistent, coherent, recognizable style. As most of coach Arnie Ramirez's players are from Latin America, it is a Latin style. The players, by and large, are at ease with the style, they know—instinctively—what they should be doing at any given moment (not always—there are plenty of errors, this is the real world we're talking about). When things click at LIU, the team is delightful to watch. When they don't—well, they're no worse than most of the other teams who are trying to do things that they don't understand, or that they're not capable of doing.

The vast majority of the players that I have seen so far—except LIU—are American-trained. And far, far too many of them *simply cannot play.*

That is a sad thing to say. It is a painful thing to *have* to say. By the Rick Davis definition, they ought to be soccer players—after all, they kick and head the ball, they don't touch it with their hands, and so on. But they are not soccer players.

During the same weeks that I have been watching college games, I have also taken a trip to Flushing Meadows Park to watch a youth game in one of the local Hispanic leagues. Boys of 17 and 18 mostly—a well-organized, exciting game, only a couple of subs used, officiating by a referee and two linesmen.

And in that game, I saw more genuine soccer talent than I saw on any of the college teams (always excepting LIU). I do not know all of the boys who played—but I can assure you that the ones whom I do know have been mercifully free from the deadening clamp of methodical coaching. All foreign-born and trained? Again, I don't know—no doubt many are. But at least one—the quickest and the smoothest forward on view—is a Dominican boy (a country where they play very little soccer) who learned to play solely in New York.

Our orthodox coaching fraternity is at liberty to (and probably will) reject my assessment. They could go and take a look for themselves. But I never see any USSF badges at such games.

The USSF, which spends a lot of money and time organizing its coaching schools (and which also makes money out of them), might ponder the matter: those schools, and their influence, are still giving us players who are inferior to players who have had very little coaching at all. Common sense would suggest at the very least a radical overhaul of what the coaching schools are doing. But the USSF has shown a marked aversion to common sense in this matter, so the betting here is that it will continue to blindly undermine its own efforts to raise the caliber of American players.

Soccer in the Heart of Texas!

Youth Tourney Features
International Sort of Football

DALLAS—Even though it takes place in Texas, the Dallas Cup is not the world's biggest youth tournament. But it does have a solid claim to being one of the world's best.

While the Gothia Cup in Sweden features 800 teams and the Norway Cup has over 1,000, Dallas is host this week to a mere 134 teams. But the Dallas Cup had to turn away 400 others, such is the reputation for high-quality soccer and superb organization that it has acquired in only 10 years of existence.

Still a precocious young sport here, soccer has with surprising strength and speed muscled its way into a state that only a generation ago knew nothing but football.

"I grew up in Abilene, where football is king," said Bill Stroube, an independent oil producer who, as the Dallas Cup director, leads an army of more than 400 volunteers. "There was no soccer; I never played the game. I think that's true of 90 percent of the people involved in the cup."

Stroube, like so many other people, was led into soccer by his children. His son, Jeff, one of more than 85,000 youth players in the Dallas area, plays on the Dallas Kicks.

A leader in the development of youth soccer here is Ron Griffith, an Englishman who founded the Texas Longhorns club 21 years ago (its most famous member was Kyle Rote, Jr., one of the first stars of the North American Soccer League) and immediately set about taking his club on European tours. From the desire to repay the hospitality of foreign clubs, Griffith conceived the Dallas Cup in 1980.

The first year there were 26 boys teams, with only 3 foreign entries. This year there are 108 boys teams and 26 girls teams, with players ranging in age from 11 years old to 19. And there are 37 foreign teams representing 24 countries from Canada to Chile, from England to Thailand, and including teams from the Soviet Union for the first time.

Each team is allowed 18 players, but overenthusiasm is rampant: the Moroccans of Widad AC Casablanca brought 25; the Greeks of EPSM Thessalonika arrived with 22. And organizational details may sometimes get lost in the translation: the saddest case was the Reineken Fusche team from West Berlin, which arrived ready to play but had to be denied a place in the tournament because it had forgotten to send in an application form.

Meanwhile, the Golden Grantham club of Lagos, Nigeria, did send in its application, and paid its hotel deposit, but it has not been heard from since.

All the teams pay their own way for the weeklong tournament—airfare, hotel, and rental of minivans to get around—and pay entry fees as well. Eight corporate sponsors also contribute, and the labor comes from Stroube's volunteers.

The foreign teams often get fan support from Dallas-area compatriots, who add color and excitement to the games. Tahuichi, the world-renowned Bolivian youth team that has won the under-19 boys title for the past two years, plays its games against a background of swirling flags, beating drums, and chants of *Bolivia! Bolivia!* from scores of devoted fans.

"We even had a call once from a group in Los Angeles," Griffith said. "They said they were Maltese, and they were coming to support the Maltese team. As it happens, we didn't have a Maltese team. All we had was a Maltese referee. And he didn't show up."

The Dallas Cup scored an international breakthrough this year when, after years of polite *nyets,* teams from the Soviet Union suddenly agreed to attend. Three under-19 boys teams—from Estonia, Lithuania, and the Ukraine—are playing in this week's tournament.

The boys from the Soviet Union, like the players from 20 other foreign teams, are staying with Dallas families.

"I'd really like all the teams to be with families," said Griffith, who traveled to 27 countries last year recruiting for the Dallas Cup, "but clubs are now serious about winning here, and some prefer to have their players all together in a hotel."

The Mapes family is host to two boys from Dynamo Kiev, and the foreign players have proved a surprise to 11-year-old Justin Mapes, who thought "they'd be boring and ignore us, and not want to learn what we do. But Igor and Alek are really nice," he added. "They're really funny."

Ann Danford, who has been a host for overseas teams for eight years, said of two other players from Kiev, Yuri and Andre: "You couldn't ask for two sweeter kids. They're tidy, they're polite—and they insist on washing their own uniforms."

Denis O'Hagan is housing two 12-year-olds from Thailand. He admits to a communication problem that requires a lot of miming and gesticulating. "We weren't quite sure what they would like to eat, but we're learning," he said. "We hold up an egg, and they nod. We show them a can of Coke, and they smile. And they love popcorn. It's a real neat experience."

The tournament is played on 16 fields in public parks on the northern edge of Dallas, and at the Lake Highland High School's stadium. The fields, Griffith admitted, were the "weakest link" in the tournament, but that problem is being worked on. Now that the tournament has become so well-established, plans are being drawn up for a soccer complex in the Dallas area that would provide the Dallas Cup with a permanent home.

The worldly atmosphere of the Dallas Cup fits in well with the city's drive for a more international image. More than 6,000 fans attended last Sunday's opening game, which was preceded by an Olympic-style parade of all 134 teams. The guest of honor was Mayor Annette Strauss of Dallas, who told the crowd that when 1994 comes around and the United States plays host to the World Cup, Dallas wants to be one of the playing venues.

And Ultimately, They Had Done It

PORT OF SPAIN, Trinidad—This was always going to be high drama, this do-or-die game. This was the Duel in the Sun; this was Death in the Afternoon.

This was Trinidad & Tobago against the United States. *All* of Trinidad, the whole country, was into this one. Everyone agreed that this was the biggest thing ever to hit Trinidad, that the possibility of qualifying for Italy had united the country as nothing before had ever done. Said T & T Soccer Federation President Peter O'Connor: "This has been unbelievable. This doesn't happen, but it's taken over the country. It's quite awesome."

Here was a tiny country that was suddenly a prisoner to soccer, that had joyfully surrendered to the sport. Soccer was everywhere, unavoidable. It greeted you with flapping banners at the airport, it jumped in front of you whenever you turned on the television, it poured out of the radio with a stream of happy soccer calypsos, it dominated the front pages of the newspapers. It was in the conversation of the people, it was in their eyes. And after a day of this astounding atmosphere, you had to believe that soccer had taken over the very soul of Trinidad.

The Friday before the game was declared Red Day. "Wear something red" was the message, and it seemed like every single person in Port of Spain, in the whole country, obeyed. Obeyed is hardly the word, for this was more of a joyful joining in. We *all* joined in, you couldn't resist, the tide of happy enthusiasm just wouldn't allow you to stand aside. Even up at the Hilton Hotel, the traditional bastion of remote, uncomprehending Americanism, there was

Originally published in Soccer America *November 30, 1989. Reprinted with permission of* Soccer America *magazine.*

plenty of red to be seen . . . and one of the larger, brighter red shirts was topped by the warm, smiling face of USSF secretary Keith Walker.

That was the other thing. Everyone was smiling. This was soccer party time, a massive happy festival that FIFA had classified as a "high-risk" event. Ridiculous! Risk of what? Of being suffocated by the kindness of these super-friendly people? Of being deafened by their relentless calypsos?

But reality will have its way, and there was another risk there all the time. Beneath the color and the celebration, a deep, insidious, corroding force was at work that ultimately undid all the hopes and dreams of the Trinidadians. Not overconfidence so much as confusion.

A confusion over what needed to be done.

Every so often, when you had time to catch your breath, to step back a little from the tumult, you had to remind yourself that the thing being celebrated had not yet actually happened. There was still a game to be played. There was still the possibility that the U.S. would spoil the party.

I did not think that likely; there were simply too many factors lining up in Trinidad's favor. One of the biggest of those factors was the home field and all this tremendous hoopla that went with it. That, surely, must work decisively for Trinidad. So I thought, as my taxi approached the stadium two hours before game time. Again, that sea of red. Red clothes, red banners, red flags, and—pouring out of the already jammed stadium—the wonderful noise of the crowd singing their happy calypsos.

Inside, the green of the field sparkled in the sun, at the eye of a swirling red storm of 30,000 delirious fans. When the Trinidad players, not yet in uniform, strolled lazily out to walk about on the field, the roar that greeted them took the breath away. This was a roar of triumph, if ever I heard one, a roar for the victors. But a roar for victors who had yet to achieve their victory.

At that moment, a vision entered my mind, belatedly but with startling clarity. The year 1950 had been much in the minds of the Americans as this game approached, and we'd talked a good deal about that year, the last time the U.S. appeared in the World Cup finals, and that famous 1–0 win over England. Now, another image of 1950 came flooding in.

This stadium full of celebrating fans, this colorful, noisy, musical, joyous celebration . . . this was the way it must have been in Rio de Janeiro on the afternoon of July 16, 1950. With 200,000 Brazilian fans acclaiming their team as world champion, with the mayor of Rio on the field delivering a speech hailing their victory . . . and with the game against Uruguay not yet played. But why worry? The Brazilians were at home; all they needed was a tie; they were in splendid form; the Uruguayans were struggling. A recipe for sure success that somehow went sour, that somehow sapped the resolve of the Brazilians and gave more courage, more intensity, to the Uruguayans. When it was over, the crowd in the vast Maracana Stadium was quiet, stunned, many in tears, and Uruguay had won 2–1. A game that produced one of soccer's memorable quotes, Juan Schiaffino's, after Uruguay's second goal had muted the crowd: "That was when I knew we were going to win, when I heard that silence."

The parallels were exact—too exact to be ignored—and for the first time, my head, rather than my emotions, told me that the U.S. could win this game. The only significant difference between Rio and Port of Spain was that it was *tiny* Uruguay that had beaten *mighty* Brazil in 1950. Now it was the mighty U.S. tilting at tiny Trinidad. But that is not a soccer argument. Even though the U.S.'s much vaunted millions of youth players far outnumber Trinidad's entire 1.3 million population, the U.S. is still a tiny country in soccer terms.

Just how small came forcefully home to Tab Ramos as the U.S. team was waiting to board its plane in Miami, waiting to fly down to a country that was aflame with soccer. The laconic announcement came over the airport PA— "Will the Miami Soccer Club please board the plane."

"That brought us back to reality," said Ramos, "because we knew we were coming to a place where it wasn't going to be like that. As soon as we got to Trinidad Airport, there were thousands of people there to remind us how big this is, and I think that got us excited. I think the atmosphere helped us a great deal."

Something else that helped a great deal was the knowledge that this game had to be *won*. That appalling performance against El Salvador in St. Louis turned out to be a blessing in disguise. Now it was Trinidad that was put in the apparently comfortable position of "needing only a tie." Seductive, fatal words.

For Trinidad, those words meant a further confusion of what needed to be done. To attack from the start? To play defensively and rely on counterattacks? To apply pressure? To lay back? What effect would those words have on a team with a natural attacking tendency, knowing that it didn't need to score a goal to "win" the game?

No such problems for the U.S. It had to win. This was a theme that came up time and time again in talking to the players after the game. Peter Vermes: "We knew what we had to do today—if you try for a tie you get scored on, it always happens. This was like a championship game—you're not out there looking for a co-championship, you want to win it all, that's the attitude we took today." Tab Ramos: "I was even glad after we tied El Salvador, because I think it would have been a lot harder for us to come down here and wait out 90 minutes for a tie." John Harkes: "The pressure on us to win actually helped us. It was a lot better having to play for a win than a tie. We knew what we had to do, we went out and we did it, it just made it that much easier for us." Brian

Bliss: "Having to win worked *for* us, because we all knew we had to do it here, or go home."

Where Trinidad was tentative in its game, the U.S. showed a spirit and a determination that had been lacking in recent performances. Perversely, a lot of that may well have been created by the very atmosphere that was supposed to sweep Trinidad to victory. Bob Gansler got that one exactly right, telling the team that this wasn't a threatening atmosphere—this was festive, and maybe they could get something out of it, too.

Gansler, finally, showed some realistic flexibility in his team selection, giving the promising John Doyle a start and—at last—bringing in Paul Caligiuri. That was a move to produce more speed in midfield than John Stollmeyer can provide, but it looked like a coaching masterstroke at 16:01 local time.

That was when Caligiuri's left foot scored what is arguably the most important goal in U.S. soccer history. And a very good goal it was, a real soccer player's goal. Caligiuri received the ball some 30 yards out, with no obvious options. His instinct (sometimes, you despair that it's a *dying* instinct among modern players) said *go forward.* He went, thinking about taking a right-foot crack at goal. That wasn't on, as a defender came at him; but Caligiuri, having chipped the ball around the defender, now found that a left-foot shot *was* on—and with the bouncing ball, it was a left-foot volley that was going to spin and dip. From about 27 yards, the shot spun toward goal, not irresistibly, but insidiously. Maybe goalkeeper Michael Maurice was screened, maybe the low sun bothered him . . . but this was always going to be a difficult shot to deal with. In it went, Caligiuri disappeared under a mountain of teammates, and the U.S. was on its way to Italy.

Yes, there was stunned silence from the crowd—but the drama that Schiaffino described of hearing the silence just wasn't there. The realization that this wasn't a true soccer crowd had been confirmed only a minute earlier when the Trinidad forward Philbert Jones had been brought down in the penalty area by a clumsy tackle from Doyle. "That was an anxious moment," Bliss admitted later. "I looked at the referee at once, but he was waving to play on." It was the one questionable call in an excellent game by the Argentine referee Juan Loustau—but what a crucial call it was. Yet the crowd never let him know what they thought of it. A real, serious soccer crowd would have roared, and would have kept on roaring in anger . . . but this crowd barely reacted.

What a hurtful thing to have to say, but this crowd was simply too pleasant, too *nice.* The whole atmosphere was too *nice.* It was lovely, it was friendly . . . but it was not the sort of atmosphere that helps win vital World Cup games. Would any other country in the world have greeted their opponents so amiably at the airport, whisked them through customs, and driven them straight to the hotel? I think not. Anywhere else, the U.S. team would have found obstacles in their path, meaningless functions to attend, endless standing about, buses that didn't arrive, drivers that didn't know the route to the hotel.

The amiability even continued on the field. Heavens, no wonder Loustau had such a good game. In this most crucial of games—for *both* teams—there was hardly a tackle that could be described as crunching, hardly even a verbal confrontation. The whole game was a prime candidate for a FIFA Fair Play Award—and as such, a most unreal exercise.

Trinidad turned out to be a toothless tiger; their Strike Squad (as they were called) had no strike. Said a weary-looking Peter O'Connor after the game: "We never looked like scoring at all." Some of that ineffectiveness can certainly be credited to the U.S.'s defensive game, but by no means all. Before the goal, Trinidad had its chances. But the chances were not hungrily snapped up. They were treated too casually, too conservatively, almost too lazily.

And when anything did look threatening, Tony Meola was there, with the wonderful arrogance of the confident player, to snuff it out. This young man gets more impressive with every game, almost with every save that he makes. This was the sort of performance that is going to bring the European scouts sniffing around.

The Trinidad chances were coming because the U.S. was taking risks in going forward. And, frankly, what a welcome relief that was. There was intensity to the attacking play, the moves so clearly sprung from a *conviction* that this was the thing to be doing, that today defense was secondary. And what a difference that made to the whole performance, what a difference from the diffident, half-hearted, ineffective performances we have become used to during the past three games.

I have to believe that it makes a difference to Peter Vermes to know that when he gets the ball, he is going to be supported in numbers *quickly,* instead of having to hold the ball and wait or try to go it alone. Certainly we saw a much more effective Vermes here, gritty, determined, skillful, a sharp aggravating thorn in the Trinidad defense all afternoon. Behind him, Tab Ramos had one of his best games yet for the national team, running everywhere to get into the action, dribbling and holding the ball with confidence, resisting tackles with his usual athletic grace. John Harkes put in his customary Stakhanovite performance . . . but how much more effective it was in the context of a team that was going forward with determination, that looked as though it really meant it.

I am talking about the atmosphere of the team, and that is vital to what was done here. I think that atmosphere was there when the team arrived in

Trinidad, it was there to be detected at the hotel before the game, it was there in the quiet attitude of the players. They said they were confident . . . but, hearing that, you always ask yourself, "Well, what else would they say?" Of course they meant it, and this time it was solidly true. This was a team that had undergone a personality change since the St. Louis travesty. I didn't pick it up, didn't realize that something different was happening here.

I might have gotten it from Bob Gansler at the pregame press conference, but Gansler is a difficult man to read; he's *always* low key and ostensibly confident. This time was no different. When asked how he saw his future if the U.S. didn't qualify for Italy, he simply replied, "I intend to win tomorrow."

After the game, Gansler gave his technical and tactical explanations of how the triumph had been achieved, but they sounded too cold, too scientific when delivered in the bedlam of a locker room where champagne and beer were squirting in all directions and the chant of *Italia! Italia!* filled the air.

No, this one belonged to the players. They had had meetings, players only, during the week of training in Florida. Rumors are that a group had even suggested, or demanded, team changes from Gansler. And ultimately, they had done it, they had won their way to Italy. And, remember, they had done it without being able to use star midfielder Hugo Perez, injured yet again.

Moving with difficulty around the chaos of the locker room, greeting one smiling face after another, I found myself sinking slowly but very surely into easy sentimentality.

Because this is such a *nice* bunch of guys. And suddenly you're thinking everything is great, they must all be great players, they're all going to do well in Italy, because if there is a soccer god somewhere, he must reward good guys like this. There was only one remedy to the will-o'-the-wisp of those thoughts: to walk a few yards to the Trinidad locker room, where surely tears and sadness must reign. Waiting to get in (I never made it), jammed against the concrete corridor wall by Trinidadians, there was, oddly, no escape from the betrayal that sentimentality brings. For these were nice people too, behaving bravely and courteously in their worst hour. There were tears to be seen, but no dramatics, and most of the faces still had a smile.

I waited for the locker room doors to open. They did—but only to let out the sports minister, Jennifer Johnson, somber and dignified. The people stood politely back to make way for her and her group.

From outside the stadium, the rhythm of the happy calypso music penetrated the stifling corridor. No, this was not to be like Brazil in 1950 when distraught fans committed suicide. This defeat was not going to plunge the country into dark mourning. The dignity and the happiness of these people was going to make sure of that.

A group of us journalists, very obviously Americans, drove back to the Hilton, passing through streets where parties and dancing were already noisily under way. No one reached out to bang angrily on our vehicle, no one shouted abuse or nasty words at us.

"It's All Over" said the local *Daily Express* front page the following morning. Yes, the World Cup dream is over for Trinidad. But life goes on, and the Trinidadians are still smiling and friendly people. And one is left to reflect, sadly, that being nice—or at any rate, being *too* nice—is no way to get to the World Cup finals.

In this competition of niceness, it was the nice young Americans who had won. The calypso we'd been listening to for days had told us "We going Italy." It was true, but it was the U.S. that was going. Going because they deserved to go, because the players had pulled off the most important victory in the history of American soccer.

When asked if this victory meant a surge of interest in the sport in the U.S., Brian Bliss replied "Definitely." A lot of work is going to have to be done to make that prediction reality, but Bliss and his teammates have taken the first step.

We have six months in which to make sure that when the airport PA makes the announcement, it's the U.S., not the Miami Soccer Club, that is going to Italy.

Soccer Federation's Goals Are Just That

The Newly Defense-Dominated Era Is Drawing Scorn, Worry, and Remedial Action

NEW YORK—Real Madrid never had any trouble scoring goals when the legendary Argentine Alfredo Di Stéfano led the team to its greatest triumphs in the late 1950s. Usually it was Di Stéfano himself who put the ball in the net—but his passion for scoring was infectious, and there always seemed to be goals for his teammates, too.

Di Stéfano became a coach in the 1970s, when defense was beginning to dominate soccer, and goal-scoring declined. He noted the rise of 0–0 ties, and poured scorn on them with a wonderfully evocative line: *A game without goals is like an afternoon without sunshine.*

That sentiment has been echoed in recent days by Joseph "Sepp" Blatter, the general secretary of soccer's governing body, the Fédération Internationale de Football Association (FIFA).

Using the group's new slogan, Blatter said: "What FIFA wants the sport to do at the beginning of the new decade, is to *Go for Goal,* so that soccer shall be an enjoyable, attacking game. Scoring goals is the most enjoyable activity on the field."

FIFA's slick slogan will be backed by tough action when the latest edition of soccer's showcase tournament, the World Cup, gets under way in Italy in June.

The referees for the competition will be told, when they meet at the end of March, that they must not allow tackling from behind in the 1990 World Cup. Such tackling has long been used as a means of cynically tripping an attacking player who has broken clear, with the defender always claiming that he was going for the ball, not the legs, and that his tripping of the man with the ball was accidental.

"We *have* to enforce this ban," says Blatter. "Referees are very knowledge-able about the rules, but sometimes they are lacking the courage to impose those rules. Defenders, including goalkeepers, who have no chance to get the ball, but deliberately bring down attackers, must be penalized."

Asked if such offenders would be ejected, Blatter replied, "Yes, there could be red cards for this. If defenders do not change their attitude, yes, this World Cup could feature more expulsions than usual—at least in the beginning."

This represents a significant change in FIFA's thinking. Seven years ago, when the English professional league tried to outlaw tackling from behind, FIFA ordered the league to drop the experiment.

Further evidence of FIFA's new attitude is its proposed change to the off-side rule (an attacker in line with the last defender will in future be onside, not offside as at present), although this will not be in force in time for the World Cup in Italy.

The message is clear. Goals are beginning to look like an endangered species. The most recent World Cup, in Mexico in 1986, produced an anemic 2.54 goals per game, the lowest average since the tournament began in 1930. And there is evidence that things are getting worse. Argentina, the winner of the 1986 World Cup, has scored only 5 goals in its last 14 games over the last year.

From the merely alarming to the almost unthinkable: a defensively ori-ented Brazil. The sight of the yellow-shirted Brazilians weaving their attack-ing magic in full cry for goals has long been one of the glories of soccer. But the Brazilians have not won the World Cup since 1970, and their coach Sebastião Lazaroni has his team playing a more defensive game.

The strategy has brought success, but low-scoring success. Victory in last year's South American championship owed much to an ironclad defense that allowed only one goal in seven games, while the attack averaged less than two goals per game.

Pelé, who is an adviser to the Brazilian national team, said afterward: "The Brazilian press did not like it, they complained to Lazaroni that 'this is not Brazil.' Lazaroni told them, 'But we won. Which do you want?' "

Lazaroni's stark choice—either entertaining soccer or winning soccer—highlights the sport's difficulty.

The era of defensive soccer began in the 1960s with the sport's entry into the world of big business. Losing a big game can cost a club a heap of money. It can also cost a coach his job, with the result that caution reigns.

Oscar Tabarez, the coach of Uruguay's national team, said, "The first responsibility is to not lose, to not give up goals."

That is precisely the mentality that FIFA hopes to vanquish with its *Go for Goal* slogan. "If you tell your players that the first thing is to avoid giving up a goal," says Blatter, "you kill the spirit of the game."

Goal-scoring provides a measure of that spirit. Giorgio Chinaglia, a teammate of Pelé's on the New York Cosmos of the mid-1970s, speaks with the certainty of a man who was once a prolific goal-scorer: "Goals are what the fans want to see. You entertain with goals, you *win* with goals. To me, a 0–0 game is always boring, even if it's a great game."

It was an appallingly tedious 0–0 game between Italy and Argentina in December that raised the disturbing prospect of a goal drought in the 1990 World Cup.

"This is the sort of soccer that we're going to see in the World Cup," said the Italian coach, Azeglio Vicini. "We must prepare ourselves."

The soccer fan, who will be asked to pay up to $105 for the opening game and up to $166 for the final in Italy, may well wonder why he should prepare himself for high-priced tedium.

As Bobby Robson, coach of the England national team, commented: "We're in the entertainment business, and it's a very competitive world. We owe the fans something." But that view is not shared by Tabarez, who said that his team owed the fans only one thing: "To win."

Tabarez believes that the problem is aggravated by a shortage of goal-scorers.

Asked to list soccer's current world-class goal-scorers, Pelé names Marco van Basten of Holland and Careca of Brazil, hesitates, then adds Gary Lineker of England—and comes to a halt. Pelé can offer no reason for the dearth, believing that this is simply "a bad moment for goal-scorers."

Chinaglia agrees: "We have to be patient," he said. "These things go in cycles."

Tabarez, too, talks of a cycle, but concedes that modern ultradefensive attitudes may be stifling the development of attacking players.

There is general agreement that the game is now weighted in favor of the defense. "Twenty years ago, forwards were quicker than defenders," Robson said. "Not so now." Not only are defenders faster, they are also, Chinaglia believes, "much more skilled today."

Tactically, the game has become enmeshed in a more defensive outlook. Where teams once took the field with three or even four out-and-out forwards, the usual number today is two, sometimes only one.

"The game is defensive-minded," Robson said. "However many forwards you play with, the other team will always have at least one more defender."

Thoughts on the Infamous Tackle from Behind

NEW YORK—I was intrigued by Peter Curtis's letter to *Soccer America* a couple of weeks back. I have never met Mr. Curtis, of Washington, Pennsylvania, but I have a feeling he may be a referee. At any rate, he certainly sounds like one.

I say this because of his comments on this unpleasant business of tackling from behind. I had written that FIFA's Sepp Blatter had told me that in the 1990 World Cup tackling from behind will be prohibited.

Mr. Curtis's point is that I am guilty of an oversight for not drawing a distinction between a legal tackle from behind and a cynical trip. This is his definition of legal tackles: "Those challenges where a defender slides in from behind and dispossesses a striker cleanly."

Obviously, I was guilty of an oversight, but not the oversight that Mr. Curtis suggests. What I should have made clear, and didn't, is that I do not believe that there is any such animal as an intentionally "clean" tackle from behind. If it happens, if—as Mr. Curtis so idyllically puts it—the player with the ball is cleanly dispossessed, then I'm heavily inclined to regard it as a fluke.

That opinion is based on over 40 years of watching the game at all levels, under all conditions, in many different countries. Experience has convinced me that the tackle from behind almost invariably results in a foul. What Mr. Curtis is giving me is a theoretical definition of an ideal technique that simply doesn't exist. (Which, incidentally, is why I suspect Mr. Curtis of refereeing tendencies—as a group, they are very good at the theory side of the game.)

Originally published in Soccer America *March 15, 1990. Reprinted with permission of* Soccer America *magazine.*

If this technique did exist, then it should be possible to coach it (heaven knows, we manage to find a way of coaching just about everything else). And if it is possible to coach it, then you can be quite certain that it will have been written up in at least one or two of the mountain of coaching books that threaten to suffocate the sport.

I have some of these stupefying tomes on my shelves, so I have taken a look at a couple to see what they have to say on the matter. First, to the one that used to be called the soccer bible—that great Hungarian epic, the dry-as-dust, unspeakably boring *Soccer* by Arpád Csanádi, Master Coach (listen, it actually says *Master Coach* on the title page, I'm not making it up). The sliding tackle, says Csanadi, "is performed from behind the dribbler in a somewhat oblique direction . . ."

Quite. The only possible explanation to put on that quaint piece of Hungarian-English is that the tackling player is not directly behind the dribbler, but possibly behind and certainly to the side of him. Which already compromises the definition of "from behind."

Here is another description, this one from *Allen Wade's Guide to Training and Coaching:* "The sliding tackle is usually employed as a desperate measure . . . when an attacker has broken clear of the defense and is running towards goal with the ball." And just *when* does the defender slide desperately in? Wade is no more helpful than "the tackler must be as near to his opponent as circumstances permit."

I could delight you with further examples from other coaching treatises, but believe me, none of them says anything different, or anything more revealing. (Well, just a moment: I can't resist this bit of advice from Herbert Smith, an English national, published in 1907: "My idea is that the back should act quickly. He should decide whether he is to go for the man or the ball. Personally, I always prefer trying for the ball.")

Because none of them is talking about tackling from behind—what they are advising is that the tackler gets into a position *to the side* of the man with the ball.

In his book *Soccer Power,* Franz Beckenbauer talks only of a slide tackle "from the side." Others talk about the tackler being "alongside," while the most lenient is Master Coach Csanádi with his "somewhat oblique direction." But even Csanádi makes it clear (for once) that he does *not* mean "behind." He says that when "the defender tries to slide into the tackle from directly behind the attacker, in most cases this will be considered an infringement. The dribbler must be approached obliquely."

Nowhere have I been able to discover any coach who recommends pure tackling from behind, or who attempts to give a technique for doing it. Which is hardly surprising. How would you coach a player to run behind a dribbler, and then—with perfect timing and accuracy—to somehow slide his foot forward between the dribbler's feet without getting entangled with them, and to sweetly poke the ball away? All to be performed while the dribbler, if he's any good, will be changing pace and direction.

Any coach who even tried to organize such a session would have to be off his rocker, as he could expect most of his dribblers to suffer injuries. For that is the other damning indictment of tackling from behind. It is extremely dangerous and quite likely to cause serious injuries. What else would one expect from a situation where the dribbler is concentrating (as he must) on the situation in front of him, while behind him an unseen opponent—quite possibly an aggrieved one whom he has just beaten—is snapping at his Achilles tendons?

The classic tackle from behind was there for all to see in the Denmark vs. Scotland game during the 1986 World Cup. With about six minutes left in the game, Scotland's Charlie Nicholas set off on a midfield dribble. Klaus Berggreen was behind him, made no effort to overtake or draw alongside him, but simply pushed his foot in from behind—and sent Nicholas sprawling. The referee gave Berggreen a yellow card, and Scotland a free kick. Charlie Nicholas was taken off the field on a stretcher, and had to sit out Scotland's next game, against West Germany.

I can't find any of my celebrated coaching authors who draw much attention to, or even mention, the danger of this type of injury. They all agree that the procedure is a risky one . . . but to the defender! They are much too busy trying to pretend that the real danger of injury is to the tackler, or that—if the dribbler is brought down—a penalty kick may be conceded.

Anyway, the real question is this: why should tackling from behind be legal when virtually everything else done behind a player's back is not legal? You are not allowed to trip from behind, or push from behind, or pull a shirt.

Shoulder-charging is permissible, but (and the rules spell this one out) not if it is done from behind.* In other words: if you are chasing a player and you want to apply a legal shoulder-charge, you must at least draw level with him. And that sounds like a pretty good idea when it comes to tackling.

The player in possession of the ball should need to worry only about those defenders who are in front of him, or alongside him—defenders he can see, and against whom he can employ his skills to avoid their challenge. There is not much he can do to avoid a defender who, probably sensed but certainly unseen, clatters into him from the rear. Allowing defenders to perform such "tackles" is yet another example of the way in which the modern game has made life much too easy for the destroyers, and much too difficult for the playmakers.

I'm talking about defenders as though they are the only culprits here. Not so. With the advance of modern tactics has come the coaching wisdom that insists that all players be able to do all things, and that forwards—should they lose the ball—must immediately become defenders. Some of the worst tackles from behind that I have seen have come from forwards chasing after defenders who have stripped them of the ball. Forwards who were desperately trying to prove that they were not neglecting their defensive duties.

I talked earlier about referee-type thinking, by which I mean the compulsion to classify complicated actions into simple, easily defined categories, and then to proceed as though the simple category, rather than the complicated action, is reality.

A perfect example of what I mean is the shortly-to-be-changed offside rule. I have listened to dozens of referees explain to me why (in the past) a player who is in line must be offside. But no one has ever been able to explain satisfactorily what "in line" means. Because, in reality, many offside calls have to be made with players moving at speed. Such a player may have his front leg, part of one arm, maybe his upper body in line—and therefore offside—but his rear end may be solidly onside.

It is not an easy call, but I don't think it helps to pretend that such problems don't exist, and that "in line" is a position that lends itself to precise definition.

Similarly with tackling from behind. To suggest that it is easy to define a "fair" tackle from behind is to confuse theory with reality. In practice, 90 percent—maybe even 100 percent—of such tackles result in fouls. But because referees are confused by the thought that such a tackle *might* be fair, a lot of these fouls are not called. And the player committing the foul can always claim that what he did was OK, because—along with his opponents' ankles—he got a piece of the ball.

Far better to do away with the confusion, to get rid of an impossible definition; to banish an ugly, destructive, and dangerous maneuver from the game altogether.

So, in case Peter Curtis, whose thoughtful letter started this discussion, is in any doubt, my position is this: I'm totally opposed to tackling from behind, and believe it should be outlawed. I hope that is what FIFA has in mind for the World Cup.

When Mr. Curtis writes that "this type of tackling is just as much a part of the game as any glorious offensive move and, when executed with correct timing and positioning, involves just as much skill," I *hope* that he is talking about tackling from the side—in which case he has put the case beautifully.

Notes:

* In 1990 the rules stated that it was an offense to charge an opponent from behind "unless the latter is obstructing." In a major revision of the rules in 1995,

the specific reference to "from behind" was dropped in favor of an overall ban on charging that was "careless, reckless or involving disproportionate force."

Controversy continues to swirl around the tackle from behind. A statement was issued by FIFA, with much fanfare, immediately before the 1994 World Cup, stating that tackles from behind would be punished with a red card. Then it turned out that FIFA meant only certain types of tackle from behind, a modification that left the rule toothless. There were eight direct red cards issued in the 1994 tournament; not one was for a tackle from behind. The matter came up again, more forcefully, before the 1998 World Cup. Again it sounded as though FIFA was banning the move outright; again this was not quite so. Only tackles from behind that "endangered an opponent." During an interview immediately after the 1998 World Cup, Sepp Blatter—newly installed as the FIFA president—told me "The idea is to ban it [the tackle from behind] completely. I will work on that."

Day-by-Day Guide to Italia '90

NEW YORK—No doubt, like everyone else, you're sitting there wondering just exactly what's going to happen in the 1990 World Cup. Right? Well, your bafflement is over. I have worked it all out, so—allowing for a few unpredictable circumstances—this is more or less what's coming up in Italy this month:

June 7: FIFA Congress opens in Rome. The Isle of Man (with 42 players, three clubs, one referee, a part-time linesman, and no stadiums) is welcomed as a full FIFA member. Unopposed, João Havelange is reelected to a fourth term as president. To save time, he is also awarded the Nobel Peace Prize, the Croix de Guerre, the Order of the British Empire, the Congressional Medal of Honor, an Oscar, an Obie, an Emmy, and the Cordon Bleu cooking certificate. He says: "Thank you for all this stuff, but my favorite honor is the FIFA Fair Play Award, which I have just awarded myself." Havelange also states that he thinks soccer should be played in four quarters.

June 8: The opening game is delayed when the parachute display team is shot down by a party of Italian hunters. A hunter apologizes, saying: "We couldn't believe it. We're used to shooting sparrows—we thought they were monster geese." Further delay is caused when the Cameroon team is lost for two hours in a traffic jam. The game is finally canceled when it is learned that Maradona cannot play, as he has an urgent press conference with a sponsor in Scotland. A tape of *Heidi* is aired instead. Nobody notices.

June 9: The United States Soccer Federation holds its first press conference in Florence. Hordes of journalists arrive, but cannot get in, as coach Bob

Originally published in Soccer America *June 7, 1990. Reprinted with permission of* Soccer America *magazine.*

Gansler has requested that the conference be held behind closed doors. The Society of Italian Wigmakers calls a one-week strike; their leader says "We will not tolerate this sort of thing."

June 10: The first high-speed, super-luxury World Cup special train departs from Rome for Florence. Ten hours later it has not arrived, and is officially listed as "missing."

June 11: English fans arrive in Genoa and are not allowed to board the ferry for Cagliari. They wreck downtown Genoa, then hijack the ferry, throwing the crew into Genoa Harbor, and sail for Sardinia, chanting "Remember Dunkirk!"

June 12: Playing against Egypt, Ruud Gullit gets entangled in his own dreadlocks, falls heavily, and reinjures his knee. The Italian Order of Public Toilet Attendants goes on strike; the impact is limited, as no one has ever been able to find a public toilet in Italy.

June 13: Against the USSR, Maradona puts the ball into his own net, but races to the referee to confess that it was the Hand of God at work again. The referee thanks Maradona for his sportsmanship and cancels the goal. The USSF holds its second press conference—the journalists are allowed in, but Bob Gansler and Werner Fricker are too busy to attend.

June 14: In the first half against West Germany, Colombian goalkeeper Rene Higuita is caught six times in the German offside trap.

June 15: The World Cup special train that left Rome five days ago has turned up—in Antwerp. The driver blames global warming and an out-of-date map. The Italian Brotherhood of Ski Lift Operators stages a mass walkout. Their leader admits that the timing may be a bit off.

June 16: Before the England–Holland Hooligan Game of the Century, a highly suspicious party of noisy ruffians is spotted trying to board a plane for Sardinia. They are flung into jail, but released when they prove that they are really English soccer journalists. Security at the stadium is so tight that no one, not even the teams, can get in. The game is called off and declared a 0–0 tie. The English and Dutch fans combine to wreck downtown Cagliari.

June 17: The Uruguayan goalkeeper, a self-confessed adherent of the Roberto Rojas school of goalkeeping, claims he was hit in the ear by a flare during the game against Belgium. Asked if he will be fit for the next game, he replies "Speak up, can't you see I have a flare in my ear?" The Firework Manufacturers Consortium goes on strike.

June 18: The USSF holds its third press conference in Florence. Nobody at all turns up. The Italian Organization of Hedge Cutters votes for strike action. Their leader says "The situation is totally unacceptable."

June 19: A Yugoslavian player is sent to the sideline for wearing his shirt outside his shorts, and told to tuck it in. He proves to the fourth official that his shirt is *not* outside his shorts, as he isn't wearing any shorts. He is re-admitted to the game.

June 20: The Scots' seven-man wall against Brazil refuses to back up more than eight yards, and the referee gives them all yellow cards. He says: "They wouldn't listen, it was like talking to a wall."

June 21: The first round is over, and all games have finished as 0–0 ties. It is decided to restage the World Cup draw to decide who advances. Luciano Pavarotti and Sophia Loren cannot come, and are replaced by The Fat Boys and Bette Midler. The U.S. is the first name drawn, and they qualify along with Italy, England, Brazil, Argentina, USSR, Austria, United Arab Emirates, Colombia, West Germany, Scotland, Ireland, Belgium, Holland, Spain, and South Korea. Maradona says the draw was fixed. Havelange denies it, and adds that he thinks soccer should be played in quarters.

June 22: A Nigerian witch doctor predicts that the United States will win the World Cup. He also predicts that a new dance, the foxtrot, is about to sweep the world, and that Hitler will soon be overthrown. It is felt that his timing apparatus might be out of whack. The Italian Confederation of Olive Pickers is on strike.

June 23: Peter "Methuselah" Shilton, England's 40-year-old goalkeeper, is severely reprimanded by FIFA after being seen, during a game, relaxing in the goal mouth in a deck chair. He says he is baffled at the rebuke: "They told me it was an all-seater stadium."

June 24: The hooligan problem is solved. After England's loss to South Korea yesterday, fans wrecked what is left of Cagliari, then hijacked a ferry and headed for Rome. There, they were put aboard one of the World Cup special trains, headed for Milan, and neither they nor the train have been heard of since.

June 25: After a 0–0 tie with the USSR, Belgium is expelled from the World Cup for being too boring. The referee fell asleep on his feet during the second half, and the snoring of the 60,000 spectators set up vibrations that threatened to bring the stadium crashing down. Dr. Havelange said he regretted the decision, but that he thought soccer should be played in quarters, anyway. The Italian Styrofoam Cup Makers Association announces an indefinite strike. "Indefinite," says their leader, "because we're not sure why we're striking."

June 26: All eight second-round games finish as 0–0 ties and have to be resolved with penalty kicks. No goals have yet been scored in the tournament, and FIFA general secretary Sepp Blatter demands action to step up the scoring rate. Secret instructions are issued to referees for the quarterfinals.

June 27: Results of a routine drug test reveal an Italian player with astronomically high level of caffeine in his blood. He is exonerated when he explains that his mother always makes him drink 10 cups of her homemade espresso before every game.

June 28: West Germany's revolutionary new 3-5-3 formation, with which it has been doing pretty well, is ruled illegal by FIFA's technical committee, which has studied the matter and says the Germans must have been using 12 players. They are ordered to play the rest of the tournament with only 10 men. Dr. Havelange says this sort of thing wouldn't happen if the game were played in quarters.

June 29: Reports from the Trans-Siberia Railroad say that a wrecked train, giving off cries of "'Ere we go, 'ere we go, 'ere we go," is making its way across the Gobi Desert.

June 30: After Argentina's quarterfinal triumph over Spain, Maradona admits that he scored one of the goals with his backside. There is no mention of God this time.

July 1: There is a sudden explosion of goal-scoring in the quarterfinals: Italy 21, South Korea 12; Brazil 33, USSR 19; Holland 25, West Germany 24; and Argentina 14, Spain 9. Coincidentally, all eight goalkeepers were sent off in the first half. Sepp Blatter praises the goal rush and denies referee complicity in the sending off of the goalkeepers—"These things happen," he says. "They wouldn't," adds Dr. Havelange, "if the game were played in quarters." It is reported that Italian school teachers have been on strike for two weeks, but as the schools are closed, nobody noticed.

July 2: The FIFA luxury World Cup helicopter, carrying all the FIFA top brass, is forced down by a barrage of gunfire from a hunting party near Naples. Apologizing, a hunter says: "We couldn't believe it—we really thought it was a giant bird, maybe a roc even." Dr. Havelange, looking stunned after his ordeal, remarked, "I think playing soccer in quarters is the most ridiculous thing I ever heard. It will never happen as long as I'm president!"

July 3: Argentina has to take the field without Maradona, who has an important publicity engagement in Japan, and loses its semifinal to Holland on a goal that Gullit punches in with one of his dreadlocks.

July 4: Having recalled Claudio Gentile to their team, the Italians take care of Brazil in the other semifinal. Three Brazilians are taken to the hospital after accidental collisions with Gentile, who says, "Soccer is not a game for ballerinas." The Italian College of Ballerinas accuses him of discrimination and goes on strike.

July 5: The referee for the final between Italy and Holland is appointed. He is Fred "Four Eyes" Notail, from the Isle of Man. "It is very important," says Sepp Blatter, "that the referee is seen to be unconnected with the finalists." This seems to be the case, as Notail has never refereed outside the Isle of Man. Notail, age 39, works as a wine taster and is married to Imelda. The couple have three sons and six Manx cats. The Italian Society of Manx Cat Owners goes on strike.

July 6: The Claudio Gentile Award for Unsportsmanlike Conduct is given to the Yugoslav who, in one tremendous sliding tackle (degree of difficulty 2.5) took out three opponents, one teammate, a linesman, five advertising boards, two members of the *carabiniere,* and laid waste to the entire bench area. Protesting the referee's red card, he said "But I got the ball, ref." The ball was, in fact, never found, and the Italian Ballmakers Union comes out in sympathy.

July 7: Argentina travels to Bari for the third-place game. Trying to capture a Buenos Aires atmosphere, the citizens prepare a special welcome of confetti made from telephone directories. They omit to tear them up, and many Argentine players are knocked unconscious by falling Yellow Pages.

July 8: Italy wins a dramatic final, beating Holland in a penalty-kick shootout that Fred Notail mistakenly organizes at halftime. As it seems a waste of time to play the second half, the Cup is awarded to Italy. Only 675 spectators see the ceremony; the rest are trapped outside the stadium in an award-winning traffic jam.

July 9: The World Cup is over. The Italian government says it was worth it, despite the thousand zillion lire worth of damage done by the hooligans, and calls a national holiday. Franz Beckenbauer says he will accept an offer, which hasn't been made, to coach the U.S. Reached via a hastily arranged telephone hookup with the States, Bob Gansler has time to comment: "We did some things well, and others not so well, we have to work on this . . ." before he is cut off by a flash strike of Italian telephone operators. The Wigmakers, Toilet Attendants, Ski Lift Operators, Firework Manufacturers, Hedge Cutters, Olive Pickers, Styrofoam Cup Makers, School Teachers, Ballerinas, Manx Cat Owners, and Ballmakers return to work. The rest of Italy, all of it, goes on strike.

Memories of a Boyhood Idol: Stanley Matthews

LONDON, England—Are childhood heroes to be trusted? Sadly, I suppose not. Leave them alone, let them be, glowing warmly in some distant past that never was, bigger then they ever were, nobler than they ever could have been.

You find out too much as you get on in years. Time does brutal things to ancient idols, strips them down to bare ordinariness. They fail any longer to inspire. They amuse, they embarrass. You are likely to ridicule them—well, better that than to ridicule oneself for ever treasuring such people. Or—and maybe this is worse—you begin to romanticize. The former hero must not be allowed to fall. He is propped up with exaggerations and fanciful achievements, and as you tell the stories of feats that never were, your listeners turn away—and you have reduced your hero to a bore.

Perhaps the kindest fate for the champions of those distant years is that they be gently forgotten, that the wonder that once surrounded them fades and they slip, forgotten, into some obscure outback of the mind.

Yet . . . that won't do. There must be exceptions, those who do what Dylan Thomas demands, who "do not go gentle into that good night," but "rage, rage against the dying of the light." Yes, I have my exception. A boyhood hero who has survived, almost intact, who seems to me to be as worthy now as the worshiping mind of a 12-year-old boy believed him to be nearly 50 years ago.

It was 1943. I had been playing soccer for some years, not at all well, full of enthusiasm, short of talent. David, a year older and a much better player,

Originally published in Soccer America *September 27, 1990. Reprinted with permission of* Soccer America *magazine.*

showed me a copy of *Picture Post,* an English version of *Life* magazine. It had Ingrid Bergman on the cover, but we weren't interested in film stars. We sat on the floor and looked instead at the pictures of Stanley Matthews.

A man I had never heard of until that moment. "The Best Footballer the War Has Produced," it said—hardly the truth, for Stan was already 28 years old, and had been a star before the war even began. There he was, in dramatic black and white photographs, poised over the ball, taunting the hated Scottish opponents. "What will he do? Which way? The crowd believes his opponent will never guess right," said a caption.

How could I resist descriptions like "a football equation without a solution," or "a whole football entertainment concentrated in one man"? David's enthusiasm did the rest, for he reminded me that Stan had been born in Hanley, and played for Stoke City, both towns only 15 miles to the north.

Just 15 miles, but these were wartime days. Travel wasn't easy, and anyway Matthews was in the Royal Air Force and rarely appeared for Stoke. A year or so later, I got my chance to see the player who had now become my hero. I read in the local *Evening Sentinel* that Matthews was turning out in an evening charity game in Hanley. My father, who hated everything to do with soccer, said I couldn't go on my own, but a soccer-loving family friend said he would take me.

Late one afternoon we took the train north to Hanley, and walked to Port Vale's ground. No floodlights, just early evening light . . . and a strange lack of spectators. The teams appeared and I shot an embarrassed glance at my companion. These were *boys*! We stayed for awhile, watching some meaningless local youth game. Not entirely meaningless—it featured a young boy named Ronnie Allen, who would later play for England. Already, with local pride, they were calling him "the new Matthews."

But I wanted the *real* Matthews. My bitter disappointment softened my father, and I was allowed to return to Hanley the following evening on my own (I had confused the dates).

Standing on the terraces—nothing but a huge mound of earth with railway ties serving as the steps, and with weeds growing around your feet—I saw my fabulous Stan for the first time.

It's funny, you don't remember the things you ought to remember. What the teams were, who won, who scored—none of that. I remember those weeds, I remember Stan looking disappointingly old—well, he was already 28 with a receding hairline—in his red-and-white vertical stripes. But above all, I remember something that, surely, I can't have experienced.

I remember the *sound* of Stan playing soccer. The soft, seductive noise of leather shoes making delicate contact with a leather ball. Not the biff-bang thumping noises that I was used to, but the neat sound of the ball being caressed. Did I really hear those sounds? Maybe I did. With all the other small boys, I stood close to the field, and this was not a jammed stadium filling the air with a deafening roar.

Maybe I did hear those gentle sounds, or maybe I just invented them as the natural sound effect to a way of playing soccer that I'd never experienced. They were to stay with me; they are with me now as I write. Tap, tap—soft little movements by knowing feet, the ball a willing conspirator in the Matthews dribbling magic.

They'll tell you that Matthews only had one trick. Take the ball up to the fullback, lean inside, then sweep suddenly away to the outside. Well, it's true. That was Garrincha's move, too. And they both got away with it for years. No defender ever really solved the problem.

And because you knew what was coming, precisely because you knew as soon as Stan got the ball what he was going to do, there was always excitement and anticipation in the air. Shuffle, shuffle, tap tap—and Stan was suddenly on top of the fullback. Sometimes the action would stop right there for what seemed like ages, the defender almost paralyzed by caution, until Stan decided it was time to sweep by him and on to the goal line. At other times, Stan would take pity and administer the coup immediately. Frequently, the fullback was left sitting on his rear.

There is a famous photograph, taken at Wembley, of Matthews at work. He is playing for England against Brazil. Facing him is fullback Nilton Santos, one of the finest in the history of the game. It is a photograph that Santos can hardly treasure—for he is lying on the ground, reduced to squirming inelegance by the Matthews magic. Matthews is past him, already preparing for the next opponent. England beat Brazil 4–2 that spring day in 1956. Matthews was involved in all four of England's goals. He was 41 years old.

Incredibly, Matthews went on playing at the top level for another nine years. A pro career that spanned 33 years. Imagine that—33 years of being pursued and tackled and hit and kicked. Yet in all that time, Matthews was never even cautioned once.

He is a strangely unemotional man. This comes through very clearly in David Miller's fascinating biography *Stanley Matthews** published earlier this year. There are no wild, saucy anecdotes about Stan. He is, if truth be told, a rather dull man. He exploded into sparkling brilliance only on the soccer field. And there, it was all instinctive improvisation. He downplayed the importance of tactics, and clearly never really gave much deep *thought* to his game. It was all golden instinct.

Miller tells of how another journalist—Ivan Sharpe, a former international player—asked Matthews how he did it, and took him out onto a lawn for a demonstration. Said Matthews: "Honestly, I can't do it in cold blood, it just comes out of me under pressure."

I watched Matthews whenever I could in the late '40s and on into the '50s. It became a little more difficult after 1947, when Matthews was traded to Blackpool, farther north. Matthews had tried to move away once before, back in 1938, but the locals weren't willing to let him go. Three thousand of them jammed the town hall, and a thousand were left outside, waving their "Matthews Must Not Go" banners. (If you read Arnold Bennett's short novel *The Card*—set in Bennett's mythical Five Towns, which were based on the Stoke area—you will find a scene where the townsfolk jam the town hall and cheer when a councilman tells them, "If I'm not mistaken, one of the greatest modern footballers is a native of this town." The player is brought back, and the local club is saved. Life and art strangely intertwined. Bennett's novel was written in 1911, four years before Matthews was born.)

It was with Blackpool that Matthews had what is remembered as his finest game. The year was 1953, and Matthews had achieved just about everything that English soccer had to offer. Except the most important thing of all. He had never won an FA Cup winners' medal. He had played in the Wembley Cup final—the crowning moment of the English soccer season—twice with Blackpool. In 1948 and 1951, and had finished as a loser both times.

Blackpool made it to the final again in 1953, and this was surely Stan's last chance. After all, the man was 38 years old (no one—except possibly Stan—could imagine that he had another 12 years of soccer life ahead).

The story has been told many times—of how Blackpool was losing 1–3 with only 20 minutes left; of how Matthews suddenly took over, played the game of his life, ran the Bolton defense ragged, and laid on the winning goal in the last minute for a stunning 4–3 victory.

I was at that game. No longer the giggly schoolboy who had stood among the weeds in Hanley 10 years earlier, but now a knowing college graduate sitting on a bench in pale afternoon sunshine. But still *listening* to the sweet tap, tap of Stan's artistry, as excited as any schoolboy has ever been, standing to cheer as dear old Stan went up to collect his winners' medal. For some reason, I still have my ticket to that game—a small, undistinguished piece of pasteboard. I couldn't tell you why that has survived, when I have thrown away so much else.

I went on watching Matthews until 1959, when I moved to New York. But there is a postscript. I was in England in 1965. I paid a brief visit to my boyhood home, then took the train back to London. Finding an empty compartment, I closed the door emphatically against intruders.

Ten minutes into the journey, the door slid slowly open. I took my feet off the seat, and nodded curtly to a smiling, plain lady who enquired if she could take one of the empty seats. She came in, followed by her husband, I supposed. I wanted to sleep, they kept talking softly, which annoyed me, and then made a terrible noise with paper as they unwrapped sandwiches.

1953: A memento that mysteriously survived when so much more has been thrown away. My ticket to the 1953 Cup final, a game that is now part of English soccer lore, the famous "Matthews final" in which Stan the Man, at age 38, finally got his cupwinner's medal.

I probably huffed and puffed a bit, I certainly stared. And there he was. Stan, drably dressed, eating his sandwiches in a second-class railway compartment.

Now I wanted to talk about him and his career, to tell him what he had meant to me . . . but Stan just smiled and changed the subject. There was a terrible shyness there, he would not talk about himself. He told me about his times in Canada, but it was all about Canada, not about him; and he told me about his son the tennis player, and he asked me what I thought of America. I didn't even ask for an autograph. He didn't mention the reason for his trip to London. He was on his way to Buckingham Palace to be knighted by Queen Elizabeth—to become Sir Stanley Matthews. When we got out at Euston station, people far more aware than I surrounded him.

I wandered off, wishing that my hero had been more, well, hero-like. But that was Stan. No dashing sex idol, he. Simply a modest working-class man who turned into a genius when he ran onto a soccer field.

Would he be a genius in today's game? It's never easy to switch a player's skills from one era to another. But I like what little Jimmy McIlroy—a Northern Ireland international of no mean skill himself, who played with Matthews—has to say in Miller's book: "He wouldn't be allowed now to train as an individual, to work on his own at sprints and breathing exercises and jogging. Now, he'd be regimented, they would demand circuit training. There's no way he would do that. *Mentally,* he couldn't exist today. But skill-wise? He'd be a sensation."

I'm sure of it. If today's game could not accommodate Stan, that is the game's loss, not Stan's. He is my exception to the faded heroes of boyhood. The man who hooked me on soccer.

Today there is a statue of Stan (well, of Sir Stanley really, but that doesn't sound quite right) in Hanley's town center. David Miller wrote the inscription:

"Sir Stanley Matthews. Born Hanley, 1 February 1915. His name is symbolic of the beauty of the game, his fame timeless and international, his sportsmanship and modesty universally acclaimed. A magical player, of the people, for the people."

Notes:
* *Stanley Matthews: The Authorized Biography.* (1989). David Miller. Pavilion Books Ltd, 196 Shaftesbury Avenue, London WC2, England.

Pelé

He Remains the Truth and Beauty of Soccer

NEW YORK—You have to use big, clumsy, ugly words to explain the situation. Statistically, mathematically, and chronologically speaking, the incontrovertible fact is that Pelé is now 50.

Well, phooey to that. Pelé has never had anything to do with clumsiness or ugliness, this most agile, most brilliant of players. How can Pelé be 50? Why, surely it was only a couple of years back that he led Brazil to World Cup victory in the dazzling Mexican sunshine?

It was longer ago than that, sadly, much longer. Twenty years have sprinted past since those wonderful 1970 Brazilians showed us soccer in all its glory. But the images of Pelé in action remain as fresh, as startling as ever. Film and tape have saved them for eternity. The joy of looking at them again is the joy that overcame John Keats when he looked at the static figure of the musician on his Grecian urn and wrote of the "happy melodist, unwearied, for ever piping songs for ever new."

Pelé will be forever playing soccer, forever new. And forever unique. There will be no "new Pelé." There are no clones in the realm of genius, no pallid photocopies up there on soccer's Olympus.

What Pelé did, he did in a way that only Pelé could, stamped with his own personality—there was character there, unmistakable, inimitable. That explosive, darting figure, such an impossible combination of ferocious muscular power and delicate, subtle artistry, those sinuous, feline dribbles, the whiplash headers, the thunderbolt shots—the unforgettable excitement of the climactic leap and that triumphant punch at the air.

Originally published in Soccer America *October 25, 1990. Reprinted with permission of* Soccer America *magazine.*

You felt that excitement on a stifling August night, 14 years ago in New York's Shea Stadium. The Cosmos against the Washington Diplomats. Pelé hovering over the ball in the Dips' penalty area, two defenders in front of him, the goalkeeper crouching alertly behind them. It took no time at all, one blink and you would have missed it. Pelé ghosted past the defenders, drew the goalkeeper, the ball was in the net . . . and Pelé was airborne, soaring high in that magical salute.

In the locker room after the game, Pelé was asked how he did it. There was no answer. Not in words. Just a shrug, a quick shuffle of the feet, a lunge, and a twist of the body . . . and a hopeful smile. That would have to do. Pelé didn't *know* how he did it. This was pure instinct at work. Highly trained, beautifully honed instinct—but instinct nonetheless. It was pure Pelé. No one else could have done that, or done it in that way.

You don't talk to Pelé in locker rooms these days. But you can often find him—just a mile or two from Shea Stadium—in his midtown Manhattan office. Pelé is a businessman now. There is work for sponsors like Umbro and Seiko, and for FIFA. And, of course, for former Cosmos owners Warner Brothers, in whose building he has his office.

Pelé springs athletically to his feet from behind his desk, and you tell yourself yet again that the guy cannot possibly be 50. He talks immediately of fitness. He has decided to make a comeback of sorts, to play for Brazil in a 50th birthday game in Italy. "I've been training," he says. "I weigh 75 kilos now—I've lost 6 kilos since you saw me in Italy. If I'm going to play, I must be fit. I was always fit. However I played, no one could ever say 'Pelé didn't run today.'"

Julio Mazzei comes in from the adjoining office. A longtime friend and counselor who now runs Pelé's New York office, Mazzei is known to all as the Professor. He is a physical-conditioning expert. He casts an approving eye at the slimline Pelé and does a quick calculation: "Now he weighs 75 kilos—that is 165 pounds."

When Pelé came to the Cosmos in 1975, he knew very little English, and Mazzei did most of the talking for him. One of Mazzei's most frequent lines from those days, the one the press used to joke about, was "Pelé—he's about, let me say, 80 percent fit now." Sometimes it went down a bit, sometimes up to 85 percent, but it never got any higher. Reminded of these past fitness ratings, Mazzei is asked to give one on Pelé, age 50. He gracefully evades the question: "Let me say that he is close to his best playing weight."

1972: Santos, Brazil—A moment during the filming of the instructional series *Pelé: The Master & His Method*. The author, in his role as writer and soccer adviser, chats with Pelé, who was always the gentleman and who never complained, no matter how many times he was called upon to repeat his skills for the camera. *Courtesy Paul Gardner*

Pelé no longer has to rely on Mazzei to speak for him. Pelé's English, once so hesitant, flows smoothly now: "The original idea was to play this game in Wembley Stadium. Because in all my career, I never played at Wembley. But there was no date free at Wembley, so now we play in Milan. Brazil against the rest of the world. I shall be ready to play for 90 minutes, certainly a full half. I want to prove to young players that if you're in shape, you can play. If you have the skill, of course."

But is it really a good idea to come back, at age 50? Pelé clearly regards the question as virtually irrelevant: "But I don't *feel* 50. I feel that I don't know what age I am. I'm doing the same things that I did at age 25—the only difference is that I'm not playing any more. I didn't change anything. Sometimes—when I look at Edinho—then I realize my age!" Edinho, his son, is now 19 years old, a goalkeeper on the squad of Pelé's old team, Santos.

Pelé says that he thinks he will have a long life, because his family is long-lived. "My grandmother died at 97, I have an 82-year-old aunt, my father is still very active at age 73. I'm going to live to be 100—the only problem will be that all my friends will be dead! At 100, I'll still be on the field, kicking out the first ball for a game in Maracanã."

It seems possible. For Pelé, that is. Not for Maracanã, which will have crumbled long before that. "If I have to repeat my life," says Pelé, "I will do everything the same again—I think I'm one of the few people who can say 'I'm a happy man.'"

The telephone rings, and Mazzei answers. He turns to Pelé—"I think you should take this." So Pelé, with a courteous "You will excuse me?" talks business in Portuguese.

While he talks, you think about his career, and realize how utterly remarkable it is that he has survived the cutthroat world of showsport apparently unmarked. For Pelé was the first true global star in soccer. It was all uncharted territory when he, at the age of 17, became the world's most famous player back in 1958. The temptations, the pitfalls, the traps, the vultures, and the sharks were all there. But nobody really understood what they were. Just a few years later, the pressures of being a superstar were to ruin the career and the life of another soccer genius, George Best. More recently, they have soured the life of Diego Maradona.

Pelé, Best, and Maradona—all from humble homes, none of them really prepared for stardom. Pelé has coped the best. Something was there from the start, something that enabled him to sense that there had to be two Pelés—one public, one private. Where Maradona decided that his wedding should be a massive, expensive, media event, Pelé quietly courted a white girl, Rosemary Cholby, and refused to allow their 1966 wedding to become a circus.

Yet the marriage ended in divorce in 1979. That, at least, is surely something that Pelé would not want to repeat in a new life?

Pelé finishes his business call. He is asked about his divorce. "No, I wouldn't want to do that again. At first it was difficult—for two years after the divorce, I had no communication with Rose at all. But now we are good friends. She lives here in New York and we talk often. After all, we had three children. Edinho has two sisters, Kelly is 21, Jennifer is the youngest, she's 12. Some people, when they get divorced, they say never again, they'll never marry again. I don't say that—but I haven't found anyone I really love. If I do—then I will marry again."

Pelé talks easily and openly about his private life, but soon switches matters back to soccer. The modern game worries him. He wasn't at all happy with what he saw in the 1990 World Cup: "The level of the game was very low. We had some good aspects—the referees did work hard to try to get *clean* games. But technically the soccer was poor. I believe the sport needs to change things a bit. Every sport in the world, even tennis—which is very old-fashioned—has changed. But soccer wants to be the same as it was 100 years ago."

Rule changes. Pelé has what FIFA general secretary Sepp Blatter has described as a "very progressive" attitude to rule changes. Pelé is not horrified by the idea of experimenting with larger goals. He believes that defensive walls should be banished from the game. And he doesn't like indirect free kicks within the penalty area. "Many times in my career, when I was brought down in the penalty area, the referee doesn't want to give a penalty kick, but he must give something. So he gives an indirect kick. You get all the opposing players lining up on the goal line, and it takes the referee two or three minutes to get them in order. No indirect free kicks in the area—they should all be penalty kicks."

Throw-ins also come under fire from Pelé. He strides smoothly and light-footedly around the office, taking throw-ins with an imaginary ball. "There is no offside on a throw—that's good. But you can't throw too far." He lets the invisible ball drop—and that cultured right foot, wearing a very expensive-looking shoe, flashes forward, to silently punt the ball toward some unseen penalty area. "Let the player kick it into play. Not from the ground—that takes time to set it up, and you have problems with players blocking the ball. Let him do this, let him do it quickly, kick it from the air, so that he can clear the other players."

Another phone call. A journalist calling from Brazil. Mazzei looks doubtful, but Pelé again asks for patience—"Do you mind?"—before taking the telephone.

So you have another little pause to think about Pelé's career again, and the comparisons with Best and Maradona. George Best was a thin, shy boy of 15 when he left Belfast to join Manchester United. Diego Maradona was an immature 21 when, already lionized as the world's top player, he left Argentina for Spain.

But Pelé didn't move around, he didn't move to a foreign country. In fact, until his move to the Cosmos when he was already 34, he had played all of his soccer for just one club: Santos. Throughout the '60s, there were plenty of rumors that said Pelé was about to join an Italian club, but he stayed in Brazil.

No doubt he lost money by that. There were repeated disagreements with the Santos board, for Pelé felt—surely correctly—that he was underpaid. But he gained much by staying at home with his family in a country that he understood, among a population that treasured him.

What was it that kept him in Brazil, Pelé is asked. He leans forward, suddenly serious, the smile gone from his face: "One thing I have to mention. I have to do something to help the Brazilian people. When I was a player I was too busy traveling. I had no time to pay attention to the political situation. But now I have to do something. Brazil is a very rich country, it has everything in resources. But there is terrible poverty there, and that is unacceptable.

"In 1994, there is a presidential election. Maybe this is the last thing in my life. To run with some group to change the situation in Brazil. We need a new group—because now there is so much corruption in Brazilian politics.

"I am a socialist, a man of the center. In all my travels, I think that in the socialist countries—Sweden, Finland, Norway—things are better there for the people. I didn't decide yet, but I have to prepare myself politically for this election. Perhaps I will work with the Socialist party in Brazil, or perhaps I will form a new group with people whom I trust. But if I go, I don't go to be some minister of something or other. I must go to be the president.

"I had to work to help my family. I had luck, everything went well. But I didn't have time to see my life until now. Perhaps that is my only regret about my life."

One wonders about a political Pelé. About Pelé tossed into a cynical world where good intentions count for little, where morality and truth bear only utilitarian value. Certainly, that is not the place for the Pelé who shouted *Love! Love! Love!* to the fans at his farewell game in Giants Stadium.

But one thing Pelé always had on the field—something he does share with both Best and Maradona—is courage. The courage that sends a player unflinchingly into the hardest action, that challenges the roughest defender, that cannot be blunted by intimidation.

Will that be enough to turn Pelé from a legend into a successful political leader? We shall see. For the moment, it will do to savor the legend, to recall the squat, powerful figure whose very presence on a soccer field supercharged the whole game, who raised the performance of his teammates and the expectations of the fans. Above all, who raised the art of soccer to heights it had never before known.

That is the duty of the great artists—to make us see things differently, more excitingly. Pelé opened our eyes to new subtleties and beauties in the craft of soccer.

Which brings us back to John Keats: "Beauty is truth, truth beauty—that is all ye know on earth, and all ye need to know." Pelé was, and will remain, the truth of soccer, the beauty of soccer. And, for the moment, that is all ye need to know.

The End-of-the-Year Post Bag

NEW YORK—Time for the end-of-the-year post bag, when I try to answer the more difficult questions that I received during 1990. These are the ones I've been putting off—but no longer. Deep breath, and off we go . . .

A funny thing happened at our game last week. We were in the 10th overtime period of a pulsating 0–0 tie when Whizzo the goddamn Wonder Dog (an ugly brute that had been performing silly tricks at halftime) slipped his leash, ran onto the field, intercepted a pass, dribbled past everyone, and nosed the ball home from an acute angle. The referee allowed the goal, and we lost the game. Is that fair?

Good heavens, yes! Whoopee! A goal, a goal, my kingdom for a goal! Yippee! (A moment please, while I recover from all this excitement.) The goal described is actually a form of og, and should be entered on the score sheet as "Whizzo, (d)og."

This is really exciting news, and you must write immediately to Siggi Schmid at UCLA.* I don't know whether they give canine scholarships there, but it's worth a try. Quite probably there's an NCAA rule against it. There is an NCAA rule against most things. Unless the dog also plays basketball or football, in which case he's home and dry and you needn't even bother about his SATS.

Originally published in Soccer America *December 20, 1990. Reprinted with permission of* Soccer America *magazine.*

I am the president of the American Bar Association, and it has come to my notice that the United States Soccer Federation and World Cup '94 now have more lawyers on their staffs than we do. We are not particularly amused by this, and call on you to stop these illegal recruiting practices.

OK, OK, keep your wig on there. You've no need to worry—I have reason to believe that this is merely a temporary state of affairs and that you'll be getting your members back in about three and a half years' time.

So we need more scoring, and they're talking about reducing the teams to 10 men or making the goals bigger. I have the perfect solution: leave the goals alone and just get rid of the goalkeeper.

You know, you must be an even bigger idiot than your stupid letter suggests. Do away with the goalkeeper? Are you mad? Have you no idea of the importance of the goalkeeper to the modern game? Do you not understand how *vital* he is to the current concept of the sport?

He is the only member of the team that the equipment manufacturers can really go to town on. With all the other players, it's just shoes, plain, ordinary, boring old shoes. But a goalkeeper can have a line of fancy gloves named for him, or a special goalkeeping hat or sun visor, or a lurid jersey equipped with all sorts of aerodynamic padding, or foam-lined pants, plus long pants (yes, *long* pants—not even referees get to wear those), even cuddly mascots to place in the back of the goal.

To say nothing of all the unnecessary and expensive training equipment that is a must for any serious club. Oh no, we must have goalkeepers. The future of soccer marketing depends on it.

I do not understand how Maradona finds the time to play professional soccer and to make all those sexy videos. Does he use a stand-in? If so, which is the real Maradona? Please explain.

I've been wondering about this myself, and I'm afraid I can't make up my mind. I am, however, rather good on anagrams, and can tell you that *Nora Adam*, or *A Roadman*, or *A Mad Roan* are versions of Maradona. If we take the full name, Diego Maradona, we can come up with *No Radio Damage*, or *I Go Mad on a Dare*, or *One Mad-Dog Aria*, or, more poetically, *O, I'm a Dead Organ*. None of them sounds likely to make the Top Ten.

A referee at one of my games called a balk on the opposing goalkeeper, and allowed us to walk in a goal. Later he invoked the infield-fly rule on one of our keeper's towering punts. I never heard of these rules—do they exist?

Yes, absolutely, in high school soccer. There are many such innovations at this level, new ideas brought into the sport by crossover officials from other sports. Look out also for: half the distance to the goal line (when setting up your free-kick wall); the drop-ball that is actually thrown high into the air; the out-of-play whistle when the player, but not the ball, goes over the touchline; the too-many-players-in-the-wall whistle (no more than four permitted); the retake of the penalty kick ordered when the goalkeeper moved, but the player scored anyway. All examples guaranteed authentic, alas.

For a doctoral dissertation that I am writing on "Socioeconomic Pluralism and the Centripetal Role of Soccer in the Collapse of Marxism-Leninism and Its Effect on the Binomial Fungibility of the Ozone Layer," I have been trying to find out how many soccer players there are in the U.S. I am getting many different answers—can you help?

Probably not, but I'll try. The USSF, which can be regarded as the horse's mouth on this matter, has developed a sophisticated method of counting soccer players. Everyone in the country between the ages of 2 and 90 has been asked: "Are you now or were you ever a soccer player?"

Initially, there was some difficulty in defining what "playing soccer" meant, but that has now been solved. You played soccer if you ever kicked a ball, or a tin can, or anything, or anybody, anywhere, or stubbed your toe on the couch, or tripped over a curbstone.

Respondents were asked to check one of the following answers: never, regularly, occasionally, constantly, somewhat, not quite, not sure, not much, infrequently, repeatedly, can't remember, don't know, mind your own business, possibly, and please call back, he just stepped away from his desk.

Correlation of the answers has produced a grand total of nearly 26 billion players. This is almost certainly an underestimate, as the USSF believes there is still a large community of closet soccer players who have yet to be heard from.

I have to tell you that the figures have been questioned on the grounds that the total is actually five times greater than the entire population of the world. But the USSF is confident that its skilled statisticians will prove that the figures are reliable—at least in a marketing sense.

Do we have a mascot for World Cup '94 yet?

Not yet, but we're not short of suggestions. Mickey Mouse, Donald Duck, Tweety Pie, Snoopy, Charlie Chaplin, Abbie Hoffman, and a Mutant Ninja Turtle, whatever that is, have all been suggested. Personally, I think we should break new ground and introduce a World Cup '94 coat of arms. I didn't get much help on this when I called the Herald's College in England—they rather snottily suggested I contact the New York City Transit Authority's graffiti department.

What I have in mind for the escutcheon is this: a gules and vert marketing contract rampant on an azure field of attorneys at bay, with the usual bend sinister. For the crest, a symbolic sponsor-lion draped in fleur-de-lis and squeezing the life out of a sable and argent soccer ball.

Finally, in response to numerous requests from all over the United States and Colorado Springs, a gift list of recent books on the sport.

Among the more unusual spinoff books from the recent World Cup, I would recommend:

- *4-4-2 and the Art of Creative Expectoration* by Frank Rijkaard (translated from the original Flemish).
- *How We Didn't Quite Win the World Cup, Again* by the Scottish coach Andy Roxburgh (also the author of a revealing travel book, *All You Need to Know About Costa Rica*).
- *Soccer for Arthritics* by Roger Milla. (There is also what seems to be a related book on the market, *How to Encourage Fragile Old Fools to Go on Playing Soccer Long After They Should Have Given Up and to Make a Fortune Treating Them When They Start to Fall Apart*, a "joint" publication of the American Medical Association (AMA) and the Original Geriatric Physios Union (OGPU—can that be right?).
- *Andy Brehme's Inter Black-and-Blue Pop-Up Foul Book*—stand well back when opening this, it's quite realistic.
- In other offbeat books, famous players give advice on related sports and activities: *The Secrets of Handball* by Diego Maradona, *Diving for Profit* by Jürgen Klinsmann, *Clog Dancing* by Andreas Brehme, and *ICBMS and Other Forms of Aerial Bombardment* by Republic of Ireland coach Jackie Charlton.
- From the United States Soccer Federation come two companion volumes on the tactical side of the sport: *The Art of Attractive, Attacking Soccer* by Walter Chyzowych and Bob Gansler (4 pages, 1 diagram, 25 cents per copy), and *How to Play Unimaginative, Boring, Dull, Mechanical Soccer* by Walter Chyzowych and Bob Gansler (3,468 pages, with

more than 3 million charts, plans, graphs, diagrams, maps, tables, holograms, drills, exercises, restarts, and set plays, $75.00 per copy). This is the definitive work on turn-off soccer, written by the acknowledged masters in the field. A musical version (tentatively titled *Don't Play for Me, Hugo Perez*) is in the making.

And that's it for 1990. Seasons Greetings to all—see you in 1991.

Notes:

* One week earlier, UCLA had won the NCAA Division I championship without scoring a goal in the semifinal or the final. Both its wins came on penalty shootouts after 0–0 overtime ties.

Messing About

NEW YORK—There is nothing so enjoyable—according to author Jerome K. Jerome—as "simply messing about in boats." As one who has been known to get seasick standing on the shore merely looking at a boat moving gently up and down, I'm not so sure about that.

But I think I know what he was getting at. This is the same guy who wrote that "it is impossible to enjoy idling thoroughly unless one has plenty of work to do." What he was saying was that we take things too seriously—and that in so doing we end up getting them wrong.

Maybe things would go better if we just allowed people to "mess about," to enjoy themselves.

So there's the connection to soccer (in case you were beginning to wonder). Because we hear so much talk from so many involved people about the curse of overcoaching of young players. *Why can't we just let 'em play?* has become a theme of youth soccer.

Almost everyone seems to think it's a marvelous idea. When was the last time you heard anyone defend heavy coaching for kids? Anyone making such a stand today would be tarred and feathered and employed as a halftime attraction at an indoor game.

Yet . . . if nobody would dream of overcoaching, why do people keep complaining about it? Because it does indeed go on—perpetrated by people who are quite sure they are not doing it. Adults, of course—straying into a child's world that they no longer understand.

Originally published in Soccer America *April 22, 1991. Reprinted with permission of* Soccer America *magazine.*

Look at that phrase of Jerome's—"messing about." It implies childishness. And childishness is always a word that we use in a pejorative sense, even when we apply it to children. Messing about is childish. It is unproductive. It is a waste of time. It must not be allowed. It is wrong.

But again, no one really expresses matters like that. It is simply that adults always feel they know better, that they can *improve* things, that by butting into the children's world they can help the little ones. That, by making play more sensible to the adult mind, they make it more enjoyable to the child mind.

So the adults—with the best of intentions—interfere. Put another way, the coaches overcoach. Structure rears its ugly, inevitable head, and messing about is banished. Children, I guess we would all agree, love to play, need to play. I don't necessarily mean at soccer, I mean just *playing* at anything. We agree—but do we know what we mean?

What is play? Play is "activity engaged in for amusement or recreation; sport, games etc.; often, specifically, the natural activities of children." That's what my dictionary says. I don't know that that gets us much further, any more than the knowledge that play can be classified as "biologically irrelevant or useless" behavior.

More to the point is the obvious fact that play has something to do with laughter and fun. In her *Psychology of Play,* Dr. Susanna Miller has this to say: "Freedom of choice, not being constrained by other people or by circumstances is a hallmark of play . . . lack of constraint from conventional ways of handling objects, materials, and ideas, is inherent in the concept of play."

It is, I think, that lack of constraint that leads—in the eyes of adults—to the dreaded messing about. A child must not be allowed to build his pyramid starting with the apex downward—I mean that's just plain *silly.* It must be explained that he's got it upside-down. Must it be explained?

Can not the child be left to find that out for himself? Is there anything more typical of childhood, more downright *childish,* than the wish to explore, to find things out? And is there a better way of learning than by exploring and experimentation? Does the fact that an adult *knows* certain things won't work entitle him to take away from the child the beauty of working it out for himself? To deprive the child of the wonderful excitement of discovery?

I'm talking in general terms, but the soccer connection is obvious. The soccer child should be allowed to mess about with the sport. Do what he likes with it. Explore the possibilities, shape them to his own abilities and to his own personality. If he doesn't have any feeling for the sport, well, he shouldn't be a soccer player and probably never will be one. That is not a crime. The crime is to insist he keep playing when he's not interested.

The young soccer player does not need—is greatly inhibited by—the presence of an adult telling him what to do and what not to do. And that is what coaches most often end up doing, however much they may protest otherwise. As I said earlier, it is all done with the best of intentions. But should it be done at all?

Consider the matter of street soccer. There seems to be a consensus in soccer these days that street soccer is the best way to produce players. Or used to be. Trouble is that with modern highways and traffic jams on the one hand, and a hundred competing recreations on the other, we don't have much street soccer any more.

Not to worry—we (read "the coaches") will simulate street soccer. Not a bad idea at all—after all, what other choice do we have? But being coaches, being imbued with the teaching, technical approach to the game, they promptly get it wrong. Street soccer must first be analyzed (in a technical sense, of course) to find out what makes it tick.

The answer is obvious, clear to everyone. More touches of the ball. The teams are, we are told, smaller so each player has more ball contact. Hmmm. My memories of street soccer involve what I recall as hordes of uncouth monsters. That was why I used to arrive early, to play with just a few kids until the older boys arrived and the teams got bigger and bigger. At that point, if you wanted any ball contact at all, you had to work bloody hard for it.

The other conclusion from the analysis of street soccer was that restricted space is important. So the coaches can now come up with the modern version of street soccer: small teams, restricted space, small goals. Add a dull, totally unimaginative name—small-sided games—and you've got it.

Or have you? I have a feeling that the coaches have ignored the vital ingredient of street soccer: the fact that it was never really seen by the participants as anything more than messing about. Sure, plenty of good players started that way—but did they take part with the attitude of "now for another training session that will help make me a better player and get me a job as a pro"? Huh? Messing about, and the fact that adults disapproved, was justification enough.

That second point is vital. I just cannot envision what sort of reception an adult, a coach, would have received had he turned up and tried to start telling everyone what to do.

Street soccer was kids messing about, they were enjoying themselves— and they were learning in the best possible way: by doing more or less what they liked, by taking the criticism or the praise of the other kids, by finding out for themselves what worked and what didn't, what they could do and what they couldn't.

Sure, by that time the world of constraints was beginning to close in, but there was still much left of the magical world of childhood fantasy and exploration. There were wonderful feats accomplished in those games, and it was mostly the personal skills that stood out. Team play there was, but it was a spontaneous sort of cooperation. It came not from any tactical plans, but from young players who were realizing that team play worked, that it was fun. Kids who developed an instinctive way of combining with other players. There was never, I'm quite sure, any deep *thinking* about any of this.

You can see, can you not, what sort of player is going to develop from that sort of atmosphere. He's going to be skilfull, and he's going to be willful. He'll know how to look after himself; he'll be confident, maybe cocky, because he's self-made and he's proved to himself that he can do it. He will have his own way of doing things. He will have learned to take responsibility for what he does, because no one else (well, no adult) has ever told him what he should be doing. He will have a unique, clear style. There will be a distinct personality about his playing.

I agree that a factor in all that will be "the number of touches" of the ball. But I do not believe it is the most important factor. Surely it must be clear that you can bring up young players solely on small-sided games with an astronomical number of touches—and that this is no guarantee at all that they will be players?

That early freedom to mess about, to be free of the crushing burden of adult wisdom—that is the most important thing. Soon enough the adults, the coaches, will arrive with their deadly somber mission. They will then—as Jape Shattuck so smugly explained in his recent chilling letter to *Soccer America*—set about "correcting" things. The coach as corrections officer.

At what age one stops being a kid—I'm not sure about that. But does anyone know? Clearly, at some point, coaching comes into the picture. But at what age? And what sort of coaching? We really don't know the answers to those vital questions.

All that we can ask of the coaches at this stage is that they stop behaving as if they do know the answers. It may, I fear, be asking too much. The whole inane structure of coaching courses and coaching badges, which gets ever more complicated and ever more divorced from the reality of the game, is working in the opposite direction.

Mark ye my words: the day will come, verily it will, and probably quite soon, when the USSF inaugurates a special course scientifically designed for youth coaches.

I shudder to think what will be taught in those courses. For I do believe that the best youth coaches are those who love the game, who love kids and respect them on their own terms, who will encourage and coax and chide and mock and laugh and gently nudge things along. That is all hopelessly unscientific, but those qualities are worth any coaching badge you can think of.

They are qualities that will *really* allow kids to play, to have fun. Or simply to mess about.

Remembering the Remarkable Sonny Carter

NEW YORK—If one could only know . . . if one could—at the time—recognize the real value of an unusual moment. I am thinking now, with a great deal of sadness, about the last time I met Sonny Carter. Sadness, and something else, something almost approaching anger. Why didn't I *know* this was the last time I would see him? Why didn't something, some little *frisson* of excitement, alert me?

It was just three months ago, at the coaches' convention in Atlanta. The banquet was about to begin, when Rick Davis came up to me, saying, "Sonny Carter wants to say hello." That was wrong, of course—I should have been looking for Sonny, not he for me. But it was typical of this almost pathologically modest man, this medical doctor, fighter pilot, and astronaut . . . and ex–pro soccer player.

We chatted briefly about the day—20 years back—when he was a young player with the Atlanta Chiefs and I had interviewed him in New York. I said, "We must talk again. Keep in touch." I believe I meant it, that it was not just an empty farewell remark.

Sonny took his seat on the platform. He gave a speech in which, typically, he mocked his own ability as a player ("I could hardly kick the ball!"), and, looking at me, he added, "You can ask Paul." I answered only with a silly grin.

Back in 1971, the North American Soccer League was living a precarious existence. Only eight teams—but even that was an improvement on

Originally published in Soccer America *April 29, 1991. Reprinted with permission of* Soccer America *magazine.*

1970, when it had been six. American-born players were a rarity. The St. Louis Stars had a bunch—straightforward, hardworking guys—but that was all.

So I noted the news that the Atlanta Chiefs had an American fullback named Sonny Carter with some curiosity, especially as the lad was supposed to have been playing soccer for only two years. It sounded like a publicity stunt.

It was not. The Chiefs came to New York in August 1971, and I went to see Sonny in his hotel. It was Room 756, I can tell you that, though I've forgotten which hotel. I found a tall, gangly young man whose courtesy made me feel uncomfortable. Every sentence finished with the word *sir*. At one point I asked him to drop the *sir*—he was making me feel old. He agreed, but went on doing it anyway.

A tall, polite young man with a dreamy, intense quality about him. A contradiction? I suppose so. He seemed as surprised as I that he was actually playing for the Chiefs: "I never played high school sport—I never went out for a sport, I was never asked." But he had a small dream: "I always wanted to punt for the football team." Ah, kicking—a hint of soccer interest? Sonny seemed doubtful, replying that he simply "enjoyed watching the flight of the ball."

He thought he might have seen a soccer game while in high school; and he did remember playing soccer informally once, with a basketball, and scoring a goal. That was it. When he left high school, he "more or less abandoned any idea of sports." He went to study medicine at Emory University (he pronounced it "Imry," and that's what I, in my ignorance, wrote in my notes). There, in January 1968, aged 20, he played intramural soccer as a right winger. There was no coaching, but his progress was watched by the Emory coach, Tom Johnson ("he emphasized guts" said Sonny), who liked what he saw and invited Sonny to join the team.

In September of that year, Sonny became the starting right winger for Emory. But he had been doing some homework on soccer. The Atlanta Chiefs practiced at Emory, and Sonny spent a lot of time watching them. There was a copy of *Goal!*—the 1966 World Cup film—available on campus, and Sonny was captured by it. "We watched it three times through—the last time, there was just me and the projectionist left. He enjoyed it, too—he was the water boy on the team."

By the end of the 1969 season Sonny was playing at right back, after the regular starter in that position had been injured. It suited him: "My strength was my heading, and I found I had a lot more room to go for the ball at right back."

Then, in December 1969, "Coach Johnson came up to me and asked me if I wanted to play for the Atlanta Chiefs. Their coach, Vic Rouse, had asked about me. I couldn't believe it. I just thought I was miles away from that level—I'd never entertained any idea of being anything other than a hacker. My father thought it was great—so long as I could continue to study at the same time."

So Sonny joined the Chiefs. I still couldn't see it—weren't the players a bit scornful of his background? "No sir, all the players have been very nice. I had started to think I was better than I was, but after about 10 minutes of the first practice I realized that I didn't have their skills. They helped me—Ken Bracewell used to work out with me for about an hour before the session started.

"One or two of them wanted me to get tougher; they'd make a point of taking the ball away from me. But I learned from that, and they taught me how to play as a fullback, how to turn players to the outside, things like that."

Well—this was 1971, so I had to ask—how did he, a young white from Macon, Georgia, get on with the black players on the Chiefs? Sonny might have found that question offensive. If he did, he certainly didn't show it: "I was at an all-white high school, it was a public military school. In 1965, my senior year, they brought in six colored boys. I got on well with them—and I get on well with the colored guys on the team."

There really wasn't too much time for Sonny to dwell on whether he was good enough or not, because his pro debut arrived with a rush in 1970: "I think it was about the third game of the season, against Washington, when I got to play for the first time. I got in pretty early, as a sub. I was scared—but I did a lot better than I thought I would."

Sonny went on doing better than he thought he would, though he clearly remained mystified by his success. He was not the only one, as he charmingly admitted: "I went to the Masters golf tournament earlier this year [1971], and I met someone I was at high school with. He'd been the big baseball star there, and had gone on to Mercer U on a scholarship. He'd read about me playing professionally with the Chiefs, and he told me 'I'd never have thought it would have been you!'"

I saw Sonny play the following day, up at Yankee Stadium, where his Chiefs went down 2–1 to the Cosmos. He played the whole game at right back, a disciplined 90 minutes of marking an opponent. Nothing adventurous here, just solid defense in the British tradition (most of his Atlanta teammates were British). As he said, he headed well. He tackled somewhat less well, but never gave up, coming back for more if beaten, remembering to stay goalside. He wasn't the smoothest mover, but neither did he ever look awkward. His play looked like what it was—a role that had been outlined for him, and that he had studied and practiced with meticulous care. I think what impressed me most was that Sonny didn't indulge in wild clearances, he didn't just whack the ball long whenever he got it. That surely would have been the hallmark of an inexperienced player on a British-oriented team.

That was the only time that I saw Sonny Carter play. It is still difficult to believe that that performance—which, if it could not be described as poised, was certainly never naive—was the result of only three years playing the game.

I guess, looking back at it, it bore the stamp of Sonny Carter's particular genius. A sensitive young man who had fallen in love with the sport of soccer. Where others would have made much noise and clamor about their passion, Sonny embraced his new love quietly . . . but relentlessly.

He worked hard at it, learning and watching, absorbing all he could, modestly getting the small things right first. A quiet, almost gentle young man who backed up his dreams with a steely willingness to do the work that would make them come true.

Sonny left the 1991 coaches' convention banquet early, soon after he had delivered his speech. A couple of weeks later, I received a mounted photograph of a spaceship launch, with a lovely personal note from Sonny written on it.

It sent me rummaging about among piles of old photographs for a picture that I had taken of him at that game against the Cosmos in 1971. I wanted to send it in return, but I couldn't lay my hands on it. So I delayed my reply.

Now, I have found the picture, but of course, it's too late. Sonny died on April 5, killed in the crash of a commuter plane. I'm looking at the picture—and, as I suspected, it's not very good. Partly my fault, partly Sonny's—whatever would FIFA say today about this player wearing the big #19, his shirt out, and his socks rolled down?

But Sonny is lithely stalking his prey, a young Italian named Maurizio Minieri, whom the Cosmos had borrowed from Lazio for the season. Minieri went back to Italy—I do not believe he made it as a player.

Sonny Carter didn't really make it as a player either. But he had other things on his mind: other dreams, dreams that soared beyond the little world of soccer. When Sonny told me he'd wanted to be the football punter at high school, I made the obvious, the unimaginative link to kicking and to soccer.

If one could only know . . . if I had known enough to see something more romantic in that wish of a boy who "enjoyed watching the flight of the ball" as it spun high against the sky . . . the boy who went on to become an astronaut.

In his 43 years, Sonny became a pro soccer player, a medical doctor, a fighter pilot, and an astronaut. The rest of us would be satisfied with just one of those achievements. We—I don't mean just soccer, I mean all of us, humankind—we have lost a most remarkable man.

The Loud-Mouthed Strutting Peacocks

NEW YORK—We start with an inarguable fact: goalkeepers are not soccer players. Sure, some of them know how to head the ball, some are reasonably proficient with the ball at their feet, but not much more.

Goalkeepers have more in common with handball or basketball or volleyball players, or maybe with baseball catchers or cricket wicket-keepers than they do with their own teammates.

Yet these interlopers—who make up only 9 percent of a team—have somehow acquired a tremendous influence on the way that soccer is played. And it is a most unhealthy, negative influence.

Their importance represents quite a change of status for goalkeepers. Things were very different back in 1958, when the poor goalkeeper got very little respect. That was the year of a famous incident in the English FA Cup final. Manchester United's goalkeeper, Harry Gregg, parried a hard shot, knocked it up into the air, spun around to catch the falling ball . . . and was charged, in the back, by the Bolton center-forward Nat Lofthouse. Gregg went down, the ball went into the net, and the referee said it was a goal.

That was the way things were in those days. Gregg had clearly been fouled (asked about the incident years later, Lofthouse bluntly replied, "Of course it was a foul"), but charging the goalkeeper was not then an unthinkable no-no, and the referee evidently felt comfortable ruling that the charge was fair.

No doubt it was such blatantly unfair decisions that swung things the goalkeeper's way. The dramatic reversal of attitude was made bitterly clear during the 1982 World Cup in Spain.

Originally published in Soccer America *May 20, 1991. Reprinted with permission of* Soccer America *magazine.*

On June 22 of that year, I had a chat with the English referee Clive White, who was to be the official that night for the game between Hungary and Belgium. A pleasant, encouraging chat in which White agreed that defensive fouling was marring the sport, and should be more severely dealt with.

I watched the game that night with every reason to hope that White would come down hard on Belgium—a team that had already shown a brutal disposition to commit tactical fouls in the opening game against Argentina. A disappointing evening. Belgium's fouling was as cynical as ever, with the speedy, skillful Hungarian forward Laszlo Fazekas as the chief victim. The low point came with 23 minutes left, when Fazekas chased a long ball at full speed. Out came the Belgian goalkeeper, Jean-Marie Pfaff, out of his area, and—according to my notes of the time—"obliterated" Fazekas.

It was a sickening foul, and one feared for Fazekas. He was lucky he was not seriously hurt. Pfaff was even luckier—all he got was a yellow card. (In the interest of fairness, I should point out that Pfaff, earlier in the game, had barreled into one of his own players, defender Eric Gerets, and sent him to the sidelines for treatment.)

I spoke to referee White the following morning, and asked him why, given his strong condemnation of foul play, he didn't give Pfaff a red card? He replied: "Oh no, we'd get into all sorts of trouble if we start sending goalkeepers off."

Two weeks later, we all saw the end result of that mentality when West German goalkeeper Toni Schumacher's criminally reckless foul sent poor Patrick Batiston off the field on a stretcher. And Schumacher got away with it—not even a yellow card!

Goalkeepers were now a highly protected species. Almost any sort of challenge on the goalkeeper was now whistled as a foul, while the goalkeeper himself could carry out a murderous mugging without even being cautioned.

Alongside this absurdly solicitous attitude of the referees came another form of protection for goalkeepers: the packed defenses of the modern game. More and more frequently, games were played in which you could count the number of shots on one hand, games in which the goalkeepers had virtually nothing to do.

They soon found something to do. They started to yell and to scream and to strut. In particular, they began that obnoxious practice of theatrically yelling at their own teammates whenever an opponent took a shot on goal. Grandstanding, letting everyone know that whatever happened, it wasn't the goalkeeper's fault.

As for the shouting—well, we all know that a good goalkeeper is supposed to help organize the defense. But go to a college game—any college game—and just listen to the goalkeepers (you won't have any trouble hearing them, I guarantee). Just listen to the drivel they're shouting. A good 75 percent of it nothing more than brainless cheerleading or worse.

Frankly, it puzzles me how defenders in college soccer restrain themselves from belting their own goalkeeper across the chops from time to time, just to shut him up. How do they put up with the guy yelling *Clear it!* and *Heads!* to them? Do they need that?

Consider today's goalkeeper. He has become a loudly dressed, loud-mouthed, strutting peacock of a player. With his personalized shirts and personalized gloves and personalized shorts and personalized padding and personalized sun visor—with all that stuff to market, no wonder there are specialized goalkeeper camps. Maybe they'd like to add something really useful—like a personalized pacifier—to that list of marketable equipment?

Sadly, the goalkeeper has also become a rather arrogant figure on the field. This business of being a protected species, of being immune to the punishments reserved for ordinary players, has clearly gone to his head.

Watch him come out to grab an easy high ball. The opposing forwards, of course, are frightened to go anywhere near him, in case they get sent off or banned for life. No matter, the goalie still comes out with his knee up, foot raised. Any other player going for the ball like that would immediately be called for a foul, and rightly so. But not the goalkeeper.

Watch him stand around, holding the ball, the main focus of time-wasting in the game. Watch him survey the field before him, as though calculating some master move—and then watch him whack the ball any old where, as high and as long and as brainlessly as he can manage.

In short, the goalkeeper has become "a bit of a nuisance in terms of spoiling the game"—that's what England coach Graham Taylor has to say about things. He's quite right, and this lamentable state of affairs has come about because goalkeepers have simply become too big for their (customized) boots.

Let us recall that there was once an idyllic time when there was no such animal as a goalkeeper. When he first appeared on the scene back in the 1870s, he was liable to be called the "custodian of the sticks," and it was clearly stated by the rulemakers that he was "allowed to use his hands in defense of his goal."

It wouldn't be a bad idea to take that definition pretty literally. And it does seem that FIFA is going to do that. How can receiving a back pass from a teammate be construed as defending the goal? It cannot, so the goalkeeper shouldn't be allowed to use his hands on those. How is standing around holding the ball "defending" the goal? It ain't, so the goalie shouldn't be allowed to get away with it.

FIFA, commendably, has landed on those two problems and has suggested that both practices be banished (less commendably, as I pointed out recently, it proposed to instigate the changes in the under-17 World Cup finals in Italy).

So things are moving in the right direction there. The goalkeeper will have to use his feet, will have to become a bit more of a soccer player. (A few more Rene Higuitas would certainly make for a more colorful game.) But more is needed before the various goalkeeping excesses can be said to be under control.

I'm not sure what we can do about all the yelling and posturing, but that is probably best handled by the goalkeeper's own teammates. They should be able to find a way to get him to pipe down. Maybe they should just keep peppering him with cries of *Dive!* and *Catch it!* whenever he's actually called upon to do anything. If that doesn't do it, the entire team could take to racing back to remonstrate (theatrically, of course) with the goalkeeper when he lets one in, and before he has time to blame it on them.

There remains another avenue to be explored, one further way of reducing the bothersome influence of the modern 'keeper. Which is to limit his area of activity. I discussed this approach briefly last July, when I was in the throes of post–Italia '90 depression and suggested that "the goalkeeper should have his wings clipped a bit by cutting down the area in which he can handle the ball."

Can it really be called "defense of his goal" when he can venture 18 yards out to grab a cross with his hands? Would it not be better if we could make the goalkeeper try to make a genuine save of any shot or header on goal that results from the cross, rather than allow him to snuff out the cross itself? Is that not, more accurately, "defense of his goal"?

If not 18 yards, then how far should we allow the goalkeeper to roam? I don't know—you have to experiment with changes of this sort. If you want to keep things simple and keep the costs down, then retain the present field markings and limit the goalkeeper's handling to the six-yard box. That seems a bit too cramped to me—but it may not be. I would suggest doing away with the six-yard box, and replacing it with a new box of either 10 or 12 yards. Leave the penalty area as it is (too many changes make everyone nervous, especially the International Board, which has the final say).

So the goalkeeper now has only a 10- or 12-yard area within which to handle the ball. Give him full protection within that area. (Though this should be a bargaining point. In return, the goalkeeper should agree to shut up, to cut out the grandstanding, and to wear less lurid shirts.)

Then, perhaps, we shall see more of the truly exciting and wonderfully athletic things that goalkeepers are supposed to do—the fingertip saves, the breathtaking leaps and dives, the sudden pounces, the lightning reactions. In short, we shall see more *real* goalkeeping.

Ending the Ennui: Soccer Can Stop the Stall

"Victory justifies the means."
Ljubomir Petrovic

NEW YORK—Just when it seemed that soccer's scoring drought couldn't get any worse, along come coach Ljubomir Petrovic and his Red Star team from Belgrade, Yugoslavia.

By playing 120 minutes of totally negative, defensive soccer, Red Star stalled its way to a 0–0 overtime tie against Olympique Marseille in this year's European Cup final. It then took the trophy—the top honor for European club teams—by winning a penalty-kick tiebreaker, 5–3.

A wretched business, because this was an eagerly awaited game between two supposedly enterprising teams. On the day of the game, *The Times* of London had hailed the game as having "the ingredients for a marvelous spectacle with a profusion of skill in midfield."

Red Star squashed that hope with its defensive tactics. Blithely rubbing salt into the wound, Petrovic made no secret of the fact that Red Star was deliberately stalling throughout the game, trying to arrive at the penalty kick tiebreaker, which he was certain his team would win.

After the game, Petrovic said, "We did not invent the present rules, and the rules include penalties and invite the use of tactics to reach the penalty shootout stage. For most of the second half, and in overtime, we were deliberately waiting for penalties."

Originally published in The New York Times *July 21, 1991. Copyright © 1991 by The New York Times Co. Reprinted by permission.*

In other words, it was the tiebreaker, the little penalty-shooting contest tacked on at the end of the game, that *caused* this debacle. In the words of Franz Beckenbauer, the technical director of Marseille, Red Star had "refused to play" while stalling for the penalties.

Aware that his tactics had turned the game into a parody of soccer, Petrovic said defiantly; "We weren't there to put on a show."

Petrovic had cynically exploited soccer's weaknesses and its rules to the full, had made a travesty of an important game, and—the most unforgivable achievement—had come up a winner. There have been other recent penalty-kick champions: Portugal when it won the under-20 world championship last month, for example, and the United States when it won the Concacaf Gold Cup last weekend in Los Angeles. But neither of these victories was the result of deliberate stalling tactics.

Red Star's tarnished victory may yet have its positive side. For it has exposed the fatal flaw of the penalty-kick tiebreaker, and in doing so has drawn attention to the deeper reason for soccer's malaise.

The tiebreaker is flawed because it consists of a totally separate event, added on at the end of the game. Whenever any form of add-on tiebreaker is used, there are bound to be teams that feel more confident of winning the tiebreaker than the actual game. A situation that will "invite the use of tactics" to arrive at the tiebreaker.

That would not matter too much if it weren't so very easy to stall in soccer. Where American sports—by the 24-second rule, or by limiting strikes or downs—have eliminated stalling, soccer, traditionally slow to change its rules, has yet to find an answer to the problem.

Rather, it has yet to *adopt* an answer that already exists, one that does not involve any rule-changing at all. Simply this: to count corner kicks gained during a game and to use them as a tiebreaker.

The beauty of using corner kicks as a tiebreaker is that corner kicks are an integral part of the regular game, not an add-on. They go to work the instant the game starts—and it is almost unheard of for a game not to feature corner kicks. In the 103-year history of the English pro league, only one such game has been recorded.

A team intent only on defense will, inevitably, give up corner kicks—but it is unlikely to gain any. The final corner kick score in the European Cup final was 7–1 to Marseille, an accurate reflection of which team had been playing attacking soccer. Red Star, which fell behind on corners early in the game, would have been quickly forced out of its defensive shell. But clearly the mere threat of corner kicks would have rendered Petrovic's defensive tactics suicidal, so that he would never have used them in the first place.

Opponents suggest that the corner kick tiebreaker would distort the game by encouraging teams to "play for corner kicks." A strange criticism, in the light of the damage done to soccer by teams like Red Star that pervert the game almost beyond recognition while stalling for penalty kicks.

The gaining of a corner kick can only come from attacking play, and once gained, a corner kick is acknowledged as one of soccer's more likely scoring opportunities.

While the corner kick tiebreaker will not solve all of soccer's woes, it will at least attack the root of the problem: stalling.

Soccer Is Not a Science

NEW YORK—The relationship between society and soccer remains a mysterious one. It has not really been explored with any great intelligence, and certainly not in a global context. I say that with some hesitation, because I'm aware that quite learned works do exist on the subject. But it seems to me they all have a major drawback.

Most of those that I have read are written by sociologists—already a big problem, as it tends to make them difficult to read, full of elaborate theories, weighed down by turgid prose and ugly, pseudotechnical jargon. But the biggest fault is that they are obviously written by people who simply do not know the sport of soccer. Or, better, do not understand the soccer scene.

So we get books where the authors—intelligent, educated people, all of them—"discover" things about soccer that most of us have known for ages, and write them about them in terms of incredulous (and ultimately laughable) wonder.

Books where elaborate studies are done on the game and this sort of conclusion is drawn: that players tend to pass the ball more to their friends than to teammates whom they don't like. That was some years ago passed off as a constructive, scientific observation that would presumably lead to a better understanding of soccer. It has its possibilities, I suppose. It might, for instance, be possible to explain the rise of defensive soccer by a sudden increase in the number of immensely likable goalkeepers.

The rise of hooliganism has not only spread mayhem in the stadiums and the streets. It has caused other damage by proving irresistibly attractive to

Originally published in Soccer America *July 22, 1991. Reprinted with permission of* Soccer America *magazine.*

sociologists, far more attractive than the soccer itself has ever been. The literature on hooliganism is now substantial, replete with all the trappings of academic learning, the footnotes and the references and the cross-references, and, of course, the ever-growing reading lists.

I read these works—both on soccer and hooliganism—and around page 10 (certainly by the end of Chapter 1), an impertinent question is demanding an answer: has the author ever actually *been* to a soccer game? Has he (or, quite likely with sociologists, she) ever witnessed hooligans in action? The interviews with players (or self-confessed hooligans) have a suspiciously unreal air about them, as though the interviewer is being strung along, told any old thing while the player or hooligan has a good laugh at the stupidity of it all.

The problem being that the vast majority of the sociologists are ignorant of the roots and traditions of the sport. They don't know what questions to ask, and they have no way of intelligently assessing an answer, of deciding whether it is meaningful or simply nonsense. But the sociologists go ahead anyway. There is an arrogance about education and book-learning that insists that it be taken seriously, even when (or especially when) it is at its most pretentious.

As if the academic sociologists were not enough, soccer has also been invaded by the popularizing sociologists, the sport's equivalent of those with-it clergymen who like to invite rock groups into their church. You will find that branch of learning at its most elaborate in Desmond Morris's book *The Soccer Tribe* (which I was much alarmed to see on *Soccer America*'s recent list of bookshelf essentials). A superbly produced work, full of beautifully reproduced photographs, and—it must be admitted—one or two interesting insights into the game. But on the whole, the book is stuffed with eminently silly twaddle.

I am particularly fond of Morris's chapter on "The Triumph Displays," in which he attempts to classify all the various ways that players celebrate scoring a goal. The British never used to do much of this, but learned it from the "emotion-free Latins." That is Morris's phrase, not mine. It ought to mean someone who has no emotions, but it doesn't, not when Dr. Morris uses it (sociologists are not great respecters of language). It means someone who shows his emotions freely, as opposed to someone who (like the British) is emotion-shy.

Having established that, Morris goes on to a hilarious listing of the triumph displays. Well, I think it's hilarious, though I have a sneaking suspicion that we're supposed to take his various categories seriously. We have The Arms Aloft (not, please, to be confused with The Leaping Fists-Aloft), the Back-Tilt, the Multi-Embrace, and the Horizontal Embrace, and many others.

In The Embrace Invitation, we are told "the players run toward one another with their arms stretched out sideways as far as they will go, signaling 'I am about to embrace you' . . . sometimes there is an obvious conflict between inviting an embrace and raising the arms aloft, with the result that they point diagonally upward."

Another of Dr. Morris's startling discoveries is The Frontal Leap-Cling, and its more suggestive cousin, the Rear Leap-Cling: "Occasionally, the leap-cling is performed from behind, in which case the couple are likely to topple over backwards and come to rest on the ground in a confused heap." Wow!

Among other original revelations in Morris's work, you can learn that "when overcome by dejection, players adopt a heads-down posture." And Wow! again.

All that is merely laughable, and can surely be seen to be laughable by anyone who has his head screwed on correctly. Things get trickier when the sociologists start to educate us on aspects of soccer in which, maybe, they do have expert knowledge. In Morris's book, he talks about the social life of players, and declares "footballers make better than average family men and excellent parents partly because, like soldiers at war, they value the quiet moments at home more than other men, and partly because, having fought hard on the field, they feel less need to throw their weight about when they return to their families at the end of the day."

Logical enough, in a pedantic sort of way, and one's inclination, I suppose, would be to accept it. After all, it comes from a sociologist, and they're supposed to know about that sort of thing. But is it true? Morris cites no evidence whatever to back up his claims.

It is difficult to believe that this combination of piffle and vague assertions comes from a man who is one of the world's leading experts in human and animal behavior. I think there might be a common bond here between sociologists and businessmen: put either of them anywhere near soccer, and they immediately lose all the intelligence and acumen that have made them successful in their chosen fields.

Part—quite a large part—of the problem when sociologists write about soccer is exactly the same one that arises when the modern academic teacher/coaches get to work. Suddenly, everything must be defined, a term must be invented to describe every move and every action. And the tighter, the more strict the definition, the better (by definition, if I may use the word) it is considered to be.

If I dismiss Dr. Morris's demotic definitions (rear leap-cling indeed!) as just plain silly, it is not so easy to get rid of much of the coaching terminology. There, the devotees would defend this matter of definition as scientific, an attempt to produce accuracy.

The danger, as I see it, is this: strict definition carries with it the stamp of inflexibility, of rigid thinking. In the true sciences, no doubt, everything *can* be categorized, must be categorized. But soccer is not a science, it is a most unruly slice of human behavior that does not, will not, lend itself to easy definition. If it is to be classed as some sort of discipline, then it is a very sloppy discipline indeed.

It has a shape of sorts, I suppose, but it is one that is constantly altering. It changes, just as a team formation changes on the field, according to circumstances—if not from day to day, certainly from year to year. Any attempt to impose scientific certainty on such a protean entity is bound to lead to distortion.

If you want to hear the true voice of soccer, capture the real atmosphere of the game, then the only way is to live in the world of soccer—to be there at the games, talk with the people who are involved, the players and the coaches and the managers. The other trick is that you have to know enough to sort out the truth from the BS. Not easy—not even journalists get it right all the time!

I started by talking about books on soccer, and have been denigrating the sociological works. An alternative is books by players and coaches, but here again one has to be careful, because so many of these are written more to make the author look good than to throw light on the sport itself. If you want a glowing exception to that rule, try Eamon Dunphy's *Only a Game?* (I was delighted to see this one on *Soccer America*'s essential reading list).

What Dunphy gets over, with wonderfully simple language, is the gut feeling, the sounds and the sights and the smells, of what it is like to be a professional soccer player. The book is not meant to be either scientific or glamorous—it simply is what it is. As such, it tells much more about the relationship of soccer to society, and maybe about the soccer player's merits as a husband, than all of your sociological treatises.

Dunphy's book has its limitations, because it deals mainly with the English scene. Alas, I have read no similarly down-to-earth book from another country.

Time to make peace with the sociologists. Herewith the exception to the rule; a well-researched, well-written book by a sociologist who obviously knows a thing or two about soccer: Stephen Wagg's *The Football World: A Contemporary Social History.* This one really does set soccer in its social context, without the obscurantism of sociological scholarship and jargon. It has the same fault as Dunphy's, in that it is essentially English in outlook. But an immensely worthwhile read, for all that.

New World Meets the Old
Under-17 World Cup–1991

MONTECATINI, Italy—A beautiful little town, this—but an odd choice as the site for a youth tournament. The prevailing atmosphere in Montecatini is one of respectability, of sedate old age, of retirement. You walk around the delightful little streets, and it comes to you that you really are strolling—moving slowly with the rest of Montecatini, patiently making its way along the crowded sidewalks.

Middle-aged and elderly people, well-dressed, respectable people. Many of them, of course, visitors here to sample the supposedly health-giving waters of this spa town. You notice quickly that almost every other building seems to be a hotel . . . but what hotels! Stately affairs, with huge lobbies and landings, high ceilings, marble walls, polished wood floors, and glistening chandeliers.

The lobbies are cool and quiet, apparently empty. But waiters stand watching, every now and then gliding forward to attend to the needs of the elderly clients who are hidden in the huge high-backed chairs. A sudden sharp click of a heel on the floor, the staccato rattle of spoon against saucer, a soft but persistently echoing conversation are the only sound effects.

Into this lazy atmosphere of strolling senior citizens and hotel lobbies where it is forever Sunday afternoon comes the under-17 World Cup, the violent noisy world of international soccer. Bands of hooligans yelling obscenities in the tidy little streets? Mobs breaking up the sleepy lobbies?

No, no. In this meeting of two different worlds, it is the old, the prim and proper, that has triumphed. You can tell where the soccer world starts . . .

Originally published in Soccer America *September 2, 1991. Reprinted with permission of* Soccer America *magazine.*

and almost at the same time, where it ends. As you wander around, you notice that a few of the hotels have little groups of bored-looking cops standing around the entrances. The hotels where the teams are staying, of course. Maybe the cops are there to keep the hooligans out, maybe they are there to keep the teams in. But mostly, it seems, they are just *there*, with no function other than to talk to each other.

The boys eat in the hotels, they take large buses to the practice fields, they sleep . . . and they even hang out in the sacred lobbies. Above all, they are well-behaved. Little is seen of them in the town—an occasional group of players in track suits is about all you get, and the good citizens of Montecatini stare for a moment, then get on with the business of contented strolling.

The exception occurred on the day before the tournament started. Chaos in the center of town, traffic brought to a standstill in the tiny Piazza del Popolo by a yelling mob, appeals for calm over the PA, finally the arrival of the police to restore order. Causing all the trouble, at the center of the pushing, shoving crowd . . . Pelé, taking it all in good humor, smiling and carefully signing, one after another, the pieces of paper being waved all around his head.

You look at the excited crowd, you watch with your heart in your mouth as an old guy with shining gray hair clambers laboriously to the top of a small concrete post for a better view, and it hits you that these are not youngsters—this is a temporary derangement of these same people who stroll up and down the streets in such a well-behaved way.

Nowhere is that well-behaved atmosphere stronger than in *La Pace* Hotel. It seems to be the headquarters not only of the under-17 World Cup, but of old Montecatini, too. The FIFA dignitaries fit right in here, sober in their dress, dignified in their bearing. A notable exception, as far as the dress code goes, is USSF president Alan Rothenberg, glaringly visible in shorts and a garish World Cup '94 T-shirt. A piece of new-world brashness that is clearly not appreciated by the traditionally minded FIFA biggies.

Hardly something that is going to bother Rothenberg in his present mood. The U.S.'s Gold Cup victory was fresh in everyone's minds when news arrived that the United States had won the championship of the Pan American Games. Rothenberg, whose attractive smile is almost enough to blot out a tasteless T-shirt, received congratulations from all sides.

More. That same night, as Rothenberg left for the race track, Concacaf secretary Chuck Blazer slipped him $100 to place a few bets—on the theory that everything Rothenberg smiled on was turning to gold. Rothenberg's first horse was a wire-to-wire winner, and he returned to the hotel that evening to present Blazer with his winnings.

There was more success the following day, as the United States defeated Italy 1–0 in the opening game. And more *gaucherie* from the United States—

this time from United States Youth Soccer Association (USYSA) chairman Bob Contiguglia, seen jumping up and down loudly in the VIP section. Leading to further raising of FIFA eyebrows.

There is not much jumping up and down in the world of FIFA, where things are done slowly and quietly. Generally speaking, that is—for the under-17 World Cup, as it happens, had to be put together in a tremendous rush. The decision to move the tournament from its original site, Ecuador (because of the cholera epidemic in neighboring Peru), left the committee in Montecatini with only five months to organize the whole thing, to arrange hotels for 16 teams, and to set up the 32 games to be played in six different cities.

A complicated operation, and an expensive one, too. One that will end up costing FIFA—or its marketing arm, International Sports, Culture and Leisure Marketing AG (ISL)—about $2 million. Worrying figures, for they cast a cloud over the future of the tournament. There is virtually no television income for this tournament, and a look at the attendance figures for the first few games tells you that ticket sales are not going to be a major revenue producer.

The opening game, featuring the home team, Italy, drew only 3,254 spectators, and things got worse after that: 350 people for China vs. Argentina, 146 for Congo vs. Qatar, 798 for Ghana vs. Cuba, only 80 for Sudan vs. United Arab Emirates. The alarm bells start ringing loudly when you see that only a few hundred turned up on a perfect evening in Massa to see Brazil play Germany. All this with eminently reasonable ticket prices, ranging from $3.50 to $12.50.

It is alarming, and it is sad, because there is so much good soccer to be seen. China and Argentina put on a wonderful 80 minutes of skill and speed and sportsmanship. The Argentines, in particular, were on their best behavior. Their performance in the under-20 World Cup in Portugal in June is generally agreed to have been a disgrace, and they are certainly being closely watched by FIFA. A conspiracy of silence surrounds the team. "Problems?" says the Argentine federation president Julio Grondona. "There are no problems with the team." One persists: but surely, after Portugal, and with the same coach, Reinaldo Merlo, still in charge . . . ? No, Grondona does not budge: "Merlo is a gentleman. The only problem we had in Portugal was with Señor Juan Esnaider (the young Real Madrid player banned from international competition for one year for trying to strike a referee).

The day after Argentina's 2–1 victory over China, Merlo himself appeared relaxed, and talked freely in his hotel as his players assembled for the evening meal. I remarked on what a clean game it had been, with only three physical fouls by Argentina, none of them violent. Merlo smiled and said "Yes." And, I continued, none of his players had argued with the referee. Another enigmatic smile from Merlo: "In Argentina, the players are used to arguing, but it

1991: Montecatini, Italy—Argentina has just clinched third place in the under-17 World Cup, and 15-year-old Marcelo Gallardo gives his version of their win over Qatar. Seven years later, at France '98, I watched Gallardo again, this time starring for the full Argentina national team. *Copyright Paul Gardner*

is something we are trying to correct. Perhaps we have been successful?" Was he under pressure to produce a superclean team? "No, no one has put any pressure on me."

Later, a couple of Argentine journalists insisted to me that it is not true, and that there had been a meeting in which Grondona had made it clear that Merlo's job was on the line if there was any trouble.

Whatever the reason, the new trouble-free Argentina was a delight to watch, with 15-year-old Marcelo Gallardo a wonderful embodiment of superb ball skills and poise. But the Argentines are a young team, average age 16 years, 4 months. The Italian coach, Sergio Vatta, still smarting from his team's 1–0 loss to the United States, looked ahead to his next game and declared that he was not afraid of Argentina, whom he described as "relatively naive, the youngest team in the tournament."

An interesting observation, for the official figures show that Ghana (16 years, 1 month) and Congo (16 years, 3 months) are younger. When this was pointed out to Vatta, he merely shrugged—surely a mute acknowledgment of what many still feel to be an awkward truth: that the ages of the African and Asian teams are suspect.

Suspect or not, it is Ghana that is exciting the most comment. A narrow 2–1 victory over Cuba does not reflect the dazzling play of the Ghanaians. The day after the game, a group of Ghanaian officials made it clear why the margin of victory was so narrow: "The referee!" said one of them in an extraordinarily loud voice. "The referee!" He banged the metal table so loudly that even the old hotel dog, sleeping peacefully in the afternoon sun, raised its head for a brief moment. "A penalty denied, a good goal canceled . . . and why did he caution our player when he should have given the Cuban a red card? FIFA should send that referee home."

The star of the Ghana team is the remarkable Nii Odartey Lamptey, who is already a first-team player with the Belgian first division team Anderlecht. It is rumored that he has been targeted by Marseille, the center of an as-yet-unannounced $15 million transfer deal.

Lamptey has competition here—from the Brazilians, of course. If there is an award for the goal of the tournament, it is likely that it has already been won by the Brazilian Adriano, with his superb solo effort against Germany. At the end of the first half, a poor German clearance landed suddenly at Adriano's feet, just outside the penalty area. It is more accurate to say that the ball struck him. But he was ready. The ball was under control in an instant, and Adriano was threading his way, with physical power allied to delicate touches of the ball and incredible balance, past *four* closely packed German defenders, right down the heart of the German defense in the middle of the penalty area.

The sparse crowd was already rising to its feet and yelling as Adriano twisted clear of the knot of defenders to confront the goalkeeper. With one elegant sway of his body, Adriano dismissed the 'keeper and rolled the ball sweetly into the goal.

A moment of breathtaking soccer, made all the more beautiful by the sight of a couple of the German players softly applauding.

Roasted Cuckoo Crumbs and the Certainties of Coaching

NEW YORK—We shall begin today, logically enough, with the death of Charles II of England, in 1685. The poor man was suffering from some sort of kidney disease. The doctors—there were more than a dozen of them—tried just about everything that they knew. Which was, at one and the same time, too little and too much.

They cut off his hair and plonked blistering poultices on his bare scalp, they applied plasters of pitch and pigeon dung to the soles of his feet, they poured emetics and purgatives down his throat, and to be on the safe side, gave him enemas as well. Antimony, zinc sulphate, spirit of human skull, Peruvian bark, cowslip, manna, and mint, and God knows what else went pouring into the unfortunate king. Above all, as was the generally accepted practice in those days, they bled him, removing pints of royal blood at a time.

Good King Charlie, a mere 55 years old, withstood the therapeutic onslaught for five days, then conked out, probably from loss of blood. A historian later remarked that the doctors had denied him only three things: light, rest, and privacy. Not quite. The king was also suffering from convulsions, so the tireless medics could have blown crumbs of roasted cuckoo up his nostrils, a practice that was once considered a surefire cure for epilepsy.

My purpose in relating this elevating tale is to undermine the experts, to cast doubt on their solemn word, to throw scorn on the certainty with which they speak. The point being that the doctors who committed the above-mentioned excesses were not just any old doctors, they were the cream of the

Originally published in Soccer America *November 11, 1991. Reprinted with permission of* Soccer America *magazine.*

English medical profession. They represented the pinnacle of the profession, all that was best in medical wisdom.

They were not, of course, trying to bleed their patient to death. They were trying to bleed him to life. They were doing the *right* thing. Bleeding was how you removed all sorts of nasty humors and pernicious distempers from the body. How else would you do that than by draining off the fluid that was carrying them? It was logical, and it was backed up with a good deal of persuasive reasoning and theory. Persuasive, that is, in the sense that hardly anyone could understand it, so that it must therefore be immensely clever.

History is full of such examples of the high and mighty making fools of themselves. Quite possibly, history is nothing but such examples. Because the scope of knowledge does widen, we *do* know more than our forefathers, we *can* see how primitive were their methods. Roasted cuckoo crumbs indeed!

We like to think that we learn from the past, that we will not repeat old errors—so no more cuckoo crumbs. Well, OK, that seems reasonable (though I, for one, am not betting against a cuckoo crumb revival). But the cuckoo crumbs are not what matters: they are the easy target, and in sweeping them so contemptuously aside we tend to overlook the real lesson.

Which is the experts themselves. If we assume that all experts are intelligent people (not, I fear, a reliable assumption, but let's go with it), then we have to admit that the proven inadequacy of bygone experts was not the result of stupidity. It was the result of ignorance (strange thing for an expert, no?) and of arrogance.

As those ancient sages did not, could not, know what we know now, the ignorance is excusable. The arrogance is not. Yet it is the arrogance that persists. It persists because it is encouraged to persist—by the likes of you and me. We all tend to be impressed by knowledge, willing to accept unquestioningly the views of those who are alleged to know more than we do.

Television has cashed in on this subservience and created a whole industry of instant experts. Experts for everything that can possibly happen. It could be that as I am writing this, somewhere in the United States a precocious French poodle is sitting down at the piano to rattle off the first-ever canine performance of Beethoven's *Moonlight Sonata.* If that be so, then tonight, on the tube, we shall have Professor Somebody-or-other, the well-known expert in doggy pianistics. In fact, we'll get at least three professors, one for each network. And we'll hear more of *them* than we will of the pooch pawing the keyboard.

The essential thing about the experts will be their certainty. They *know.* Well, that's what they're for, isn't it? If they start humming and hawing and hesitating, I mean, what kind of an expert is that? We want unarguable facts from our experts, not wishy-washy maybes.

Lost in all this is the one lasting lesson that history has to teach us: that there are very few, if any, eternal certainties. Eternal? Someone might want to do a study on the shelf life of certainties (damn, I've just created a new expert, the Professor of Certainties). He'd no doubt find that, around the time that Charles II was being cured to death, a certainty probably lasted at least 100 years, far longer than anyone lived, which meant that a certainty was a certainty. Change was slow, and by the time it arrived, everyone who remembered way-back-when was dead.

But today, good grief, such is the pace of new scientific discoveries that a certainty is likely to be debunked within 10 years, if not 10 minutes. A process that ought to have resulted in a healthy questioning of the experts' claims to superior wisdom . . . but which has had, if anything, the opposite effect. As the traditional certainties crumble before our very eyes, we've discovered that we're lost without them. So new certainties are created, and are fervently accepted. Many of them, probably most of them, will prove rather quickly to be nonsense. In short, the roasted cuckoo crumbs have never gone away— they have just changed their name.

Said Claud Cockburn, one of the most brilliant of journalists: "It is almost always fatal to pin any faith to the belief that the professionals in any line—from newspaper proprietorship to field marshals—have much idea of what they are up to." To that group I would add architects (the worst of the lot) . . . and soccer coaches.

I fear that in soccer we have more than our fair share of experts, and of cuckoo crumbs. I was reminded of this the other morning, while watching an Italian league game on television. Alessandro Bianchi of Inter was shaping up to kick the ball, when he collapsed with a sudden muscle pull. Late in the game, Lothar Matthaus left the field, also with a pulled muscle. The commentator was going on about Inter's problems, suggesting that some of them might be caused by the players not warming up properly.

Warming up is, of course, one of the current indisputable certainties of any athletic activity. I'm sure I do not exaggerate if I say that any coach who omits stretching and all that sort of stuff runs the risk of being sued should someone get badly injured. Warming up is also, at least as far as soccer is concerned, a comparatively recent certainty.

Ten years ago, I listened to former FIFA president Sir Stanley Rous telling me that he was quite certain that the number of injuries in soccer had increased over the years. He was particularly critical of injuries that happened during training, and expressed serious doubts about warming-up procedures. He made one fascinating point. In the old days (neither good nor bad, just old) hardly any players had cars, and most walked to the training sites. They arrived already warmed up in the most efficient, natural way. (A few years after that, I found out that goalkeeper Bert Williams, one of my boyhood heroes, actually walked to practice on tiptoe, believing that this increased his springiness.)

Walking is out, BMWs and Audis are in. Times have changed, so we have elaborate warming-up routines. Do they work? Not being an expert in that field, I don't know. I imagine they do, they sound logical, and all sorts of learned people support them. But beware. For they represent, can only represent, the state of current knowledge. Listen to this from *The New York Times,* just one year ago [September 27, 1990]: "Scientists are developing a new understanding of how muscles function, leading them to suspect that warming up before exercise does not protect muscle fibers from injury."

That "new understanding" should not surprise anyone who is not overly impressed by the claims of experts. Frankly, it would not greatly shock me if the next stage was for another expert to find out that warming up actually makes muscle fibers more susceptible to damage.

I have been talking about the medical field, which has some claim to being scientific, but must also operate at the popular level. Precisely because of that, it is a most fertile area for the development of pseudoscientific nonsense.

Soccer—probably more than any other sport—is right up there with it. A popular activity with a totally false claim to scientific accuracy. An activity that has become infested with "experts" who *know* what is right, who can correct everything that is being done wrong. Those experts, of course, are the modern coaches with their bloodless, draftsman's view of the sport and their interminable theories about the way the game should be played.

Over 20 years ago, I was sent, by a FIFA coach, an elaborate manuscript for a coaching book, beautifully typed, with a mass of rather fetching little drawings, all done by hand. Could I find an American publisher? I did not, though I have to confess that I didn't work too hard at it. Some 15 years later, I ran into the coach again, and sheepishly apologized for my lack of success. I even felt obliged to offer a renewed effort. The coach laughed—"Oh, it doesn't matter now, it's all changed. Everything's out of date."

The book had seemed to me fairly sensible. But the vast majority of soccer theories are pretty worthless, certainties that will be soon forgotten, replaced by other, equally spurious notions. You could call that progress, except that it doesn't get anyone anywhere. If anything, it tends to obscure the basic truths. Because these vapid theories about the "real" nature of soccer, the "inside" game, the "only method," and so on are always advanced with the most extraordinary fervor. They are laid on us as the ultimate truth, and we are damned if we don't worship the light.

Humbug. All such theories should be subjected to a remorseless scrutiny. Most of them will simply not withstand such treatment. I am hoping that such a process is going on at the USSF right now, where they are supposed to be rewriting the syllabus for the coaching schools. Because the coaching schools have been allowed to degenerate into centers for doctrinal certainties and party-line thinking.

If the schools feel they must deal in certainties, they can seize on the only one we have, and its elaboration should provide them with enough material for all their courses. Namely, that the game of soccer is only as good as the players. All the rest is roasted cuckoo crumbs.

New York, New York, It's a Soccer Town

NEW YORK—Don't get me wrong. I loved the Cosmos, and everything they did for soccer—all that excitement and all the great players and games they brought to New York. I loved every second of it, I get childishly sad when I think about those days, I wish it could all come back. . . .

But it was never quite right, the Cosmos scene, never exactly a soccer setup. I have to admit, I never liked the Cosmos Cheerleaders (heavens, that's done it!), and I secretly resented all those glamorous showbiz types who paraded about in the locker rooms after games. I definitely despised the artificial turf, and I used to seethe at the superior know-nothing experts, big journalistic names from other sports who occasionally condescended to turn up in the press box.

There *was* an unreal quality about it all—but it was fun, and I don't remember complaining too much at the time. But if you've got the idea that the New York Cosmos and New York soccer were one and the same thing—no way, no way.

There are guys around, pretty old most of them (I mean, even older than me), who will tell you about games in the 1920s that used to draw thousands and thousands to Yankee Stadium, and indoor games in one of the old Madison Square Gardens, in the same era, that competed with six-day cycling events.

I guess they're right, but the figures and the exaggerations don't really matter. The point is, there's a history, a tradition, of soccer in this city. Real basic soccer, Sunday afternoon stuff played in the wind and the rain or the withering sun, played where people stand around the touchline and yell obscene things at the ref and players alike, played on fields where the ball

Originally published in Soccer America *November 25, 1991. Reprinted with permission of* Soccer America *magazine.*

keeps being kicked over the fence, where there's barely room for a whole team to get into the locker room at the same time.

It was the devotion of the fans who went to places like that that led to the Cosmos. Every so often, the promoters would bring in a top team, and the diehards would turn out in large numbers. They brought in Liverpool in 1948, and 18,000 turned up at Ebbets Field. Who do you think they were? Yuppies? Youth soccer types? No sir, they were the same longtime soccer people who turned out 15 years later when Bill Cox started his International Soccer League (ISL) up at another baseball ground that's since been turned into a housing estate: the Polo Grounds.

That's where I got my introduction to the New York soccer fans, ethnics mostly in those days, the ones who used to come to cheer for the flag. I also saw how they loved to be entertained, and in 1960 Bill Cox had a wonderful Brazilian team, Bangu, that entertained everyone. It was fun, and it was soccer. And, of course, it didn't last. The Mets arrived to claim the Polo Grounds, so the ISL got shunted over to Randall's Island.

It wasn't bad in those days, and the crowds continued to come, and Bill Cox continued to come up with great little teams. In 1961, there was Dukla Prague, with four players who would play on Czechoslovakia's World Cup team the following year (they were beaten in the final by Brazil), including the captain, Ladislav Novak, and Josef Masopust, European Player of the Year in 1962. Dukla also had a youngster called Rudi Kucera, a darting, quicksilver little forward who scored a hatful of goals (he got five against Shamrock Rovers one night). Tragically, Kucera was soon out of soccer, victim of a serious head injury. No one who saw him can doubt that the world lost a potentially great player.

In 1963, England's West Ham United arrived—so we saw Bobby Moore, Geoff Hurst, and Martin Peters as young players—and three years later they'd be leading England to the World Cup. By then, the ISL was dead, and it almost sounds like that's the way the sport goes in New York, like it doesn't last.

But it does, of course, because way beneath the Cosmos level, not so far beneath the ISL level, lies the world of the Sunday leagues. Amateurs, semi-pros, old-timers, kids, and referees—they're all part of it, the true soccer people who turn up every weekend at dozens of little fields, wedged away in unlikely parts of the city.

Let me tell you about one of those fields. . . .

The poor guy had only uttered a two-word question. But he had produced shock and a stunned silence among his listeners—a group of New York soccer people, staring at him like he should do the decent thing and shoot himself.

Out in Maspeth, Queens—hemmed in by abandoned warehouses and factories, but with the Manhattan skyline as a majestic backdrop—sits the heart and soul of New York City soccer: decaying, dirty, rundown Met Oval, as it was in 1962. Sadly it was no better in 1998, but that year a concerted move to save the Oval was begun. *Copyright Paul Gardner*

He had been told that tomorrow's game would be "at The Oval." And he had asked, "What oval?"

What Oval? What Wembley? What Maracanã? Met Oval, that's what Oval. Metropolitan Oval, in Queens. Sounds great, doesn't it? Well, in all honesty, it's a dump. But a lovable, living, vital, essential dump. Lord knows what New York soccer would do without the Oval.

I'm not going to tell you how to get there, because I can't. It sits in the middle of a maze of little residential streets, and I'll swear that every one of them is 60th something-or-other: 60th Street, 60th Drive, 60th Avenue, 60th Road, 60th Lane, 60th Court. A nightmare for the mailman, and for anyone looking for The Oval.

When you get there, if you get there, you find this battered sign that says *Soccer Games Every Sunday.* That must have gone up when they opened the place (in the 1920s). Now they have games on weeknights, too, since they put the lights in. They're not very good lights, yellowish and patchy—there are some who swear that visibility at The Oval gets *worse* when they turn the lights on—but they fit the general run-down feeling of the place.

I first went there 30 years ago, and hardly anything has changed. It's not worse, and it's not better. If you stand on the terracing behind the east goal, you can—on a clear day—see the whole midtown Manhattan skyline. And it's a safe bet that during the past 30 years, that skyline has changed more than The Oval has.

People tell me there used to be grass on the field. Ben Boehm, who coaches at the Gottschee club these days, used to play there in the '50s, but he only remembers little arcs of grass around each corner flag. The rest was dirt—but it was, Ben assures me, a smooth, sandy sort of dirt. So I guess that's worse, because today it's coarse and there are stones to cope with.

So when it's hot and dry, Met Oval is a dustbowl; and when it rains, it's a mudbowl. They play anyway. It's an all-weather surface, and they get a lot of use out of it. You might get up to 1,500 people there. Thirty years ago it was teams like the German-Hungarians who drew the crowds. That club still owns the field, but today, it's the Greek and the Hispanic teams that have the following.

The local residents don't think much of the Met Oval. Not that there's any rampant hooliganism, but it's a noisy place and a fair amount of illegal drinking goes on there. And after night games, well, do you want rowdy soccer fans relieving themselves in your front yard or against your car?

On the south side there's a decaying shedlike structure, under which there used to be a sort of table. Maybe it was meant for the press, not that it matters—it's gone, burned one particularly cold afternoon, I'm told, to keep the fans warm.

Like I said, it's a dump. But we'd be lost without it. It belongs in New York, of course, because it's shabby and unkempt and dangerous. You love to see the teams come in from Long Island or some other suburby sort of place where they have glossy grass fields, and you love to see their faces as it slowly dawns on them that they *have* come to the right place, and that this is the field they're going to have to play on.

Thirty years ago, that poor guy would have been OK with his "what Oval?" gaffe. Then we had Eintracht Oval in Astoria, and another one up in the Bronx. They've gone. The Met is the lone survivor. There are other soccer areas, like Flushing Meadows Park. That's a wonderful sight on summer weekends with seven or eight fields crammed together, all in constant use. It's home to the Hispanic leagues, and it's livelier and more colorful than Met Oval will ever be. But it's owned by the city.

It's a far cry from the glitz of the Cosmos, but if you're looking for a field owned by soccer people, used by soccer people to play soccer on, then all we've got is dirty old run-down Met Oval.* God bless it.

Note:

* In 1998, Met Oval, as shabby and overused as ever, owed over $100,000 to New York City in real-estate taxes. It seemed to be doomed. But local soccer leaders, supported by the United States Soccer Federation and by sponsors, formed a foundation to save the Oval.

World Cup Pup Visits Plaza

In Search of a Name

NEW YORK—Here we are again at New York's Plaza Hotel, back in the Terrace Room, which seems to have become World Cup '94's favorite haunt. It was here, two years ago, that we were given the famous non-event press conference. The one that was supposed to kick off the whole event, but merely announced a "historic marketing agreement." One that—something they didn't tell us—hadn't even been signed at the time.

Then we had all the activity of the World Cup Draw in December last year, and now we have this major superevent, the launching of the contest to name the World Cup mascot. Don't ask me who organized this—the Terrace Room was awash with harassed-looking minor executives, all darting about with that look of martyred self-importance that spells "ORGANIZER" in capital letters.

I later discovered that one of the reasons for all the anxiety was that Pelé had threatened to put in an appearance, and no one could work out what would happen if he did. One of the harassed-looking agency-type women was heard to say "Well, in case Pelé turns up, what does he look like?"

Pelé did not turn up, so we were all able to concentrate our attentions on the mascot in search of a name. To be fair to whoever the organizers were, the invitation did not actually *say* that this was a press conference. It just invited us to be present as the mascot needed "your help to get his campaign message out to the public."

As it happened, the press were largely ignored. We had the usual speeches telling us, for the millionth time, that soccer is the most popular sport in the

Originally published in Soccer America *September 14, 1992. Reprinted with permission of* Soccer America *magazine.*

world (yawn, yawn), that it is played all over the world by six hundred billion people (zzzzz, zzzzz), that 50 trillion kids play it in the United States (snore, snore), and that the worldwide television viewing figures for the last World Cup were . . . (loud crashes throughout the Terrace Room as heads slump downward among the coffee cups and assorted Danish pastries).

While I'm on this matter of mindless repetition of huge numbers, I think there's a question that needs answering here. The going figure for the number of people playing soccer in the U.S. is 16 million. That was what we were told here, and it is a figure that USSF president and World Cup czar Alan Rothenberg uses constantly. The question for Mr. Rothenberg is this: if we've got 16 million players, how is it that the USSF membership is only 2 million something or other? Someone at the USSF must be doing an awful job to let that many players go wandering around unregistered. Fourteen *million*? A scandal, if ever I met up with one.

Anyway, after all that statistical stuff, we got Andrew Shue, a pleasant young TV star who used to play midfield at Dartmouth, and he welcomed the mascot, which appeared accompanied by a heavy bimbo factor—one on each side, actually. This is the new-look mascot. They've changed it around a bit since it first appeared in January.

It's no longer wearing a shirt with rugby stripes; it's got shorter—and presumably sexier—shorts, and it's got socks. And it's had that enormous snout reduced by about half. But it still just stands there, along with the bimbos, grinning inanely at everything. We were told in January that it wouldn't have a voice, and it's never been heard to utter a word. Just Mr. Vapid Grin.

Now we've got some cutesy-pooh biographical stuff on the mutt. We're told that its current residence is Dog House, World Cup U.S.A. 1994. I shall refrain from the obvious comments on that address, and tell you—so that you can see the depth of thinking that has gone into this—that the mascot's favorite song is "Hound Dog," its favorite food is hot dogs, and its favorite reading is *Sherlock Holmes and the Hounds of Baskerville,* a book that is probably better known under its real title, *The Hound of the Baskervilles.*

The mascot is the perfect beast to answer questions about that pile of inanities, because it can't say anything. All you get is the moronic grin. So the photo opportunities started immediately, with mascot and Shue and bimbos and Barbara Fife, a deputy mayor of New York, blinking under the assault of the flashbulbs. Also on the platform was the U.S. national team captain Tony Meola. Somehow, they forgot to ask him to be in any of the pictures. ("Well, jeez," as one of the harassed organizer-women probably said, "you can't think of *everything*.")

Shue said he thought the mascot should be named Underdog. Later he explained: "Yeah, I like that, it's a modest term, it's fitting for the U.S. national team." Tony Meola, who might have objected to that but didn't, showed greater conformity to the party line, preferring Sidekick, one of the four officially suggested names—Sweeper, Striker, Champ, and Sidekick. Meola is actually getting quite good at the party line, finding a way to mention "our ten official sponsors" in every third or fourth sentence.

Each of those World-Cup-U.S.A.-sanctioned names came with a little bio, describing what the term meant. Gawd help us. The description of "sweeper" must have been written by the lady who wanted to know what Pelé looks like.

Listen to this: "Sweeper: the soccer team's all-purpose player, the do-everything competitor. He lays out the offensive structure, but is also to defend against attacks from the opponent's leading scorer or striker. No challenge is too great for this 'team leader.'" He lays out the offensive structure? He marks the opponent's leading scorer? (OK, I know it doesn't say that, but how else would you interpret "defend against attacks from the opponent's leading scorer"?) He's the team leader?

Drivel, utter drivel, all of it. I'll not burden you with the other definitions, which are only marginally better. Fortunately, you don't have to use one of those four names. You can write in your own suggestion. So here, milling around in a corner of the Terrace Room, we have some 12-year-old kids in soccer uniforms, the Cherry Hill Hawks from New Jersey. Maybe they have some ideas.

They do indeed. First of all, did they recognize the creature as a dog? Chris said he thought it was a mouse, and Jeff said he thought it was an experimental rat. Both later claimed they were joking, and that of course they knew it was a dog. How were they so sure? We'd seen the drawings first, said Chris.

Anthony, the smallest player on the team, piped up that he had a name, and then couldn't think of it. Richie punched the air and volunteered Sudden Impact. Bill said it should be Cup Pup, Chris liked Perfect Weapon, while Jeff offered Satan the Super Kicker.

Pookie, said Haile, because he has an aunt who calls everyone Pookie. Yeah, that's good, said John, but it's spelled Poogie. No, it's Pookie, Pookie, Pookie, insisted Haile, Pookie sounds more professional. Someone else said they were both wrong, it was pronounced Poodgie. Billy the Kicker, said Ryan; Spike, said Devin.

Little Anthony pushed his way forward again and said he'd remembered the name: Super Kicker. He then went off to join the crowd trying to score goals on the experimental rat that was playing goalkeeper in front of a small goal. As it positioned itself with its legs wide apart, this proved to be remarkably easy.

The mascot has difficulty moving its legs once they're in position, because it wears what appear to be deep-sea diving boots—massive expanses of black that seem to cry out for some sort of logo. The question was raised (not by me, I would never notice *that* sort of thing): why were there no Adidas stripes on the shoes, or for that matter no commercial signs anywhere about the beast's person?

Probably I shouldn't bring this matter up. The mascot people do seem to have a habit of following my design suggestions. Maybe the next appearance of the thing will have it sitting in the back of a GM truck, operating a Canon duplicating machine while taking photographs with Fuji film, while shaving with a Gillette razor, while drinking Coca-Cola, while eating a Big Mac and a Snickers bar (listen, the thing has four paws, you know), with a MasterCard sticking out of its shorts, and . . . heck, I've forgotten what it is that Philips and JVC do, but don't worry guys, we'll get you in there somewhere.

Festoon it with sponsor significance—now *that's* what I call a mascot. On the other paw, what I don't find acceptable at all is this idiotic drawing of the thing being hit—pow!—right in the mouth with the soccer ball. What is that supposed to tell us? Is that something that happens in soccer? Is it something that makes the game enjoyable?

Brad Rothenberg—yes, he's Alan Rothenberg's son—works for the World Cup '94 people, and has special responsibility for the mascot. "It makes it fun," says Brad, "showing a dog at play, it's something that dogs do, catching things in their mouth." Hey, there are plenty of things that dogs do that they presumably find enjoyable that you wouldn't want your World Cup Pup doing. Being smacked in the kisser seems one of them to me.

If, that is, you have some sort of notion of the game of soccer at the front of your mind. The fact is that people don't get hit in the mouth very often. It's not part of the game. Besides, it doesn't do much good for the image of the sport to show someone having his teeth splattered, it's not the sort of thing parents want to see. I'm being too literal, says Brad, parents won't look at it that way.

Anyway, all the drawings were approved by soccer people, it seems, so they must be all right. In which case I want to see an Olympic poster with a javelin player skewered to the track with his own spear—I mean, how hilarious can you get?

By now, the press conference, or party, or rap session, or whatever it was, was dragging to an end. The kids had tired of putting penalty kicks past the experimental rat, and were now besieging Tony Meola for autographs. Another harassed-looking type appeared (male, this one), hovering around the edge of the crowd, telling another dyspeptic face that "We need to get Andrew and Tony over there for a few sound bites—or we'll never make the . . ." At that point Mr.

Dyspepsia swallowed hard and forced his way into the Cherry Hill Hawks to purloin Tony Meola.

I surveyed the dwindling crowd, wondering if that agency-woman was still scurrying around looking for Pelé. No sign of her. But there is Charlie Stillitano, the deputy World Cup venue director for this area. No Pelé, certainly, but a very good player in his Princeton days. What could be in that rather grubby, oddly bulky bag that Stillitano is carrying?

Stillitano grins sheepishly—"I'm going down to Princeton after this, they're working out." He unzips the top of the bag and furtively exposes a soccer shoe. A real one, with mud on it! And suddenly, surrounded by the chandeliers and the thick carpets and the mirrors of the Plaza, jostled by the gray suits of the sponsors and the harassed agency types, you can sense and feel the game of soccer. For the first time all morning. Does that make sense at a World Cup gathering?

Farewell to the People's Captain
Bobby Moore (1941–1993)

NEW YORK—Of course, I'd heard the stories from colleagues in England, that Bobby Moore was pretty sick, that it didn't look good. Then came his own announcement. He had cancer. "I have a battle to win," he said, and asked that he be left alone to fight it. A short, dignified statement. No drama, no adjectives. Ten days later, he was dead. At the cruelly early age of 51.

His moment had come in 1966, that sunny moment in Wembley Stadium when his teammates raised him on their shoulders, and he raised the World Cup. England, champions of the world. I was in the stadium that afternoon, however long ago it was. Yes, it does seem like yesterday, but it's light years away, too.

Because it's unlikely that English soccer will ever have another hero like Bobby Moore. A Londoner, born in 1941, in the middle of the blitz. A working-class boy. He remained that, a working-class Londoner, who stayed close to his roots. He never moved far from his birthplace in Barking. He spent virtually all his career with the local club, West Ham United. When he did move, much later, it was to spend the final playing years with Fulham . . . another London club.

No, we don't have heroes like that anymore. Not in soccer. People move around too much for local loyalty, the money they make strains at those class roots.

Those roots must have been important to Bobby. Very likely, they had a lot to do with the quality that everyone noticed about him, on and off

Originally published in Soccer America *March 15, 1993. Reprinted with permission of* Soccer America *magazine.*

the field. He never got upset, always seemed confident, imperturbable. Unflappable.

No wonder they made him England's captain at 22. Everyone he played with had a story about his coolness. Martin Peters, his teammate at West Ham and for England, once wrote: "You can swear at him, kick him, and if you're feeling in a particularly sour mood, take the mickey out of his golden-boy image, but you would still be struggling to get a positive reaction from him. When the coach gives him instructions, he listens in that composed, matter-of-fact way of his, and if he nods his head that's as much as you can expect."

The stories have been flowing recently, of course—especially the one about the time when the referee got knocked unconscious, but the game was going on . . . until Moore bent down to pick up the referee's whistle and blew a long blast to stop the action.

One of the most astounding examples of Moore's *sangfroid* came in 1970. Just before the World Cup in Mexico, England had been in Colombia. As they prepared to leave for Mexico, Moore was arrested by the Colombian police on a trumped-up charge of having stolen an emerald bracelet from the hotel gift shop.

The team left, Moore stayed behind, under "house" arrest, with the charge pending. A few days later, the charges were dropped, Moore flew to Mexico and resumed his life and his position as England captain as though nothing had happened.

But perhaps the most fitting description of the unflappable Moore came from the West Ham physiotherapist Rob Jenkins. Asked to run down the list of West Ham players and reveal what they were like from his point of view, he told a tale of players who worried about little injuries, players who didn't like pain, players who never noticed pain, and so on. Until he came to Bobby Moore, when Jenkins replied "No trouble" and passed quickly on to the next player.

Most fitting, because it is short, unadorned, no nonsense. No drama, no adjectives.

I first met Moore in New York in 1963. West Ham United was playing in the International Soccer League at Randall's Island. A young team, it included not only Moore, but Martin Peters and Geoff Hurst. Three years later, all three would be members of England's World-Cup–winning team.

But Moore was the one who stood out in '63, because of his appearance—his glinting blond hair, his superbly tanned skin. And because of his play. Neat, unhurried, elegant play. How many defenders are there whom you want to watch, because everything they do is a work of art? Very few. Carlos Alberto and Franz Beckenbauer, certainly, but they did their share of attacking. Moore was strictly a defender. But a joy to watch.

Above all, his tackling. Moore was the best tackler I ever saw, quick, firm, clean, effortless. Surprisingly for an English player—how they love to slide!—

1963: Randall's Island Stadium, New York—Bobby Moore (left), only 22 but already captain of West Ham United, exchanges pennants with Dukla Prague captain Ladislav Novak. Three years later Moore would lead England to victory in the 1966 World Cup final. *Copyright Paul Gardner*

most of his tackling was done standing up. It was all about confidence and timing. Bobby Moore, said Pelé, could play on any Brazilian team, any time, "and that is no light compliment."

I interviewed Moore briefly at the time. Not wildly successful. He was courteous, but he didn't open up, the answers didn't flow. Funnily enough, I remember most that he kept asking me questions about the other teams in the tournament.

My sharpest memory of Moore is not of Wembley in 1966, but of Randall's Island on August 11, 1963. West Ham United against Dukla Prague. Some good players on the field that afternoon. Dukla had Ladislav Novak, Svatopluk Pluskal, and Josef Masopust, who had played for Czechoslovakia in the 1962 World Cup final. West Ham had Moore, Peters, and Hurst, who were to star in the next World Cup final.

It finished 1–1, and Moore, playing at centerback—what would today be called a covering centerback—was the dominating figure. A majestic figure, almost. No, I can't recall any specific tackles, or headers, or anything like that.

The vision I have is of Moore, his hand up to his eyes as he looked into the bright sunlight, standing still or moving slowly forward, pointing, giving some instruction to a teammate. Not a very dramatic image, but it sticks, it means something. Moore the unhurried leader, Moore the authoritative captain.

It did all seem so effortless for him that it's a shock to be told that he didn't come by all that talent naturally. As a boy he played just once for Essex Schools, a team that has produced a crop of stars over the years—including the man who would be his coach in 1966, Alf Ramsey. When Moore left school, all his friends were already with pro clubs, and he seemed to have been forgotten. Then he got a call from West Ham.

Everything happened quickly after that—within 10 years he was the world champions' captain. In 1967 he received an honor, they gave him the OBE, the Order of the British Empire. An upper-class acknowledgment of a commoner's skills.

After that, there was nothing very much. When he retired from playing, he tried coaching—but only with small clubs. Southend United, an Essex team, still almost local, and Oxford—maybe 50 miles west of London, as far as he ever ventured from home.

Neither stint was successful. He played in the old North American Soccer League—a season for San Antonio in 1976, a couple of games in Seattle in 1978. In 1976, there was a strange rebirth to his international career, which had officially finished with his last game for England two years earlier.

The NASL organized the Bicentennial Cup, and invited England, Italy, and Brazil. They formed a team to represent the U.S. from the league's stars. It included Giorgio Chinaglia, Pelé, Tommy Smith, and Bobby Moore. It lost 3–1 to England.

Moore turned to various business ventures, but again none was exactly a triumph. One of them brought him to New York in April 1982. I got a call from a Bill somebody, who said he worked for IC Holidays. Did I want to interview Bobby Moore? Well, when? He's here in the office now, said Bill. So I trotted over to Madison Avenue.

Also not the best interview I ever had. The problem this time was that Bill of IC Holidays was sitting in. Moore was working for them. He was running his own soccer schools in England ("Monday to Friday, 10 till 4 P.M., 30 hours of tuition, 33 pounds a week") and he was helping IC to form groups of English kids who wanted to come on soccer-camp holidays to the U.S. So he felt obliged to talk about that program, which wasn't of much interest to me.

Bill got on the phone, so I asked Moore about his childhood. Yes, he'd played in the street, right outside his home. Did the kids still do that? Moore grinned. "I visit my mother every week, she still lives in the same house. You couldn't play in the streets there now, you'd be killed. The traffic . . ." No cars in his day, then? "Not for me anyway! To get to training, I had to take three buses, then a one-and-a-half-mile walk."

Bill got off the phone, and Moore slipped effortlessly back into his job-talk: "The biggest problem for American kids is the training—in my opinion, people here are impressed by complication. It should be simple, football, it's all about controlling and passing and delivering the ball right. That's what we do in my advanced course. . . ."

A bit later we got back to his early days. He praised Malcolm Allison. "He was very influential for me, he was always full of great ideas and new things, so enthusiastic. Great personality and charisma. When I was 16 years old, he was the West Ham captain. I saw him every day; he put me on the right road."

Would he like to coach? "You look at it, you know, and you think if the opportunity is right, you'd love to be involved and see if you can do it. I enjoy working with players. Yeah, I'd consider it if the right opportunity came along. I had the FA's full coaching badge by the time I was 21."

He wasn't happy about the way English soccer was going, it was getting expensive to attend, the games were poor. "I watched Arsenal against Middlesbrough. You think, Christ! . . . we used to get goals and excitement. Now it's more about coaches than players. There's a lack of good players now."

Talking of good players, I got in a question about him. And his tackling. Looking at him as he sat there, his thick thighs threatening to burst the seams of his pants, I had to remember those powerful legs that seemed to win every tackle they went into. But Moore didn't talk about strength: "It's all about sizing up the situation, reading the situation. I was never a physical-type player."

No, he wasn't. He was often accused of being slow—those heavy legs, you see. But that wasn't true. He thought so much more quickly than anyone else. That formidable tackling skill was often not needed, because Moore got there first to intercept. Whether he had some natural soccer genius, an inbuilt soccer brain, I wouldn't know. It must have been something like that, because he made it all look so easy.

Those were the words that kept cropping up last week when his old teammates talked about him. Coolness. Calmness. Dignity. Class.

It was a working-class dignity that Moore brought to soccer. Simple values, simply applied. The same sort of values that Stanley Matthews gave us. It all sounds a bit dull, but it wasn't. Not on the soccer field. Matthews was a winger, they're supposed to excite. Moore's triumph was to be an ordinary guy—"the people's captain," West Ham United called him—who turned defending into something beautiful and exciting to watch. Pure, distilled soccer. Soccer with no adjectives.

A Team for the Ages

Más Alma! Más Alma!

NEW YORK—I have been asked to act as a coach. Just for a short while, you understand. Believe it or not, a sponsor has shown some interest in my opinions. This is a new experience for me. I can state quite categorically that it has never happened before, my previous contact with the breed having been limited to oozy-charmy PR ladies or caustic letters from CEOS.

The new sponsor-friendly era of my life began with a letter from American Airlines. They want me to make a list of players, candidates for the all-time, all-great, all-everything World Cup team that they are working on.

Hey—a soccer sponsor working on an out-and-out soccer theme, asking a soccer writer to help—well, you can see that the novelty of the thing is bound to attract. Even better: the request contained a lot of sensible guidelines for the task. Soccer brains have been at work on this.

So first of all I have to make a list of players. Well, I'm rather good at making lists. I do a lot of it in my advancing years. I make shopping lists that I leave on the kitchen table when I go out. I make lists of people to call that I leave next to the telephone; then I move the telephone and lose the list. I make lists of things to do, which get buried under all the other things that I'm doing.

So I made my list—40 players—and then sat down to think about making a team out of that. Picking a team, just like a coach. As I usually find that what coaches do is incomprehensible to me, I shall begin my short tenure by doing everything backward.

Originally published in Soccer America *March 22, 1993. Reprinted with permission of* Soccer America *magazine.*

The conventional coaching wisdom (and how's *that* for gross misuse of a word?) is that you build a team from the back. You start by forming a strong defense. Bah!, sir, and bah! again. I shall start with the attack.

Because that's the most exciting part of the team—and because that's where the handful of can't-leave-outs play: Di Stéfano, Pelé, and Maradona. Alas, those know-it-alls at American Airlines are a jump ahead. They know he never played in a World Cup, so I can't pick Di Stéfano.

He didn't play when he was an Argentine citizen; after the Spaniards naturalized him, he traveled to Chile to play for Spain in the 1962 tournament. But he was nursing an injury, and he never got on the field, not one single second of World Cup playing time. (While I'm talking of absentees, George Best is another nonstarter for the same reason: never played in the World Cup.)

Pelé is there, because—oh because of a million reasons, because he's Pelé most of all. But which Pelé? Pelé the Younger, Pelé the Brave, who could dribble right through the heart of clogged defenses, swerving past brutal body checks, leaping over scything tackles, a deadly package of soccer dynamite, exploding with that ferocious shooting on goal? Or Pelé the Elder, the 30-year-old Pelé of 1970, slower, playing more in midfield, commanding, controlling, coaxing his teammates to the heights?

It'll be the younger Pelé, because I want him up front. Maradona, left-footed Maradona, will go into midfield, sort of, that indeterminate role of falling back as a playmaker, and bursting forward as a goal-scorer that another Argentine #10, Mario Kempes, did so well in 1978. But Maradona is the master.

I suppose I have to explain my tactical setup now. Reading from front to back, it's a 2-2-1-2-1-2. It's a formation designed to accommodate the players I want to select. Would it work on the field? Look, keep that sort of question until after the game, will you? How the hell do I know if it's going to *work*? Ask the players.

Reading, as I promised, backward, I have: two forwards, two attacking midfielders, one central do-everything midfielder, two outside wingbacks or flank players or whatever they're called (you know the ones, they zoom up and down the wings, fullbacks one minute, wingers the next, well that's the theory), one defensive midfielder, and two centerbacks. And a goalkeeper.

Two forwards. Pelé plus . . . another Brazilian, the man who carried in his little body the whole soul and history of Brazilian soccer: Garrincha. Oh yes, Garrincha *must* be there. If I can't find a forward spot, I'll stick him in midfield, or at full back, or in goal for that matter. But I'll take him as the most brilliant example of that most exciting soccer player, the winger. Fast, tricky, artistic, powerful, a dribbler, a goal-scorer—everything. Above all, a soccer presence, a small indomitable figure who must have been born for one thing only: to delight and amaze soccer fans. And how he did that.

Attacking midfielders: they'll have to work out for themselves which part of the field they want, because I've got two totally left-footed players: Maradona and Rivelino. More artistry from Maradona, more power from Rivelino. Extraordinary dribbling from both, marvelous swerving and dipping and curving free kicks from both. Rivelino on the left, I think—where he can release those raking long passes out to the right . . . where Garrincha lurks.

Admittedly, there's not much heading power in midfield. Maradona is no master in the air, and Rivelino was hardly ever seen to head the ball in his entire career. So what? We'll be keeping the ball down. If we need heading power up front, Pelé was one of the sharpest headers ever (a skill taught to him by his father Dondinho—Pelé once proudly told me how his father had headed five goals in one game). And that little tyke Garrincha—ask the English defenders, and you know how good they're supposed to be in the air—about that 1962 World Cup and how he flew above them all to head a goal for Brazil.

Right behind Rivelino and Maradona, doing anything he likes, all over the field, the wiry Johan Cruyff. I imagine him as the conductor, pointing, passing, *influencing,* the brains of the whole outfit.

The flank guys. Carlos Alberto on the right—all he has to do is repeat his performance in the 1970 World Cup final, and I'm satisfied. If he finishes it off with a goal only half as stunning as the one he scored then, we'll all be in seventh heaven. On the left, one of the earliest of the overlapping breed, Brazil's Nílton Santos: polished, positionally superb, tireless. His presence exposes one of the problems of creating these all-star teams: the players who get left out. Santos, brilliant as he was, was taken apart by England's Stanley Matthews during an England-Brazil international at Wembley in 1956. Yet I can't find a place for Matthews, and I'm not about to replace Garrincha.

Defensive midfielder: I never saw Obdulio Varela play—just some old black-and-white newsreel shots, but this was the man who was the driving force behind the most astonishing World Cup upset ever. The final in 1950. That pulsating afternoon when Uruguay, against all the odds, against the deafening roar of over 200,000 delirious Brazilian fans, packed into Maracanã, beat all-conquering Brazil 2–1. Sweating and straining in the Rio heat, keeping his teammates playing, shouting encouragement, was the captain, Varela. It was Varela who raced around, tugging his own Uruguay shirt, yelling *Más alma! Más alma!* at his players. Difficult to translate . . . more heart, probably. I wasn't there, I didn't see it. But I can't believe there has ever been a greater example of *alma* on the soccer field.

Centerbacks: stopper and sweeper? Maybe not, because I've got two players who like to go forward. They can work it out, who covers whom. Daniel Passarella and Franz Beckenbauer. A wonderful, error-free, defensive organizer, the elegant Beckenbauer. An incomparable soccer brain, allied to silky skills and smooth movement. Never a motion wasted, never a ball played in haste. And all right foot, too.

Alongside him, his opposite, the left-footed scrappy street fighter Passarella. The Argentine brochures listed him as 5'10", but he always seemed shorter to me. What mattered was that he jumped like he was on springs, his timing was perfect—it was a rare occasion to see Passarella beaten in the air. Plenty of *alma,* too. Passarella was the youngest player to captain a World Cup winner, in 1978.

Goalkeeper: no contest here, it must be Gordon Banks. You talk about goalkeepers radiating confidence—Banks did. Not with swagger, not with size, not with acrobatics. Probably just because he was as close as you can get to the born goalkeeper, and it came through. He made the routine saves, he made the difficult saves, and when he had to, he came up with the impossible save. Remember Pelé applauding in 1970 after Banks had somehow kept his sure-goal header out?

The captain . . . hmmm. I'm going to give it to Varela.

Actually, that's not quite the end my coaching career. Because I'm supposed to pick a coach to take care of that lot. That's the easiest part of the lot. No hesitation, no pause for thought. It'll be Telê Santana. He never won a World Cup, but in 1982 and 1986 he gave us two superb Brazilian teams, faithful to the spirit of the Brazilian game, full of sparkling skill and delightful soccer.

He was unlucky both times. But think of what he did for the sport, how many hearts he sent soaring, how many youngsters he inspired, how many dreams he ignited with his brilliant, uninhibited teams.

Hold on, this coaching thing is addictive. I'm not quitting, not quite yet. I guess I'm allowed to assemble a reserve team, so let's take a look at all the talent I've left out of the first team.

Up front: two places—and Gerd Müller, Eusébio, Jairzinho, Tostão, Stanley Matthews, or maybe Ferenc Puskas to choose from. I'll go with Eusébio for sheer scoring power, Tostão as the cleverest center-forward I ever saw.

Puskas can come back into midfield, along with Gérson. Two more left-footers. So is Tostão, come to think of it. The cunning old fox Gérson (one condition, he'd have to give up those cigarettes on the bench), and the quicksilver Puskas. Playing the center-midfield role, Bobby Charlton—ever ready to accelerate forward on those exhilarating slalom runs of his, leaving defenders staring at nothing, with the climax of the cannonball shot.

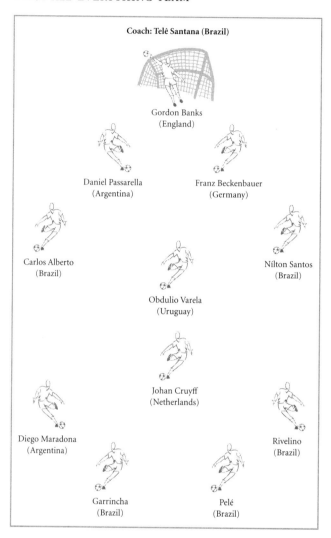

Coach: Telê Santana (Brazil)

Gordon Banks
(England)

Daniel Passarella
(Argentina)

Franz Beckenbauer
(Germany)

Carlos Alberto
(Brazil)

Obdulio Varela
(Uruguay)

Nílton Santos
(Brazil)

Johan Cruyff
(Netherlands)

Diego Maradona
(Argentina)

Rivelino
(Brazil)

Garrincha
(Brazil)

Pelé
(Brazil)

On the right flank, Giacinto Facchetti—those long legs eating up the distances, sure in the tackle and taking him forward to score vital goals. A bit of theater over on the left, the colorful Francisco Marinho, shining blond hair flowing as he streaks forward and races back. Those athletic, loose-limbed legs, the right one especially, that could bomb in free kicks that practically looped the loop before they got to the goal. Flaky, yes, but God, how exciting.

Mário Coluna gets the defensive midfield role. Never out of position, strong tackler, good marker if necessary—and plenty of attacking skills.

Bobby Moore at stopper—a rock, class and skill combined, an immaculate craftsman of the defender's trade. Ditto, ditto, ditto for the sweeper: Gae-

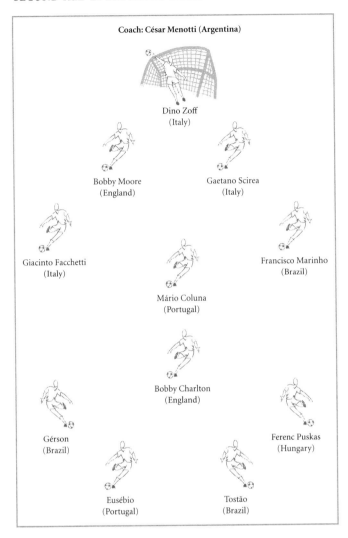

Coach: César Menotti (Argentina)

Dino Zoff
(Italy)

Bobby Moore
(England)

Gaetano Scirea
(Italy)

Giacinto Facchetti
(Italy)

Mário Coluna
(Portugal)

Francisco Marinho
(Brazil)

Bobby Charlton
(England)

Gérson
(Brazil)

Ferenc Puskas
(Hungary)

Eusébio
(Portugal)

Tostão
(Brazil)

tano Scirea. The key to Italy's 1982 World Cup win, an Italian sweeper who had learned to take the role out of its Italian defensive mode and give it the glamour that Beckenbauer had discovered.

It'll be another Italian in goal: Scirea's captain in 1982, Dino Zoff. If you can touch the heights of unspectacularity, then Zoff did that. But he could fly about like a panther when he had to.

The coach of the reserves will be César Menotti. For the way that he gave us, in 1978, an exciting Argentine team, full of attacking players, that logically, spent all its time attacking.

Where Are the Swarming Coaches?

Arsenal Pushed to the Fringes of the System

NEW YORK—Mumblings and grumblings in these parts have for some time contained an anti-California flavoring. People look at the rosters of the various national teams, and they don't see any players from New York or New Jersey. They do see plenty from California. Eight of the 20 players offered contracts by the USSF and a place at the Mission Viejo national team camp were Californians. Eight of the 20 players on last year's U.S. Olympic team roster were from California. A total of 13 different Californians.

Can that be justified? Oh yes, quite easily. Let's take the record of a California club team: Arsenal, from Alta Loma. In 1990, the Arsenal boys went to Europe and won the under-16 Dana Cup in Denmark, and the Keele Classic in England. In 1991, they won the under-16 title at the Dallas Cup. Last year, they took the national cup at the under-17 level.

Earlier this month they were at the Dallas Cup again. Along with eleven other American teams, they played in the super under-19 division, with youth teams from pro clubs like Fiorentina, Real Madrid, West Ham United, and Nacional. Arsenal was the only American team to advance to the quarterfinals. Not only did they advance: they won their group, ahead of West Ham (whom they tied 2–2, after leading 2–0), and went on to win 2–1 over the Slovakians from Tatran Presov in the quarterfinals. In the semifinal, Arsenal went the distance with Argentina's Boca Juniors, eventually losing 1–2 in overtime—a result that could so easily have gone the other way.

Originally published in Soccer America *April 26, 1993. Reprinted with permission of* Soccer America *magazine.*

Whatever, the point is clear. Arsenal was—by quite a substantial margin—the best of the American teams in Dallas.

So we have a highly successful youth team from the soccer-fashionable state of California. By a process of straightforward and unarguable deduction, we can therefore predict that this team—Arsenal of Alta Loma—must be loaded with players who are part of the national team development program. (Or is it the Olympic development program?—I have never quite cottoned on to the terminology.)

Yet a look at the Arsenal roster reveals only one player who has ever been on a U.S. national team: goalkeeper Kyle Campbell. He was the starting goalkeeper for the U.S. in the 1991 under-17 World Cup in Italy (and did well enough to be elected to the all-tournament team). But when Campbell was picked for the U.S. squad, he was not an Arsenal player; he was then with the La Jolla Nomads.

An odd state of affairs. It gets odder and odder the more you probe. How about if we take a look at all those college coaches who must have been swarming around this team? I mean, they *must* have been swarming, for these unarguable reasons: apart from three juniors, the boys are all seniors, and they all have good grade point averages and SAT scores.

The college coaches have duly swarmed around goalkeeper Campbell—he will go to Division I power North Carolina State. There has also been plenty of college interest in forward Matt Winecki, but he wants to try his luck as a pro in Belgium.

For the rest, there has been no swarm. When I put it to Arsenal coach Pete Gunby that this must be a little disappointing, he smiled and shook his head: "I would put it stronger than that. It's *very* disappointing. I call coaches, they say they're very interested; some coaches have called me, but for all the chat it never leads to anything. Yet eight of these boys played on high school champion teams this year."

The puzzlement in Gunby's expression intensifies when he thinks of stopper Reuben Tavares: "This is the player the opposing coaches always, to a man, praise. They come up to me and say, 'That Reuben's a great player.' I just cannot imagine how a player like that cannot be looked at."

Yet Tavares did not get looked at—until just a couple of weeks before the Dallas Cup, when St. Louis University coach Joey Clarke saw him in the state playoffs and took an interest. Scholarship offers? Captain Art Temblador is going to Cal State Fullerton—a local school, if you like, the nearest Division I school. Mario Sanchez is going to Fresno State. That's it.

Defender Rodney Lee has had a partial scholarship offer from Santa Clara. If he doesn't get a full offer from somewhere, chances are that he will switch sports—he is also a wide receiver.

Alex Sanchez (no relation to Mario), Kevin Posey, Eugene Brooks, and Al Partida remain without college places. So too, with a GPA of 4.13 and an SAT score of 1120, does Diego Bocanegra.

Might not national power UCLA be interested in all this talent in its own backyard? Another wistful smile from Gunby: "I'm not sure anyone from UCLA has ever seen this team."

Just what is going on here? Is there some hidden key to this peculiar state of affairs, some common thread that will explain matters?

There is, and it is a highly unpleasant one. Take a look at those names: Partida, Bocanegra, Sanchez, Tavares, Temblador. Mexican-American names. It is these boys who are being overlooked. Mexican-American players, the ones who give Pete Gunby's team an unmistakably Latin style.

That style, that way of playing, is one that almost took Arsenal to the Dallas Cup supergroup final. It is one that was universally admired by everyone who saw it there. Foreign journalists from Italy, Argentina, and Bolivia were greatly impressed and clearly somewhat surprised. Relieved, even. During the tournament, they had seen plenty of games featuring American teams—straightforward, hard-running up and down the field sort of stuff.

This was different. This was recognizable as intelligent, flowing soccer, played by boys with above-average technique. And it was winning soccer. I said it was admired by everyone who saw it. I guess I have to modify that.

I cannot speak for the college coaches present. I became aware during the week of various players—on teams other than Arsenal—who were being recruited. I also found out from the coach of one of the English teams present that several of his players had been approached by college coaches and "offered scholarships." I saw these players who are being recruited so enthusiastically. And I saw the Arsenal players, who are not being recruited. Gawd help us. No wonder so much of college soccer is pedestrian rubbish.

I'm not aware that there was anyone from the USSF's glamorous new superduper player-development unit on hand to watch. There may have been (they have three full-time coaches now, you know), but it wouldn't have mattered. Because Pete Gunby's Alta Loma boys are not the sort of players who have ever been of any interest to the constipated clique that has got its clammy tentacles all over the USSF's coaching and player-development departments.

So these Mexican-Americans are pushed to the fringes of the "system." I have, of course, fallen into the trap of calling them Mexican-Americans. It is a clear way of defining them and the style that they represent. But it should not be necessary. These boys are Americans. They are American players. They were born here, they went to high school here, they learned their game here.

All of that is something that our Eurocentric coaching community finds difficult to accept. Nay—they *cannot* accept it, because it totally undermines their image of "the American player." That image came up several times during conversations with college coaches during the Dallas week. I was told more than once (as I have been told many times in the past) that my idea of a Brazilian-type style for the U.S. was a pipe dream because it did not fit the "characteristics of the American player."

That is: the American player as defined by the college coaches. The American player as defined by that narrow-minded ussf clique in Chicago. The white suburban athlete. Physical condition: perfect. Willingness to listen to coaching drivel: unlimited. Skill level: anything from excellent to negligible will do, providing the first four criteria are met.

As long as you have that image in your mind, what on earth are you going to do with a player like Arsenal's Al Partida? Latino, lower-middle class, small stature, doesn't charge about all over the place during a game, but gets on with it in his own instinctive way. After I'd seen Partida back in 1991 and had been considerably impressed by his skill, I wrote in this column: "You'll be hearing more about this young man."

What I meant was that he was sure to turn up on some national team roster. It might have been the phase of the moon, perhaps I'd been at the elderberry wine—I'm at a loss to explain just how I could have been so utterly stupid and naive. Of course the Partidas of our soccer world won't get near the national teams.

As it happened, Partida did, somehow or other, manage to make his regional team. This almost sounds like an aberration—remember, you are dealing with regional coaches who use expressions like "He's a horse" to describe their favorite players. But the money wasn't there to send him to the regional tournament in Florida. That, of course, is another "characteristic" of the American player: that his family can afford to send him off to the numerous trials and camps that the ussf's celebrated "system" puts so much faith in.

Pete Gunby, who coaches these Arsenal boys, happens to be English. I am delighted to announce that he does *not* hold any license or diploma of any sort from the ussf's overblown coaching schools. The club had already been named Arsenal before Gunby got there in January of 1992. As a lifelong Everton fan, he's not totally delighted with the name, but he'll live with it.

It hardly matters, for the style of his team has nothing to do with English league soccer. Says Gunby: "I've always liked the idea of mixing Latin with European styles; I've always been against the 90-mile-per-hour longball stuff. The Latin kids are used to dribbling and short-passing, they're not out there to chase people aimlessly. They won't play this up-and-down stuff that we throw at them, so they get a reputation for being difficult. They can play, they can adjust to whatever's out there. But the style they prefer is better to watch, and it gets results."

Might as well bring it up, because we know what the traditional knocks on the Latin player are: temperamental and lazy. Arsenal's results are proof enough to demolish that—but there's more. On its way to the national title last year, Arsenal was more or less written off at the regionals. They went there with only 12 players. They played seven games in six days, and, incredibly, they won . . . with 12 players.

Not all of them were Hispanic. I need to stress that Arsenal is a mixed team—Hispanics and whites, one black player. I don't find it particularly edifying to categorize in that way. As I said, they are—all of them—American players. But it is necessary to describe them ethnically in order to define the problem. Soccer in this country has always been a tightly knit pro-European sport. No, the focus is even narrower: it has always been controlled and run by Northern or Eastern Europeans.

The mentality that comes with that outlook is not what is needed in this multiethnic society. It is utterly disgraceful that the sport of soccer—your sport, my sport, *our* sport—should have become so warped in this country that excellent American players find it difficult to claim college scholarships, and virtually impossible to get into the national team program.

Pete Gunby has been with Arsenal for just over a year. Of course he's enjoyed it, there's been a lot of success. But "the only disheartening thing is that I thought there would be college coaches knocking down doors trying to get at the players. It hasn't happened."

Nor will it happen for a while. The prejudice against the Latin players runs very deep in American soccer, just as the prejudice in favor of large athletes who charge about dominates college soccer. For that to change, it needs a brave, clear statement, followed by brave, clear action, from the top. From the sport's leaders in Chicago.

We have there, as I said, three full-time coaches who devote their attentions to coaching and player development (or so I am told). The man in charge is Bob Gansler. Don't hold your breath on this one.

Of Doubleday, Ellis, and McPenalty

Does Mythmaking Continue?

NEW YORK—There was a story that circulated a few years back about the origin of the penalty kick. Invented, according to this yarn, by someone called McPenalty.

The sort of tale that does the rounds on April 1. Obviously silly—I mean, who's going to believe that? McPenalty indeed! But maybe it doesn't pay to be quite so scornful, because there are several sporting legends, widely believed, that are not much less silly.

I'm talking about big-time legends, so important that even governments get involved in the mess. In 1969, the U.S. Postal Service issued a special stamp to commemorate the centenary of the birth of the game of football—which, it was proclaimed, had all started on November 6, 1869, at a game between Princeton and Rutgers.

Wrong. What the two colleges played in 1869 was actually soccer—a game based on the rules published six years earlier by the London Football Association. It was not soccer as we know it today, of course. But it was, more or less, soccer as played at the time in England, a sport in the process of defining itself. The sport of "football" in 1869 was still a mixture of many different elements that, within a few years, would sort themselves out more clearly into the two sports of soccer and rugby.

What has misled people about the Princeton-Rutgers game, no doubt, is that those early soccer rules allowed players to catch the ball (which was round) with their hands. But they were not allowed to run while holding it.

Originally published in Soccer America *May 10, 1993. Reprinted with permission of* Soccer America *magazine.*

A far more spectacular and elaborate piece of creative nonsense surrounds the origins of baseball. "We should all be grateful to Abner Doubleday. Little did he or the group that was with him at Cooperstown, New York, in 1839, realize the boon they were giving the nation in devising baseball." That was the president of the United States, Franklin D. Roosevelt, speaking in 1939—the centenary of the great occasion.

There was a special postage stamp then, too. Strangely, wisely, it did not feature a likeness of Doubleday. Because Doubleday did not invent baseball. He never said he had, and he died without ever being aware of the unlikely fame that was to gather about his name.

The Doubleday story was pure fiction. It was put about in 1907 by a special commission—the Mills Commission—that had been set up to investigate the sport's beginnings. Not quite—the real reason was to prove that the sport was of sturdy American origin, and not an offshoot of the effete English game of rounders. That point was duly "proved" with the invention of Abner Doubleday.

At the very moment when the centenary celebrations were in full swing, an annoying librarian, Robert Henderson of New York, was proving that the whole thing was nonsense. He had, among other things, a woodcut showing boys playing baseball (or was it rounders?) on Boston Common that had been published in 1834—five years before old Abner was supposed to have had his brainwave.

But Henderson was too late; his meticulous research didn't matter, nor, apparently, did the truth. The National Baseball Museum had already been established in Cooperstown, so there was to be no turning back.

To associate the name Doubleday with the beginnings of baseball is, in reality, every bit as silly as believing that McPenalty invented the penalty kick. But the Doubleday legend lives vigorously on.

I shouldn't give the impression that only Americans are susceptible to this sort of sporting fantasy. There is a pretty good example in England, where they have a wonderful tale about the "invention" of rugby football. The sport has its own McPenalty, its own Abner Doubleday. William Webb Ellis by name.

If you go to the town of Rugby in the English midlands, and visit Rugby School, you'll find a commemorative stone there that bears the inscription:

> This stone commemorates the exploit of William Webb Ellis who, with a fine disregard for the rules of football, as played in his time, first took the ball in his arms and ran with it, thus originating the distinctive feature of the rugby game. AD 1823.

Note the date: 1823—40 years before the first official, codified rules that started the split into soccer and rugby. Everything we know about the sport in the 1820s suggests that the word *football* then described an assortment of games in which kicking and dribbling and catching and running with the ball were all permitted. There were various versions of the sport played at different schools throughout England; it is quite possible that Rugby had its own rules that did not permit running with the ball. But other schools did.

So William Webb Ellis did not do anything new. In fact, he did not do anything at all. The evidence for his involvement in the sport comes from a report by a committee that was set up in 1895 to look into the sport's birth. Not really. Just like the later Mills Commission in baseball, this committee was interested in proving a point.

It was composed of Rugby School alumni who were determined to prove that—despite what some malcontents were saying—the sport of rugby had, too, been invented at Rugby by William Webb Ellis. The English journalist J. L. Manning investigated their work and came up with an extraordinary tale of deception and outright fraud.

The first thing the committee did, before it had heard any evidence, was to trot off to a local mason and order the commemorative stone with the inscription quoted above. It then set about ensuring that the words it had ordered carved into stone would be correct. Virtually everyone who might have had firsthand information was dead. Ellis, by then a clergyman, had died in 1872. Like Doubleday, he had passed on in happy ignorance of his name being hallowed and cheered by lusty athletes.

Someone who was awkwardly very much alive was Thomas Hughes, author of *Tom Brown's Schooldays,* a Rugby School alumnus, and a respected judge—the sort of man whose evidence you don't ignore. He said he'd never heard of Ellis as a football player.

The committee also got some bad news from Reverend Thomas Harris, an 83-year-old, the only man alive who had been at Rugby with Ellis. He claimed to remember Ellis . . . as an outstanding cricket player. The committee tried to pressure the old man; said one member, "I should press him—he must remember Our Hero doing something unusual."

He didn't, but luck beamed down on the committee. By the time it was ready to issue its report in 1897, both Hughes and Harris had been called to their maker. So the committee simply suppressed their evidence. The report confirmed that William Webb Ellis had shocked the onlookers in 1823 with his action in picking up the ball, that he had thus invented rugby. The prestige of Rugby School was upheld.

Later, the Rugby town authorities named a street Webb Ellis Road, and a school in the same street was called Martin Bloxam School—after the guy who had first dreamed up the Webb Ellis tale.

The sport of rugby got its own association, the Rugby Football Union, and its own rules in 1871. When centenary time arrived in 1971, the RFU perpetuated the Ellis myth by producing a film entitled *William Webb Ellis, Are You Mad?*

One thing should be clear from all that: having your sport built on totally false legends is no bar to success. Baseball and rugby did not exactly wither away when the Doubleday and Ellis myths were exposed. Both sports are doing very nicely—so, for that matter, are both myths.

The only thing that leaves one feeling a bit uncomfortable is this: if Doubleday and Ellis did not do what was later ascribed to them, then who did invent baseball and rugby? If no one invented the sports, how did they begin?

A matter for the seekers of wisdom and truth. We can acknowledge that the real inventor of the penalty kick was William McCrum, an Irishman from Armagh—a goalkeeper no less—who came up with the idea in 1890. But then he was never in danger of being eclipsed by McPenalty.

The apotheosis of Abner Doubleday meant obscurity for Alexander Cartwright, a New York bank teller. In 1845, he headed a local committee to bring some order to the game that he and his pals were playing. The rules that Cartwright's committee laid down were the basis for the modern game.

The situation with rugby is less clear, as carrying the ball was something that was quite widely done. But one of the witnesses to the rugby committee (he, too, died before the report was issued, so his evidence was ignored) swore that credit for the first rugby rules should go to another boy at the school, Theodore Walrond.

Football doesn't seem to have suffered from having a rudimentary soccer game as its parent, either. A more likely "first football game" was the one between Harvard and McGill universities in 1874. This featured the use of the egg-shaped rugby ball, and the players were allowed to run with it.

Quite possibly, football has swiped the game that gave birth to college soccer. Something for the Hall of Fame people to look into, along with another little task I have for them.

Is it possible that United States soccer is about to come up with its own Doubleday, its own Webb Ellis, its own McPenalty? I quote from the USSF's *Newsline:* "The founder of soccer in America . . . the late Gerrit Smith Miller, founder of America's first organized soccer club in 1862 . . ."

Again, just as with William Webb Ellis, it is the date that raises one's eyebrows. The sport of soccer did not exist, officially, in 1862. It was not until the following year that the Football Association's rules were published, and the word *soccer* came into existence. Before that, yes, people were playing "football"—but it was that mixed sport that featured a lot of what subsequently became rugby.

What did Mr. Miller's team play? We have another of those commemorative tablets to look at, this one set up on Boston Common (that same Boston

Common where boys played baseball in 1834, five years before it was invented). This tablet reads:

> On this field the Oneida Football Club of Boston, the first organized
> football club in the United States, played against all comers from 1862
> to 1865. The Oneida goal was never crossed.

How is it that "first organized football club" has come to mean "soccer club"? Look at that last sentence: "The Oneida goal was never crossed." By 1862, those who wanted to play a more soccer-oriented game already had goalposts, and they talked of goals being scored, or won, or obtained, or gained. There was no mention of lines being crossed.

It was those who played the more rugby-oriented game, running with the ball, who scored when the player with the ball ran across the goal line, who talked of "crossing" the goal line.

The chances are high that Mr. Miller's Oneida boys were playing a game much closer to football than to soccer—in which case, the football people have more right to claim Gerrit Smith Miller as a founding father than the soccer people.

And, as far as U.S. soccer is concerned: if not Mr. Miller, then who?

Where It Never Rained

Farewell to the Terraces

LONDON, England—It has been, this past week, a time for the ending of eras. As the first-ever Premier League season closed here, it drew the curtains on Brian Clough's colorful 18-year reign at Nottingham Forest; it marked the last-ever game at The Den, the rusty old stadium where the south London team Millwall has played since 1910; it was supposed to mark the end of Graeme Souness's short, unhappy reign as coach at Liverpool; and, very likely, it sees the end of The Kop, the legendary terraces where Liverpool fans have stood since 1906.

None of the exits went quite according to plan. Clough, one of the great characters of the English game, hung on too long. His last season was a disaster, with Nottingham Forest finishing bottom of the Premier League and Clough forced out by a vote of the directors. The same fate surely awaited Souness—yet against all the predictions, he got a last-minute vote of confidence and will be back at Liverpool next year.

But there will be no reprieve for The Den or The Kop. With their disappearance goes a chapter of English social history. The Saturday-afternoon society of the terraces was for so long the lifeblood of English soccer. It was the concentrated essence of male, working-class England—the society that gave English soccer its personality and its values, its faults and its virtues . . . and all of its players.

Most of my early soccer memories are of afternoons spent on the terraces in the 1940s and 1950s. Inevitably, they are happy memories, tinged with the warmth of nostalgia, colored by the eagerness of youth.

Originally published in Soccer America *May 24, 1993. Reprinted with permission of* Soccer America *magazine.*

How I used to love those Saturdays, the mornings already charged with a sense of excitement, the lunch gobbled down, then the coach or the train or the walk to the ground. As you got near, you could hear some sort of music, usually it was a recording of a military brass band pumping away, sometimes it might even be a real live band, often the local police band.

The brass band music was only part of the soundtrack to those games. It weaved its way in and out of the noise that the assembling crowd made—the shouting, the laughter, and that amorphous, insistent, rustle of moving feet.

Hovering over it all was the pungent fragrance of cheap tobacco, the smoke from thousands of Wills' Woodbine cigarettes, puffed in happy ignorance of yet-to-be-discovered dangers. At games in the industrial midlands, factory workers came straight from Saturday morning shifts, their greasy overalls adding the heavy, sweet odor of oil to the Woodbine smoke.

There was a program to buy, if you could afford it; then you pushed your coins at the man hidden behind the metal grill. The massive metal turnstile gave that wonderful, heavy, decisive click behind you, and there you were, racing up the steps, plunging through an opening into the stadium, then swooping down the concrete terraces, down toward the goal, down to the front where you got closest to the action, where you had a ground-level view of things, and where the goalkeeper towered above you and might even wink at you.

For the next two hours or so, you were safe in the soccer womb, safe on the crowded terraces—there always seemed to be enormous crowds in those days—safe among the coarse, good-natured, male crowd. There was more than soccer involved here, though I don't suppose many of us knew it. One who did know was the writer J. B. Priestley. This is from his novel *The Good Companions:*

> . . . it turned you into a member of a new community, all brothers together for an hour and a half, for not only had you escaped from the clanking machinery of this lesser life, from work, wages, rent, doles, sick pay, insurance cards, nagging wives, ailing children, bad bosses, idle workmen, but you had escaped with most of your mates and your neighbours, with half the town, and there you were, cheering together, thumping one another on the shoulders, swopping judgments like lords of the earth, having pushed your way through a turnstile into another and altogether more splendid kind of life, hurtling with Conflict and yet passionate and beautiful in its Art.

Looking back, it all seems so wonderfully innocent, the football so attractively simple. Of course, it couldn't have been that way, not entirely. I know my memories are warped—I know because I cannot recall ever standing on the terraces in the rain. English weather being what it is, I must have done so, plenty of times. Yet I have no memory of it.

The sun always shone, the people always smiled. Allow me a quote from another English novelist, Somerset Maugham, who shared the fantasy: "I do not know if the English climate was better in those days or if it is only an illusion of youth, but I seem to remember that . . . the sunny days followed one another in an unbroken line."

The illusion of comfort on the terraces goes even deeper; I don't even recall feeling the cold there. I do have one memory, one only, of freezing cold at a game. My sister suddenly developed an interest in soccer, and wanted to come to a game with me. I disapproved, but of course I lost the argument. So I did something I had never done, I reserved two seats. Stoke City against Arsenal, in 1947. The worst winter ever, the winter when disastrous coal shortages almost brought the government down.

So we bought our game program, a single sheet of blue paper with "Fuel Emergency Edition" stamped on it, and we sat, and we slowly turned as blue as that program. Can it possibly be that the only time I ever got cold at a game was the one time when I sat down? It's possible. On the terraces you were swathed in human warmth—and you could move around a bit, you could stamp your feet.

Possible, as I say, but unlikely. I know I have a rosy view of the terraces, and I am desperately sorry to see them vanishing. Sorry to see the last of The Den, on whose terraces I passed many hours in the 1950s. It has been replaced by a new, all-seater stadium—the first new soccer stadium to be built in England since Wembley in 1923!

The Kop is going, too—if not this year, then next, victim of new safety regulations that call for all-seater stadiums by August 1994. The Kop, we are told, is the most vibrant of all the terraces, the most passionate, the most typical.

Certainly, it has become the most famous. As for the rest of the hype, I wouldn't know. I never stood on The Kop. Just one of those things; I wasn't avoiding it, I just never got there. By the time I might have chosen to go, The Kop had become famous, and it didn't appeal to me.

In the 1960s, Liverpool broke through into the consciousness of England, and the world. Thanks largely to the Beatles, but there were other groups too—like Gerry and the Pacemakers, who had a hit with "You'll Never Walk Alone," a mawkish number from the Rodgers and Hammerstein musical *Carousel* that The Kop adopted as its unlikely anthem.

Yes, it was wonderfully colorful, all that waving red and white, and The Kop in full song was a stirring sound. And, let's face it, The Kop had plenty to be noisy about, for Liverpool became the most successful team in England, probably in the world.

For all that, there was something about the phenomenon of The Kop that was deeply disturbing. Because this was not terrace life as it had been. Where easygoing tolerance and fan-mingling once reigned, you now had a solid mass of stridently partisan fans. Where once you had a collection of individuals, you now had a crowd mentality—a crowd that seemed determined to be noticed, to strive for attention.

Did J. B. Priestley's fans go to games to be noticed? Or to escape from notice? Quite a difference. The Kop continued its raucous life, basking in the praise it always received. We were regaled with tales of how witty the fans were, though I never heard an example of that wit that seemed any funnier than the corny old lines we used to bandy around in the '50s.

Social forces that no one understood were burrowing away. Soccer was being tugged away from the working class, the working class itself was undergoing radical change, the big cities—Liverpool foremost among them—were losing their vitality as deindustrialization took a grip.

Did anyone know what was coming? I don't think so. I knew only that I was frightened of mobs, any sort of mob, and I thought I saw the beginnings of mob mentality on terraces that were becoming increasingly fanatical.

I continued, on regular visits to England, to go to Arsenal's North Bank, or to West Ham or to Spurs, always on the terraces, but it wasn't the same. The journeys to the stadiums were fraught with fear as large menacing groups of loutish fans invaded the trains and the buses. At the stadium, the fans were separated, then virtually caged. And everywhere, watchful, nervous, menacing, the police. The police . . . who had once welcomed us to soccer grounds with the harmless oom-pah-pah of their brass bands.

I finally met up with The Kop in, of all places, Italy. Rome 1984, the European Cup final between Liverpool and Roma. I watched the behavior of the Liverpool fans on that occasion—particularly outside the stadium. The mob was already there, ticking ominously away. The ghastly explosion came one year later at Heysel.

Then came Hillsborough, the ultimate tragedy, awful beyond imagination. Tragedy, and heavy irony. For it is Heysel and Hillsborough, more than anything, that have led to the all-seater regulations that are going to kill off The Kop and all the other terraces.

Yes, I greatly regret that. A world that I—and surely hundreds of thousands of others—loved is being swept away. Of course The Kop is not to blame. The Kop was merely the noisiest, the most brash, of the terraces, the cutting edge of a new mentality. In fact, the terraces as I remember them were probably already dying in the 1950s, victims of the social changes that were beginning to revolutionize English society.

So a fond, nostalgic farewell to the terraces, another "bastion of male privilege" that has fallen to the unanswerable advance of progress. I suppose, like most things, like most people, the terraces eventually outlived their purpose. If they were to be nothing more than a breeding place for mobs, then they deserved to go. Future fans will enjoy their soccer while seated, and we shall have no more violence. I hope they are right about that.

But those terraces that I remember from sunlit Saturday afternoons, those terraces where it was never cold and it never rained . . . they deserved something better. For me they live on, a beautiful illusion of youth that will not go away.

Indoor Soccer Loses
Its Relevance
Too Trite to Have Widespread Appeal

NEW YORK—The summer solstice has just recently passed our way. Lately, the event has been marked in England by various groups of loonies descending on Stonehenge. They perform strange and elaborate rites and then go away.

We now have similar evidence of midsummer madness to offer here. The devotees of indoor soccer have switched from the winter to the summer solstice, and are gathering at various Astroturfed Stonehenges around the country to watch their pagan game played out under artificial lights and, presumably, air conditioning.

What else goes on in those rude temples of soccer heresy, I wouldn't know. It's been quite a few years since I last fled the Nassau Coliseum, driven out by the sheer hysterical, high-volume, brassy artificiality of it all. The New York Arrows, wasn't it? They were supposed to be pretty good at whatever it was they were doing. Possibly. They gave me nausea and acute soccer-withdrawal symptoms.

We have been told, repeatedly and insistently, that indoor soccer is good for the game, that it has kept soccer alive, that it is exactly the type of soccer that Americans want, that it is the wave of the future, that it is just the thing for the training of young American players, and quite probably that it will cure cancer and solve the Somali crisis.

Well, we've had 15 years of this human pinball stuff—ample time, methinks, to make an assessment of its achievements. Unfortunately, that is to say fortunately, we do not have one of those elaborate surveys by the Soc-

Originally published in Soccer America *July 12, 1993. Reprinted with permission of* Soccer America *magazine.*

cer Industry Council of America (SICA) that could tell us that 50 billion people played indoor soccer at least once for 10 seconds during the past 15 years.

So, in the absence of the usual SICA scientific accuracy, you'll have to put up with my own impressions on the matter. Your undivided attention, please. We shall commence with a definition of indoor soccer.

First of all, what it is not: I am not talking about the sort of game played in gymnasiums around these parts, for instance, in the winter. This is merely a way of playing soccer when it's too cold to do it outdoors. The game is, by and large, an attempt to retain the features of the outdoor game in a condensed form. Ersatz soccer, but better than nothing, a stopgap until the real thing can start up again.

The indoor soccer I'm talking about is the one that was created by the old North American Soccer League and taken over by the Major Indoor Soccer League. For the MISL, there was no question of this being an adjunct to the outdoor game; MISL soccer was to be a separate entity, in competition with, *and better than,* the real thing. This was MISL soccer, with its boards and its penalty boxes (I should pause here, for a moment, so that you can digest those two elements and reflect on the degree of original thinking that went into the pinball game).

That's what I'm talking about, the MISL-style game. And I'm going to assess it on the basis of what it has done for the real game of soccer, the outdoor game. Those who raise howls of protest that this measurement is unfair can shut up right now. All I am doing is listening to the many, many, indoor voices that have told me so many, many times about the vital contribution that indoor soccer has made to the overall strength of the game.

So what has MISL-style indoor soccer done for the outdoor game? The official results of my 15-year survey will not be published as a full-blown research paper. They can be summed up in one word: nothing.

Nothing. As far as the outdoor game, the real game, goes, indoor soccer has contributed precisely nothing. Where, for instance, are all the national team players who were going to become so brilliantly skilled by playing "under pressure" and in "confined space"? (Again, these are not my definitions; they have all been put forward at one time or another by the defenders of the pinball faith.)

Where are the players? There aren't any. None. Zilch, zero, forget it. Promising young American players do not grow up bursting with a desire to throw themselves headfirst into the pinball maelstrom. They grow up with the desire, common to all budding sports stars, to learn as much about their sport as they can.

That has never been easy in this country. But you have to be soft in the head to imagine that the MISL and its various teratoid spinoffs have made it any easier. (Hey, maybe I've hit on something here: it seems quite possible that head-softening could be a problem for those who have spent many years in the plastic confines of indoor soccer, deafened by loud soundtracks and screaming announcers, subjected to penetrating laser beams, strange miasmic mists, and the as-yet-undetermined long-term effects of overexposure to artificial turf.)

So any young player who seriously wants to perfect his game never even considers going anywhere near the indoor game. Nowadays, the only realistic option is to head for outdoor soccer in Europe. A considerable risk, a considerable adventure . . . but one that an increasing number of young guys consider worth taking.

That has been the answer to the troublesome question: how many good young players has indoor soccer swallowed up and distorted to the point where they could never be outdoor stars? How many potential national team players have been lost? I am satisfied that the answer to that is none. Bright young American players recognize a trap when they see one.

Of course, I'm being extremely charitable to our indoor friends when I say that they have contributed nothing to the game. The fact is that they have been, right from the start, a damaging influence on the game. Inevitably. The indoor game was always going to be a fungus growing on the body of outdoor soccer. The only question was whether the two activities could sustain parallel and mutually helpful lives, or whether indoor soccer would be a parasitic growth.

That question was settled almost at once by MISL founder Earl Foreman's hostile and scornful attitude toward the outdoor game. The two were in competition. Indoor soccer would be a parasite, taking as many top players and as many college draftees as it could grab. I don't doubt that many of the MISL coaches did want to cooperate with the outdoor game, did feel that they were keeping things going as the NASL collapsed (a collapse substantially expedited by the rise of the MISL).

But look at what happened. The attempt to qualify for the 1986 World Cup was bedeviled with arguments over whether national team players with MISL clubs could be released or, if they were released, how long it would take them to make the transition from indoor to outdoor soccer. If, indeed, they could manage it at all.

For me, the hopeless incompatibility of it all came to a hilarious climax at a press conference in Los Angeles in June 1985. National team coach Alkis Panagoulias was sitting on the dais, looking even more distracted than usual, complaining about the problems he was having with indoor soccer—"this ridiculous sport" he called it. Sitting among the journalists, a painfully bemused expression on his face, was the archpriest of indoor coaches, Ron

Newman. He was bemused because the USSF, trying to show that all was well between indoor and outdoor soccer, had just made the spectacularly sappy move of appointing him assistant to Panagoulias.

Of course it didn't work, and the U.S. was bounced out of the 1986 World Cup qualifiers by Costa Rica. Since that time, indoor soccer has become increasingly irrelevant to the future of soccer in this country.

Last year we had the sight of the MISL finally collapsing under the weight of its own banalities, after which indoor soccer should really have done the decent thing, fallen on its sword and disappeared. But it won't, of course. The birth of the Continental Indoor Soccer League (CISL) proves that. How interesting to hear Tim Harris, the manager of Los Angeles United, admit that the indoor game has run out of stars, and that the CISL (which could be, but probably isn't, pronounced chisel) will feature a lot of "workers."

Well now, doesn't *that* make it sound irresistibly attractive? Indoor soccer without skill. Rather like a funeral service without the jokes. Quite possibly those who can't get tickets for the demolition derby will make the CISL their second choice. If soccer played by workers represents the pinnacle of thinking over at CISL headquarters, then you have to feel sorry for them. They have learned nothing.

For years, for decades, for as long as anyone can remember, the outdoor soccer bosses in this country have been trying to tell Americans that they must be crazy not to like soccer . . . while at the same time presenting them with a dull, unimaginative version of the game that was guaranteed to bore the pants off everyone. Soccer played by workers. If there is any excuse at all for the indoor variation, it surely doesn't include the right to repeat the most egregious of the outdoor game's errors.

But this isn't something to fret about. If there are people around who enjoy seeing workers charge aimlessly about, crashing into boards and each other, if they're willing to pay to watch it, then so be it. Let them enjoy themselves. All I ask is that they, and the rest of the indoor tribe, stop making out that what absorbs them has anything to do with soccer.

MISL-style indoor soccer—whether played by stars, or workers, or by trained rabbit-eared bandicoots—has long since ceased to have any helpful relevance at all to the development of the game in this country. It can now be seen, clearly, for what it was always likely to be: a nuisance.

It represents a distraction, a sidetracking of energy, money, and potential talent from the real game. I guess we're going to have to live with that for the foreseeable future.

There was a time when I would wake up sweating in the dead of night and babbling about boards, and blue lines, and body blocks and stuff like that. Not any more. I sleep soundly these nights, quite certain that the hustle and bustle of the indoor game are simply too trite to have widespread appeal to those who know their soccer.

The sports have split asunder, and I perceive at least a tacit acknowledgment that their interests are different. By this time, they may well have produced two different sets of fans. I certainly hope they have.

What is needed here, to clarify the air and dispel any residual confusion, is a new name for indoor soccer, one that doesn't include the word soccer. Until the new name arrives, it would be a good idea to replace "soccer" with "something." In this way the activity of indoor something can go its own sweet, summer solstice way, headed by that latest temporary haven for workers rather than players, the Continental Indoor Something League.

Drawing Conclusions

African Teams Show Promise
at Under-17 Championships
(Under-17 World Cup–1993)

TOKYO, Japan—If, as Wordsworth has it, the child is father to the man, then there are some highly fascinating conclusions to be drawn from this latest under-17 World Cup.

Here we had the children—from Europe, from South America, from Africa and Asia, and from the United States, too. What sort of men will they become, what sort of soccer will they give us in six or seven or eight years' time, these child players?

The Asians are the most difficult to pin down. Qatar, a tiny country, no soccer tradition, the sport imposed almost artificially where the weather conditions aren't suitable. But coaxed along by Brazilian coaches. So you would expect, and you get, pretty good ball skills. You get too, according to coach Humberto Redes, commitment and intelligence, a great willingness to learn.

So Qatar was taught—ironically, by a Brazilian—how to play the offside trap. They made it work well, they had the discipline to do that. But it fell apart badly when the United States geared its game specifically to beating it. The commitment remained—even when down 1–5 and playing a man short, Qatar kept coming. But there's no real sense of style here yet.

China, yes. Powerful, athletic, quick, good skills. Ball on the ground mostly, short passes, much running. If I have an image of an Asian style, it goes back to North Korea in 1966. Nonstop buzzing around, a dizzying whirl of passes. China was definitely in that mold. But it is all, at the moment, a bit mechanical, probably played too quickly to admit any of the needed subtlety. Too much bodily speed, not enough thought. And all that haste means that

Originally published in Soccer America *September 20, 1993. Reprinted with permission of* Soccer America *magazine.*

goal chances are not taken coolly, they are part of a rather overwrought approach, they tend to get missed. That China finished bottom of its group had a lot to do with poor finishing; it managed to score only one goal.

The Japanese were similar to China, but better at what they were doing, because in Nobuyuki Zaizen they had an excellent organizer, a player who did always seem to have time to do what he wanted, a real soccer brain at work. The nonstop energy of the Japanese game was matched by considerable sophistication and skill. The J-League has some promising youngsters coming along.

South America showed us nothing new. Not necessarily a problem that, for the Latin game at its best is still the cream of what the sport has to offer. Colombia bristled with remarkable ball control and the usual telepathic passing. But nervousness seemed to be a problem. How else to account for their 1–3 defeat by the RCS (Representatives of Czechs and Slovaks), a greatly inferior team?

By all that was logical, the speed of thought and execution of the Colombians should have taken the RCS apart. But the ponderous RCS players had the better of it. Not so when they met another South American team, Chile, who did indeed take them apart, 4–1. The Chileans were always looking, in the South American way, to *play* the ball forward, to work it out of defense, even under considerable pressure. It meant a lot of ball possession, and it meant plenty of chances for the dynamic little Frank Lobos to weave his soccer magic. He wore, inevitably, #10, and was decidedly left-footed. I counted two other predominant lefties on the Chilean team. A factor? Quite possibly, but how to assess it?

The thing about South American soccer is that it is unswervingly skill-based. And that is a basis that is always capable of almost endless development.

The Europeans? Oh dear. I didn't see the Italians, but the RCS and Poland were just about as depressingly ordinary as you could imagine. Big, strong, athletic, powerful headers and long kickers, yes, all of that. Too much of that. Subtlety, skill, creative or dribbling ability? Hardly any of that. A case in point: I watched Poland three times—two hours of soccer—and I recorded just *four* occasions when a Polish player passed the ball with the outside of his foot.

A statistic that is not as meaningless as it sounds. You couldn't watch, for example, any Brazilian team, at any age, for more than a few minutes without seeing four outside-of-the-foot passes. It is essential to their smooth-flowing, artistic game, it allows players to run, naturally, at full speed, and to pass without breaking stride.

The Poles (and for that matter the RCS) live almost exclusively on a stunting diet of inside-of-the-foot passes. No player yet heard of can pass with the inside of his foot while running naturally. Inevitably the game is jerkier, less subtle, less pleasing to the eye, more predictable.

That's just for starters. Unlike the Chileans, the Polish and RCS defenders rarely looked to play the ball out. When they were around, the stadium resounded to big, solid whacks as the ball flew forward 40 or 50 or 60 yards. The Poles were saved from total nothingness by Maciej Terlecki, a ball handler of considerable skill. How much more at home he would have looked playing for Chile! The Europeans, in short, looked old-fashioned, which is bad enough. But they were also boring, which is unforgivable.

And so to the Africans. To deal first with a perennial problem: the suspicions and the rumors about the age of their players are still around. The Italians, in fact, while not going so far as to lodge an official protest, have drawn FIFA's attention to the "difficulties" of playing in this under-17 age group.

There is no easy solution to this one. I can't think how it can be solved, short of an infallible age test on the players' bones or other tissues. I'm going to ignore it, because it's irrelevant to the matter of playing style. And what a wonderful contrast the Africans presented to the jaded game of the Europeans.

As skillful as the South Americans, yes—though in a different way, with the artistry of the Latin game replaced with an extraordinarily gymnastic quality. Fitter, stronger, and faster than any of the others. Above all, with a freshness to their game, an ability to play the sport with a smile, to infuse the game and the spectators with the feeling that this an enjoyable experience.

Is this the soccer of the future? Let us hope so. These sparkling, light-footed players must get better and better. The Poles, methinks, are likely only to get heavier. And duller.

And what of the U.S.? There was no new lesson to be learned here. The situation was similar to that of two years ago: the quarterfinals were achieved, and it all got a bit too difficult at that point. The jump from quarters to semis is substantial—not just in the caliber of the play. It's a different world. The final four in Japan featured the superior talents of Ghana and Nigeria, plus the experienced young professionals of Chile and Poland.

The American kids are, for quite a while yet, going to find it difficult to enter that world. Says coach Roy Rees: "It's a big gap, and the standard is going up all the time. We were fortunate we didn't have to go up against Ghana or Nigeria in group play. They're so far ahead, it's unreal.

"It's nice to have ambitions, to think we're going to win a medal—but they might be unrealistic at the moment, with what we've got, with our system.

"We've got to be better prepared for the World Cup arena—for the large crowds and media attention—we've got to play in places like Brazil, or Argentina, or Nigeria, to take our knocks.

"In all four World Cups that I've coached in, there have been players who have looked great all the way through the preparation and the qualifying stages . . . then in the finals you think 'Where the hell are they?' They're out there, but they've frozen, they're just standing around with their mouths open. There's a social problem here. Some of our kids have never heard the word *no*.

"I'm not talking about playing in front of 50,000 people, just maybe 5,000. We need to try to reproduce that atmosphere before the real thing. I think we should think seriously about staging the Concacaf qualifying games."

Déjà vu with a vengeance. I recall Angus McAlpine, who coached the very first U.S. entry into the under-17 World Cup in China in 1985, lamenting the lack of experience of the U.S. players and their inability to handle the big occasion. He, too, wanted preparation games played before large crowds. But where do you find such pressure games for youth players? Anyway, this is hardly a problem that only the American kids have to face. Youth soccer does not draw big crowds anywhere in the world.

Put simply, the American kids are pampered and naive when compared to any other team that is likely to reach the final four. They know little of the realities of the high-level international game. Where would they have learned about that? By playing in the Niotis Cup, or for Olympic Development Program (ODP) regional teams?

The USSF hasn't exactly helped the running and selection of the team. Here we have an ostensibly professional setup—that is what the USSF is now supposed to exude, a new professionalism. So the under-17s travel with an assistant coach, a physio, an equipment manager, a secretary, a press officer, and a national team director. All of them no doubt very professional, all of them full-time employees of the USSF.

The joke is that the guy who should be the most important one of the lot, the coach—Roy Rees—is a part-time employee! As such, his life has not been easy when dealing with the new professionalism of the USSF.

Asked if he wanted to continue as coach of the under-17 team, Rees paused before replying slowly and carefully: "My future? I would hope that I do have a future with the under-17 team—but only if I can coach it in the way that I feel the game should be played, without interference from Chicago.

"There's been a year of tinkering with the team from that end. I don't want a repeat of that. I should be the one who decides the way the team plays, and selects the players and the support staff. That's the only way that anyone can run a soccer team. That's what happens elsewhere throughout the world—and in other sports in the U.S.A."

I talked earlier of the naivete and the lack of real international experience of the young U.S. players. One can make excuses, reasonable excuses, for that.

And one knows that people, good people, are aware of the problem and trying to do something about it.

But there are no excuses at all to be made when the same sort of naivete is repeated at the top level, the adult level, of this new, professionalized USSF. Worse: who up there is aware of the problem? Who is trying to do something about it?

Havelange Rules in Vegas Wonderland
Rothenberg Promises Grand Pro League

LAS VEGAS—It is 07:30 and I am wandering through the Flamingo-Hilton Hotel looking for the coffee shop. To get there—as, indeed, to get anywhere in Las Vegas—you have to pass through huge halls jammed with row upon row of shiny, slick slot machines.

It is 07:30 in the morning, and there are people here pouring their money into these things, smoking themselves sick as they do so. Nobody looks very happy.

None of it makes much sense to me, but it all fits nicely into the unreality that is Las Vegas. Fake volcanoes, fake sphinxes, fake pirate ships, fake statues that come to life and talk . . . where do you find reality in all this?

Now, that should be easy to answer. I didn't go to Las Vegas for the fantasy, I went for the World Cup Draw. A genuine, high-powered soccer event, with all the world's soccer heavies on hand—that's pretty real, no?

Don't ask. I'm still confused, still trying to work out whether anything that was said during the proceedings really meant what it seemed to mean. Or was it all—like the volcanoes and the statues—glittering surface, with nothing underneath? Or were there secret meanings hidden below the public facade?

You had to start feeling like Alice, wandering in her intriguing Wonderland:

> For, you see, so many out-of-the-way things had happened lately, that Alice had begun to think that very few things indeed were really impossible.

Originally published in Soccer America *January 17, 1994. Reprinted with permission of* Soccer America *magazine.*

What, for instance, to make of Alan Rothenberg's masterful performance at the press conference where he announced the details (or some of the details) of the new pro league, Major League Soccer? A league, he said, that "will soon rank with the finest in the world." Heavens, no wonder FIFA was impressed.

This was a very convincing presentation, carried along with a sweeping, smiling buoyancy that left little room for doubters. Anyone not caught up in Rothenberg's spirit of go-get-'em optimism had to be some kind of sourpuss.

Rothenberg is a brilliant orchestrator on these occasions. He touches on everything, doesn't dodge issues, answers questions sensibly and articulately. But how *real* was all this? I feel pretty certain that Rothenberg left most people genuinely believing that major investors were falling over themselves to get into the new league. True or false? Or simply the potential truth that becomes reality through faith?

From one sort of unreality to another. We were asked to believe that it was OK to have the Draw with the likes of Barry Manilow and Evander Holyfield and Robin Williams (and how many soccer games do you think that lot have attended in the past 10 years?), but without Pelé.

Obviously, that couldn't be. Everyone *knew* that Pelé had to be present, had to be there up on the platform. Pelé, the one name that instantly means soccer in this country—how could you leave him out?

Yet the rumors were flying that FIFA president João Havelange didn't want Pelé to take part. A squabble between two Brazilians, with Pelé accusing the Brazilian soccer federation of corruption. With the crucial complication that the federation is headed by Havelange's son-in-law.

Even so, surely this could be worked out. Alan Rothenberg, racing from meeting to meeting, stopped for a brief second or two to pant, "Of course, it *has* to be worked out." At the first press conference—Havelange not present—FIFA general secretary Sepp Blatter smiled and said "Pelé will be with the FIFA family in the hall on Sunday—where he will be positioned, we shall see."

Now, that all sounded reasonable enough, but the reality turned out to be something quite different. There was a second press conference, and this time Havelange was present. Wasn't he ever. It started four hours later than scheduled, and one glance at Blatter as he took his place told you that something was not right. Blatter looking red-faced and bemused? Blatter with his normally sparkling, alert eyes reduced to a numbed glaze?

Evidently Havelange had been showing everyone just who was who when it came to FIFA decisions. Stony-faced and cold-eyed, Havelange toughed it out when the questions about Pelé started. He answered, as he always does in this country, in French.

> The Queen turned and said to Alice "Speak in French when you can't
> think of the English for a thing—turn out your toes when you
> walk—and remember who you are!"

I don't know about the toes, but Havelange certainly left no doubt as to who he was. His answers were really quite extraordinary. FIFA owns the World Cup, he said, and will decide who participates. Informed that Rothenberg had publicly stated that he would be disappointed if Pelé didn't take part, Havelange bluntly and abrasively replied: "Rothenberg would be disappointed if we withdrew the World Cup. He has all he wants."

To a third question, Havelange—still staring icily in front of him, still not uttering the word Pelé—countered: "I have already said that FIFA will decide how we are going to proceed. The persons who participate are unimportant to FIFA. What is important is the result of the draw. The presence or absence of one person in no way affects this."

> "I have answered three questions, and that is enough,"
> Said his father. "Don't give yourself airs!
> Do you think I can listen all day to such stuff?
> Be off, or I'll kick you downstairs!"

And we were, all of us, kicked downstairs by this formidable man. But the unreality persisted. After the conference, FIFA press officer Guido Tognoni said he thought that Havelange "had left the door open"—a mighty generous interpretation of Havelange's implacable stand.

The Italian press reported that, backstage, there had been an almighty row between "FIFA and the Americans" over Pelé's presence. Well, there should have been—but I was informed that, in fact, there was no row, and that everyone, presumably including Rothenberg, had agreed with Havelange's decision.

> "I can't believe *that!*" said Alice.
> "Can't you?" the Queen said in a pitying tone. "Try again: draw a
> long breath, and shut your eyes."

So we all shut our eyes, and it was true. No Pelé. But in a way, Pelé had the last laugh. He did attend the Draw, sitting in the auditorium. His entry was marked by a mad rush of journalists and photographers and TV crews, some of whom had to be literally strong-armed away from him, as their antics threatened to delay the start of the proceedings.

More unreality. No Pelé on the platform meant that there was no South American representation. Here is a continent that has won half the World

Cups, that has given the game more than a fair share of its greatest players—and FIFA and the United States organizing committee simply *forget* to acknowledge them?

So we listened to the dreary Barry Manilow, the aging James Brown, the uninspired Stevie Wonder, and we watched what appeared to be an out-of-focus home video of Rod Stewart. Said an exasperated and loud-voiced English journalist: "What the f— has all this got to do with football?"

Quite so. The game itself did manage to intrude for a moment or two when we got some fleeting action up on the screens with Roberto Baggio scoring two of the worst goals he's ever scored (tapes presumably supplied by the same guy who masterminded the Rod Stewart footage). That was it. It would have been possible—wouldn't it?—when each team was introduced, to show some action footage, a goal or two, some celebrations?

Much too imaginative, that. We got static slides, just team pictures. A colleague insisted that the team picture of Colombia was actually Ecuador—but how could you tell? It was on and off in a flash.

> "I see nobody . . ." said Alice.
> "I only wish I had such eyes," the King remarked in a fretful tone. "To
> be able to see Nobody! And at that distance too! Why, it's as much as
> I can do to see real people, by this light!"

The Draw procedures, which seemed logical to me, had already been explained by Blatter in a dry run two days earlier. "I don't know if you like it," he said. "But this is the way we shall do it."

Blatter duly performed his duty with the colored balls and the glass pots, and those who had been insisting that the whole thing was fixed were left in some disarray. If this was fixing, it was very strange fixing. I mean, Mexico in the New York group (but playing in Washington and Orlando)? The United States in with Colombia, Switzerland, and Romania? And wasn't Ireland supposed to be a surefire bet for Boston? ("All it proves," said one unrepentant believer in skullduggery, "is that FIFA can't even get the fixing right.")

"What is important," Havelange had said, "is the result of the draw." But, of course there was no result. Or was there? The rumor mills started up again. Havelange, they insisted, had really blotted his copybook this time and would certainly be challenged when the presidential election comes around next year . . . it could be the Union of European Football Associations (UEFA) President Lennart Johansson, or maybe the Belgian Michel D'Hooge, or the Cameroon Issa Hayatou, or maybe even Blatter himself.

"Contrariwise," continued Tweedledee, "if it was so, it might be; and if it were so, it would be; but as it isn't, it ain't. That's logic."

And if it's not, it's the best we can do. You'll just have to allow a little time for the Las Vegas madness to wear off. By then the real games will have started and the unreal Draw will have been forgotten.

A King Unworthy of
a Crown Jewel?
How Does the United States
Measure Up as the Host Nation?

NEW YORK—The World Cup in America? Preposterous! The very idea has greatly upset football's traditionalists. Why should the sport's crown jewel be given to a country with no soccer traditions? A country where—such is the myth—they do not even like the game?

FIFA made the decision on the very American day of July 4, 1988. Only three countries had submitted bids to host the 1994 tournament. Brazil's, flimsily prepared, had already come under withering attack from FIFA president João Havelange, himself a Brazilian. Morocco's bid was based on stadiums, hotels, and roads yet to be built: "The World Cup is not a development program," was the FIFA general secretary Sepp Blatter's dismissive comment.

The U.S. had done its homework. Its bid was full of the statistics, projections, and guarantees that FIFA wanted to hear. The U.S. it had to be.

FIFA emphasized the adventurous aspect of the decision: the conquering of the final frontier. Critics, mostly European, particularly British, saw nothing but the hand of Mammon at work. They envisaged a sport sold out to the most crass of commercial interests.

British reports on World Cup '94 preparations flogged the word *razzmatazz* to death.* The accusation was clear. The Yanks, with no tradition of soccer, no sensitivity to it, would let slip the dogs of sponsorship and cry havoc all over the sport. Football would be cheapened; it would be a Disneyfied, Mickey Mouse World Cup.

Originally published in The Guardian *(London) June 17, 1994. Copyright © The Guardian. Reprinted by permission.*

World Cup '94: Cup winner Brazil takes the field in its hand-holding chain formation. Those who poured scorn on the idea of the U.S.A. hosting the World Cup were choking on their own words as the tournament played to packed stadiums everywhere and set a new record for the total number of spectators. *Copyright John McDermott*

And so the rumors grew: "the Americans" were trying to change the rules; they wanted larger goals, demanded television timeouts, and were insisting on stratospheric ticket prices.

The truth? FIFA has made some rule modifications, not to appease the Americans, but to counter the negative football widely seen at the last World Cup. There will be no television timeouts, they were never requested. The ticket prices, in this rich country, are relatively high.

"It will be the greatest World Cup ever," is the constant refrain of Alan Rothenberg, the U.S. '94 organizer. No doubt he is right: every World Cup is the greatest, better than the one before it.

But when it comes to filling the stadiums, Rothenberg has proof. Over 3.5 million tickets have been bought, far more than ever before. It is a virtual sellout.

Even that does not convince the doubters, who see stadiums packed with Americans wandering about buying hot dogs, while they wait for the scoreboard to tell them when to applaud. But no passion.

Hang on. The idea of the U.S. as a soccer wilderness is another myth to be dispelled. Official estimates of players go as high as 15 million, an exaggeration no doubt. Halve it, and at 7.5 million one has still got twice the population of Ireland. Most are young and not yet organized enough to carry the political and cultural clout the numbers suggest.

But football—soccer—knowledge and appreciation is now widespread in this country. Americans are not yet fanatical enough to paint their faces, wave flags, and let off flares, but the huge ethnic populations here know all about that.

Look no further than the recent crowds: 91,000, mostly Mexicans, in the Rose Bowl to watch U.S. vs. Mexico; and 73,000, mostly Colombians, at Giants Stadium to watch Colombia vs. Greece. Huge, beautifully well-behaved, genuine football crowds. If Americans lack the spice of passion, it will be supplied by ethnic groups and visiting supporters.

One group of foreign fans has already made a massive contribution to the success of World Cup '94: the English. By not coming.

Forget all the kind words from the American organizers about regretting the absence of England. The hooligans, or just the threat of the hooligans, would have been a nightmare for the U.S., blackening the image of the sport in American eyes and adding millions of dollars to security costs. The organizers should consider erecting a statue in honor of Graham Taylor.

World Cup '94 will not be a failure. It will be, as every World Cup has been, a spectacular event capped by the crowning of a world champion. That is assured. There will be—as always—embarrassments and stupidities and cock-ups, but this time with an American accent.

The massive commitment of American know-how and resources will not allow failure. The blue-chip sponsors—Coca Cola, McDonald's, General Motors, MasterCard, Gillette, American Airlines, Mars, ITT Sheraton—have put up their money and, by and large, have kept their hands off the sport.

But this American version of the World Cup needs to be successful twice over. Domestically as well as globally. It is supposed to sell the sport itself to the great American public and lay the groundwork for a professional league to start next year.

Not so easy in a country that—in baseball, American football, basketball, and ice hockey—already has four major-league professional sports whose seasons overlap to take up the whole year. On July 18, the day after the World Cup final, the really difficult bit begins.

Note:

* This story appeared in the English newspaper *The Guardian* and was given a rather negative heading, which I do not feel reflected the spirit of my article. On the same page, illustrating another World Cup '94 article, was a large picture of the Macy's Thanksgiving Day Parade in New York, with the Cat in a Hat sitting on a huge soccer ball. The caption—without irony as far as I can see—read "the Cat in the Hat is right on the ball as the razzmatazz gets into full swing . . . "

Nigeria's Roughhouse Play Belies Team's Skill, Potential

NEW YORK—In 1982 it was Cameroon that first displayed the beauty, the power, and the skill of African soccer on the World Cup stage. The enormous potential was confirmed in Italy in 1990, again by Cameroon, when it got through to the quarterfinals.

Cameroon is in the Cup again, but below its former strength. The great hope for Africa is, instead, Nigeria. During the last decade, it has been one of the most powerful nations at the youth level, winning the under-17 World Cup in 1985 and 1991. The Nigerians are now ready for the adult game.

In their first match in the U.S., the Super Eagles tromped all over Bulgaria with an awesome display of muscular-but-skillful soccer. Rashidi Yekini, a 31-year-old veteran, looked like everyone's idea of a true goal-scorer—big, bold, and brave. Even more impressive was the young midfielder Daniel Amokachi, 22, who took command of the game with an authority that bordered on arrogance. Add the speed and dribbling skills of Finidi George and Samson Siasia, and there exists one of the most exciting teams of the tournament.

The teasing promise of African soccer has always been that it will approach perfection by finding the answer to a question that has baffled coaches for decades: how to combine the artistry of Brazilians with the power of Europeans.

Nigeria would seem to have all that is necessary to do that. Its players possess uniformly excellent ball control and speed, and the strength and versatility of gymnasts.

Originally published in USA Today *June 28, 1994. Copyright © 1994 Paul Gardner.*

The excitement such a mixture could produce was seen in flashes against Bulgaria. But it was a different story when Nigeria met Argentina. In that game, the unacceptable face of African soccer appeared: a tendency—at times, it seemed almost like a compulsion—to commit reckless fouls.

At halftime, the unofficial foul count was Nigeria 24, Argentina 2. Every player on the Nigerian team, except goalkeeper Peter Rufai, had committed at least one foul.

These were not all minor offenses. Augustine Eguavoen's scything kick at Claudio Caniggia's legs had the stadium roaring in disbelief. After the game, Argentine coach Alfio "Coco" Basile grimly remarked that five of his players, including Diego Maradona, would need treatment for kicks received during the game.

It was precisely this flaw of impetuous, dangerous tackling that spelled defeat for Cameroon in the 1990 quarterfinals. Playing superbly and leading England 2–1, Cameroon threw the game away by giving up two penalty kicks.

The soccer that Yekini, Amokachi, George, and Siasia and their teammates play is full of skill and beauty. But it is undermined by a self-destructive, roughhouse element. To succeed at the World Cup level, Nigeria—and African soccer in general—must clean up its act.

Genius Betrayed: Diego Maradona

NEW YORK—FIFA thought about it, then changed its mind. No sudden death in the second round, they decided. In the first round, sudden death didn't apply. They couldn't know that the sudden death of Diego Maradona was looming.

Could any of us have imagined that the man who was once the sport's greatest star would commit soccer suicide by taking ephedrine? Most of us have probably taken ephedrine at one time or another, it's in a lot of those common cold cures. It opens up your bronchial tubes, makes breathing easier.

But it does more. It acts like adrenaline, it stimulates the central nervous system, gets your heart pumping more vigorously, prepares the body for urgent physical activity. Yes, it must be considered a performance-enhancing drug.

It seems we are at the sad, bitter end of the tortured Maradona story. Surely, this must be the end. This inspiring, depressing story of talent gone wrong, of genius betrayed, has worn us all out.

It was 18 years ago that the reports started to come out of Argentina telling of a wonder boy, a 15-year-old of surpassing talent. He didn't make the 1978 Argentina World Cup winning team—too young, too inexperienced, said coach César Menotti.

Maradona arrived at a moment when the sport of soccer desperately needed a superstar. He was never going to be allowed to develop slowly and naturally. He was swept aloft on an irresistible tide of publicity and sponsor-

Originally published in '94 Cup Daily *July 1, 1994.*

ship and agents and huge contracts. The boy from the large poor family—he has seven brothers and sisters—was suddenly fabulously rich.

I once spent a morning with Diego's father, going round the Museum of the Communist Revolution in Beijing. A dreadfully boring display, nothing but tedious details of Mao Tse Tung's life. After several hours of this, near the exit, I found myself standing next to Papa Maradona as we stared into a case that contained an empty pot, unlabeled. "What is that?" I asked. "That," replied Papa, "is the pot that Mao Tse Tung used to piss in."

An earthy man, with a lovely sense of humor. If only Diego had stayed with those roots. But how could he? Too young, too inexperienced, Menotti had said. He was talking of soccer, but it applied to Diego's life as well.

Soon he was off to Spain, and the hangers-on gathered. The Maradona clan. Then on to the madhouse that is Napoli. Nightlife, a parenthood lawsuit, rumors of Camorra links, and cocaine. The quiet young boy with the innocent face and the big appealing eyes ought to have been crushed by all this. For me, that never quite happened.

The boy was always there. It was the boy in Maradona that confessed at one point that he was tired of soccer, that all he wanted to do was play soccer with kids, away from crowded stadiums.

Superstars don't get that sort of luxury.

Moneymaking is an infectious disease, and Maradona caught it big time. Why not? He'd never had any money; now he could lavish it on his family. He was always faithful to them.

His talent was so superb that it stood up to the constant psychological bombardment of a brain awhirl with strange and damaging ideas; it resisted the insidious deterioration of a body that was slowly being allowed to slide; it conquered the roughness and the brutality that he met from opponents on the field.

The climax came in 1986 in Mexico. Maradona led Argentina to victory in that World Cup, and he dominated the whole tournament. In that one marvelous game against England, you got the awful contradiction that is Maradona. That hand-ball goal, and six minutes later—as though Diego himself felt that he needed to atone for his cheating—one of the most marvelous goals in World Cup history.

He has given me as much pleasure as any player I've seen in over 50 years of watching soccer. Yes, he was a cheat, that remains part of his flawed character. But, of course, I shall not remember him as a cheat.

I shall recall him as a soccer genius. I never knew him as a young boy, but it is as a lively kid that I shall remember him. I had two long interviews with him—the last one 10 years ago—and I remember those bright and youthful eyes. Mischievous, boyish eyes. I suppose I've created my own Peter Pan of soccer, and now I've seen it destroyed.

We can't take any more of this, Diego. Please, no recriminations, no talk of plots and vendettas. Go with dignity.

Not with the dignity of mature adulthood. You never had that. But with the simple dignity of a modest boy who once loved soccer more than money and fame.

Closet Dribblers Can Out Themselves
Golden Age of Dribbling?

NEW YORK—In April 1993, Scotland traveled to Portugal for a crucial World Cup qualifying game. The Scottish coach, Andy Roxburgh, was quoted before the game as saying that he felt that the game would be decided by set plays.

But the Scots, however brilliant their set plays may have been, failed to score at all. The Portuguese scored five times—and none of the goals came from a set play.

In fact, the rout had its origins in something that is the very antithesis of set plays. It owed everything to the inventive skills of Paulo Futre, who put on one of the most dazzling shows of uninhibited dribbling that I have seen in quite a while.

Unless you happened to be Scottish, Futre was a joy to behold, unstoppable that evening, a teasing, darting will-o'-the-wisp who brought a spellbinding magic to the game. The magic of dribbling.

A magic that has not been seen nearly enough in recent years. Odd, is it not, that the sport's crown jewel should have been forgotten, frowned upon, almost scorned? When George Best appeared on the scene in 1963 it was said of him that he "had brought dribbling back to the sport." Even then, 30 years ago, it was not fashionable to dribble.

This sport, which had once, in its very early days, been defined simply as "the dribbling game," had horrendously lost its way.

It wasn't just that dribblers had somehow gone out of fashion, that the natural progress of the game had rendered them irrelevant. That was a

Originally published in Soccer America *October 24, 1994. Reprinted with permission of* Soccer America *magazine.*

process that *had* happened—with wingers. The modern game could not accommodate players who waited out on the touchline, too little involved until the ball was fed to them, players who were not prepared to fall back and help out on defense. So in the 1960s, the position of winger withered away. That was sad enough, but it was not just the position that disappeared—it was also the skill that had been such a prominent part of the winger's game: dribbling.

Dribblers, wingers or nonwingers, were no longer wanted. The modern game was all about first-time passing. The pace was too high for dribblers, who tended to slow things down. Worse, they might lose the ball, cough it up in a dangerous area of the field. The game was too important, too much money was now at stake to run that sort of risk.

Another thing: the game was now too organized. Coaches had arrived, swarms of them, to plan and to control and to impose their wills and their tactics.

Tactics, said a player from a bygone era, are "what you do when you don't have the players." Not any more. Now, tactics were for everyone. Even the teams that had the best players needed all manner of tactics.

If nothing else, it was certainly a marvelous way of increasing the importance of the coach. And decreasing the value of the dribblers.

Once the field had been scientifically divided into thirds, it went without saying that no one, but no one, was permitted to dribble in his defensive third. Much too risky. Midfield presented problems, too. Better to move the ball with quick passing—or maybe to follow the requirements of the direct-play school: cut out the midfield altogether, and hoof the ball straight up to the forwards, or forward, who could now, with total accuracy, be called a target man.

Up front a dribble or two might be allowed, but that often proved a vain expectation. Because there was suddenly a shortage of players who knew how to dribble.

Supply and demand at work, I imagine. With coaches making it plain that they didn't want dribblers, what would be the point of developing the skill?

There was another, more sinister factor at work. The game got faster, surely, but it also got more intense and more competitive, or so we're led to believe. Though I'm not really sure about those last two adjectives. It had always seemed pretty intense and competitive to me. What was new was the immense amount of money now involved.

Whatever, the game unquestionably got more defensive . . . and it got dirtier. Defenders were allowed to get away with, if not murder, then certainly assault and battery. By some strange perverted alchemy of the soccer gods, the disappearance of the skill of dribbling was "balanced" by the disappearance of the skill of tackling.

The object of a tackle was once clearly definable as winning the ball. Now the idea was to stop the player in possession: stop him passing, stop him dribbling, stop him playing. The best way to do that was to barrel into him and flatten him.

To be "caught in possession" was worse than "giving the ball away," because you were likely to get kicked up in the air by thuggish defenders.

Given all that, who would bother to learn how to dribble? No one, you might think. But it hasn't worked out that way. Dribbling lives on, a brave subversive movement in the age of tactics and set plays, but one so vital and so natural to the game that it cannot be wished away.

I should explain: by dribbling, I mean the skill of moving with the ball, and working it—by whatever trickery and sleight-of-foot—past tackling opponents. To be distinguished from running with the ball—which is the act of moving the ball forward into space, often at speed, but when not under immediate challenge. Bobby Charlton was superb at running with the ball, as was Franz Beckenbauer. But neither was a dribbler.

Maradona was a dribbler, Pelé too. Today? Paulo Futre, obviously, but take a look at Romário, at Faustino Asprilla, at Alen Boksic, at Gianfranco Zola, at Ryan Giggs, at Marco Etcheverry. During the World Cup, one of the things that made the Argentina-Romania game so exciting was the dribbling of 20-year-old Ariel Ortega.

Evidently, there is something irrepressible about the urge to dribble a soccer ball. It is deeply imbedded in the game, an absolutely fundamental element. While it may be stretching things too far to say that soccer *is* dribbling, the skill is certainly at the heart of the sport. Soccer is not soccer without it.

Dribbling is the most intricate, the most exciting, the most wondrous of soccer's skills. It is the creative player's chance to express himself, to add his own touches and flourishes, to inject his own personality into the game. You can see that it is a highly enjoyable skill, both for the dribbler and for the spectators. And it is the most intimate, the most personal of the sport's skills. Dribbling is the body language of soccer, and inevitably no two players dribble alike.

Stanley Matthews shuffled his way past his markers. Pelé was a powerful, muscular rapier who seemed to play the ball off his opponents' legs as he cut through defenses. The diminutive Maradona, with his jerky twists and turns and acceleration, kept defenders constantly off-balance, while the tall Boksic bends and sways to a slower, more elegant rhythm. Etcheverry is apparently able to move opponents out of his path with the slightest of feints, almost by just looking at them. And Romário . . . well, who knows how he does it?

And that's the point. Dribbling is not an explicable skill. It is a living, unpredictable thing, an instinctive art that springs from within a player. It exists only in the flesh, on the field. It dies when transferred to paper or blackboards. It cannot be explained by charts and diagrams. It is not at all easy to put into words.

Some 20 years ago, I was at a game in which Pelé scored yet another remarkable goal. One second he was poised, motionless in the penalty area, his way to goal blocked by two defenders; the next second he was past the defenders, and the ball was in the net.

In the locker room afterward, I asked him how he had done it. He grinned, began to mumble an answer, then simply swayed his body and moved his feet . . . he grinned again. *That* was how he had done it. Words wouldn't serve; his body had to speak for him. At the intellectual level, it was clear that Pelé did not know how he had gotten past those two defenders.

Now, how do you coach that? Impossible—so what is a coach to do? Logically, he must concentrate on the things that he can coach . . . tactics and, of course, set plays. And with equal logic, whether he intends it or not, he will end up exaggerating the importance of those aspects.

Andy Roxburgh's belief in the importance of set plays is shared by many, probably a majority, of today's coaches. The word has been around for some time now that many—nay, *most*—goals are scored from set plays.

Whenever I ponder that, and think back to games I have seen recently, I find it to be nonsense. During this summer's World Cup, I attended 14 games in which 33 goals were scored. How many came from set plays?

I'm going to subtract the five penalty kicks, which are not exactly set plays that call for any tactical cleverness. So, 28 goals . . . and only four of them came from set-play situations. Which works out to a measly 14.3 percent. And if you're looking for tactical cleverness at the free kicks, forget it. It was individual skill all the way: Branco's 40-yard bomb against the Netherlands, Gabriel Batistuta's bullet against Nigeria that came back off the goalkeeper for Claudio Caniggia to score, Hristo Stoichkov's left-foot hook over the German wall, and Aron Winter's superb header from a corner kick against Brazil.

Such statistics—which I'm convinced are representative—should explode the myth of the set play. The fact that the myth lives on tells you that someone in soccer has an interest in perpetuating it. That someone is the coach.

But I confess to optimism. Dribbling has survived the combined onslaught of ruthless defenders, feeble referees, and unimaginative coaches. Things are changing. The trend is now toward protecting the skillful players—the dribblers, of all people!

It's never easy to measure the effect of a rule change, but the ban on the tackle from behind (or the nastiest of such tackles) seems to me to have had a dramatic impact. Of course defenders don't like it, so we'll get plenty of complaints from them. So be it, they will simply have to relearn the forgotten skill of clean tackling.

But what we're also getting is a new free-flowing, much more attractive game. Suddenly all those closet dribblers can out themselves, can release their skills. And if those skills cannot be coached, there is now no need for the coach to condemn them, because dribbling can now be seen to be *effective.*

That is probably how the practical coach will see it. But the rest of us can rejoice at a return of the excitement and entertainment and personality that dribbling brings.

Soccer is rediscovering its soul. The hell with set plays—here's to a new Golden Age of Dribbling.

Journey to the End
of the Convention

WASHINGTON, D.C.—Getting around at these monster soccer conventions . . . it's impossible . . . six meetings going on at the same time . . . a clinic here, a committee meeting there, a reception somewhere else . . . how can you do it? . . . well, you can't . . . it's life on the run . . . never a dull moment . . . you keep moving, you keep talking . . . there's barely a second to pause, to catch your breath . . . you scuttle from one meeting room to another . . . always arriving late . . . always leaving early . . . there's just as much going on in the corridors . . . those little groups chatting excitedly away . . . everyone hurrying to something . . . I study the official program . . . draw up a list of what I want to see . . . nice and logical . . . and the first thing that happens is that I can't find the room . . . while I'm looking, here comes Zvi Friedman with his computer analysis . . . so I get involved with that for half an hour, an impromptu demonstration . . . as a piece of computer skill it's fantastic, incredible . . . everything's there on the screen . . . who made the bad passes, when they made them, where they made them . . . who took the shots, who made the tackles, what part of the field . . . you want to know who intercepted a pass? click click click, there it is . . . who headed the ball into touch? click click click . . . it's a miracle . . . but I don't like it . . . how can that be? asks Zvi, both Bora Milutinovic and the Brazilian coach Carlos Alberto Parreira used the system . . . found it helpful . . . I'm struggling to explain what I object to . . . I don't like the idea of players becoming dots on a screen, dots that leave wiggly lines behind them when they move . . . click click click . . . it's dehumanizing . . . Zvi

Originally published in Soccer America *January 30, 1995. Reprinted with permission of* Soccer America *magazine.*

pleads innocence . . . all he's doing is supplying detailed information about a game . . . what the coach does with it, that's not Zvi's department . . . anyway, I feel certain that any coach with half an eye open would be aware of the movements and situations that the computer is revealing . . . where is that damn room? . . . I go through the nearest door . . . no, this isn't it . . . but quite interesting anyway . . . so I stay to listen to the mysteries of the Coerver techniques . . . I watch Al Galustian doing the Rivelino move and the Beckenbauer move . . . elaborate stepovers, tight little spin turns . . . no Maradona moves, he says . . . Maradona's been a naughty boy, bad for the kids to emulate . . . the room is huge, vast, cavernous . . . but it's jammed with chairs . . . Galustian is limited to a little postage stamp of floor space . . . but he's talking about "creating space" . . . I'm trying to read my program at the same time . . . where to next? . . . the Delaware Suite? . . . I've got about 10 minutes to get there . . . but I get there late . . . too much gossiping in the corridors . . . another huge ballroom, lots of space here . . . Alvin Corneal is in the middle, moving some young players around, starting them, stopping them, doing a lot of shouting . . . this is "Communication on the Soccer Field" . . . I don't know, I never understand these things . . . I'm trying to keep ahead . . . each time Corneal stops the play, I've worked out why . . . and each time I'm wrong . . . "That's why he's a coach and you're not," I'm told by an unsympathetic colleague . . . yeah, and what if I'm right and he's wrong? . . . the players are fun, there's some talent here . . . the Bethesda Wizards . . . the team was down in Brazil this past summer . . . there's an encouraging thing . . . I race off to find their coach, Graham Ramsay . . . yep, the boys loved it he says, we're going back . . . "We got clobbered 8–0 in our first game, but the boys learned so much . . . now, when we warm up it's the Botafogo warm-up they do" . . . the team's idea, not Ramsay's . . . at some point, who remembers when? I poke my nose into one of Bora's sessions . . . hear him say "It's like chess" . . . I should scream out loud . . . but I quietly leave . . . it's *not* like chess . . . it's nothing bloody *like* chess, dammit . . . if it is like chess, then it's a bore . . . but Bora does like chess . . . later I see him in the lobby, publicly, flamboyantly playing speed chess . . . where you've only got 30 seconds or whatever to make a move . . . does he give his players time limits? . . . I'm scurrying like the White Rabbit . . . I'm late! I'm late! . . . Alan Rothenberg has already started his "State of Soccer" address . . . nothing new here . . . the Soccer Foundation will be wise in its investments . . . and slow in its disbursements . . . MLS is going to happen . . . but the usual vagueness about the investors . . . the USSF's Tom King gets up and says how happy they are to have Bora as the coach until 1998 . . . really? has he signed? . . . "Not yet" says King . . . that night, or maybe it was the following night, Bora turns up in the incredibly noisy restaurant where I'm eating . . . he shouts "Contract? Is not important. I give my word" . . . they tell me there are about 3,500 coaches at this thing . . . at a coaches' breakfast, there's a table loaded down with plaques . . . there's an award for Joe Bean who has 400 wins . . . and another for a guy who has been an NSCAA (National Soccer Coaches Association of America) member for 40 years . . . plenty of awards all over the place . . . the Hermann Award ceremony is a formal affair, too formal for me . . . emcee, film clips, celebrity speakers . . . saved by Brian Maisonneuve's wonderfully natural boyishness on receiving the trophy . . . now, what's going on in this room? . . . a talking head! . . . Carlos Alberto Parreira on videotape . . . how Brazil won the World Cup . . . marvelous stuff on the preparation of the team . . . but surely I heard Parreira say something about moving the ball up to "the three forwards" . . . what three forwards? . . . Bora is in the audience . . . when the lights go up he gets more applause than Parreira . . . there are two unusual topics . . . and they overlap, of course . . . Dan Woog's seminar on homophobia clashes with the Latino coaches' meeting . . . intelligent stuff from Woog . . . I run off to the Latino meeting . . . exciting, this . . . some 60 people present, including Bora and Timo Liekoski . . . the feeling that things are going to get done . . . sure there are problems . . . the name: Latino or Hispanic? . . . will the newsletter be in English or Spanish or both? . . . what about Portuguese? . . . no matter, this could be a very useful, even powerful group . . . that's what the Division I coaches should be . . . when I've tracked down their meeting I find disagreement over the split season . . . Joe Morrone sees it killing off college soccer in the northeast . . . killing off his superb Connecticut program . . . others think he's overreacting . . . but he's still the one who does all the work . . . reelecting him chairman takes about 10 seconds . . . more confusion . . . what does "postseason" play mean? . . . does it mean only the NCAA tournament? . . . if so, then Virginia's Mike Fisher should never have been suspended from this year's Division I final . . . the NCAA guy makes it clear that the soccer tournament "is still a deficit championship" . . . $125,000 in the red . . . the coaches don't trust the referees . . . they vote that the refs should not get a pregame list of yellow-card counts for each player . . . the vote is unanimous . . . the meeting started with 60 coaches present . . . there are 13 left as it draws to a close . . . this is an easy switchover . . . I gather up my things and move next door . . . the pro leagues are explaining who they are, and where the colleges fit in . . . Richard Groff tells us about the American Professional Soccer League (APSL) . . . but doesn't tell us it's in deep trouble . . . Bill Sage says the MLS will use only three foreigners . . . "slight chance we'd go to four, but only with the USSF's permission" . . . they need to uncross their wires . . . Rothenberg says it will be four, or maybe five foreigners . . . keep moving . . . on to the Holmes Room . . .

I'm definitely flagging . . . trouble concentrating when the coaches–referees panel starts up . . . somebody says we hear a lot about the pressure on the referees, but what about the pressure on the coaches to win? . . . well, what about it? . . . a college soccer coach fired because he didn't win? . . . not too likely, is it? . . . more crossed wires . . . "We're looking for 100 percent perfection" says George Noujaim, director of National Intercollegiate Soccer Officials Association's (NISOA) National Referee Program . . . "If I, or anyone else, expects a referee to be perfect, they're whistling Dixie," says Bob Sumpter, NISOA's director of instruction . . . I never get back to my room for that promised nap . . . they've got the bar strategically placed right at the elevators . . . "What are you drinking?" . . . and in I go . . . a bunch of college coaches wrestling with a new dilemma . . . what to do about the MLS . . . apply for a job? . . . will it last? . . . where's the security? . . . a tap on the back . . . it's Alan Hinton . . . so we're suddenly reminiscing about going to games when we were kids in England . . . if it's not the bar, then it's the exhibit area . . . down the escalator . . . past a barrier of deafening music . . . to a vast wonderland of sales and marketing . . . and guys wandering around clutching plastic bags full of goodies . . . little video screens glittering on all sides . . . lots of game commentaries . . . mostly with frightful English accents . . . miles and miles of merchandise . . . but nowhere to sit down . . . keep 'em moving is the name of the game here . . . whoops, it's nearly noon . . . I zoom back up the escalator . . . waving greetings to the guys going down . . . into the ballroom again . . . now it's broken up into a million round tables . . . late again, the meal is on the table . . . chicken . . . the top table heavies are already speaking . . . the All-America banquet . . . I love this . . . not the speeches, not the chicken . . . but to see the kids all spiffed up . . . lining up for their awards . . . shifting and giggling and smiling and trying not to look awkward . . . their eyes sparkling with excitement . . . disappointment here . . . they've got the kids lining up way down the other end of the room . . . too far away . . . I can't see their faces . . . the intimacy, the warmth is missing . . . the names are read out, over 250 of them, into an echoing silence . . . much better to jam them all together up on the platform . . . actually, this convention is getting too professional . . . you notice it with the demonstrators and the clinic givers . . . they've got the audiovisual aid stuff working nicely . . . click click click . . . they've clearly been studying their teaching techniques . . . they're putting on a performance . . . it's theater . . . we've even got The Football Dance act . . . from Roger Spry . . . rhythm and movement . . . this is sort of fun . . . I guess it's an attempt to get everyone lithe and subtle and loose . . . like the Brazilians, maybe . . . so odd to hear it all done in Spry's thick English-midlands accent . . . "I think he's Scottish" an American told me . . . why are Americans so hopeless on accents? . . . the room is crowded . . . and notes are being made all around . . . everyone seems to be writing everything down . . . one convention = 10 million words scribbled on notepads . . . I have 25 pages of notes . . . will I be able to read them? . . . by Saturday night the convention is dying . . . the exhibit area is closed . . . people are checking out . . . the hotel is getting ready for the next invasion . . . shoe salesmen? gynecologists? travel agents? . . . the bar is a quieter, calmer place . . . I can get to my room by 2:30 . . . what a mess . . . how can I have collected all these papers and brochures and leaflets and folders and booklets and magazines . . . impossible . . . surely it was only a few hours ago that I arrived?

Note:

We all have our favorite writers. This one owes everything to Louis-Ferdinand Céline.

A Trip to the Moon
Where Stars Are Born

SANTA CRUZ, Bolivia—You can take a trip to the moon here—a bumpy, hazardous journey, but earthbound all the way. From the city center it takes only about 20 minutes, then the paved roads run out and you're on bumpy mud tracks, dodging huge puddles and cows that have settled comfortably down for a quiet snooze in the middle of your path.

You seem to be getting farther and farther away from everything—no houses, only trees and bushes—then suddenly there's this tremendous open space . . . and soccer players.

Maybe 200 of them in four—or is it five? or six?—groups, ranging from little kids up to quite big kids. And you can see why they call this place The Moon. The surface is a pockmarked, sandy area with a few little patches of grass. Vast, though. Way off in the distance, over a line of small, bristly bushes, you can just make out yet another group of players; you can just see their heads as they race to and fro.

This is where kids who join up with Tahuichi start their soccer life. It certainly isn't the easiest place to get to—there's a long walk from the nearest bus stop—but that seems to be all part of the training. The idea is to arrive on time, whatever the difficulties.

It is 8:30. Two little boys are walking fast, almost running toward a group that has already started training. The coach seems to have eyes all around his head. He has seen them approaching, and as soon as they are within shouting distance, he lets them have it: "You can go home, don't come over here. You have to be here at 8:00!"

Originally published in Soccer America *March 6, 1995. Reprinted with permission of* Soccer America *magazine.*

Tahuichi: The Boys from Bolivia celebrate yet another triumph in their uninhibited, joyful way. The Tahuichi youth club, founded in 1978 in Santa Cruz, Bolivia, has become world famous for its sparkling, attacking soccer. With Tahuichi, whether they win or lose, you never get a dull game. *Copyright Paul Gardner*

The kids stop, but they don't go home. They hang around talking to other banished latecomers. The attraction of the soccer is evidently too great. The coach explains to the others: "You have to learn punctuality, that's part of discipline. Without discipline you cannot play soccer."

It is tempting to look for something secret, something sensational here. Some special, unique thing that the Tahuichi coaches and the Tahuichi kids are doing, the thing that has enabled them to produce an ongoing string of good teams and exceptional players.

But nothing unusual is going on. The bigger kids are playing an 11 vs. 11 game, sploshing through the puddles, ignoring the sidelines, perhaps dribbling a bit more than one is used to seeing. The little kids are lined up in groups, doing various running exercises, some with and some without a ball.

Actually, I should note that—certainly for American eyes—there is something *very* unusual here. No parents. Not a single one. Maybe half a dozen adults, all coaches. For the rest, it's kids, kids, kids all the way.

And when kids dominate the scene, they do bring something unusual— well, if not unusual, something different. You're infected very quickly with a pervasive feeling of enthusiasm. When there's a short break in the training, the kids surround you, you're submerged by a wave of happy faces, all talking at once, all so very obviously enjoying themselves.

Now that's exactly right, too—for this site, this almost desolate area, is one on which the Tahuichi club plans to realize a dream. Here Tahuichi will build its *Villa del Niño Feliz*—the Home of the Happy Child. A soccer center with four full-size fields, a mini-stadium with lights, plus smaller fields and a complex of buildings that will eventually house the club's offices, along with changing rooms, medical facilities, a canteen, and dormitories.

It is an immensely ambitious project for a youth club in a small country, yet the chances are that it will happen. Because the man behind it is Roly Aguilera, the founder of Tahuichi, who has a habit of making things work. So the *Villa del Niño Feliz* has been carefully planned so that it can be built in easy stages.

Already, standing a little forlornly at what passes for the "entrance" to The Moon, there is the shell of a modern-looking building. No doors, no glass in the windows yet, but this is the first stage of the administrative buildings.

As financing is obtained, so the buildings will be extended, and the fields leveled and seeded. You look at this wild, unkempt landscape, and you compare it in your mind with the neat, tidy little model of the finished Villa that sits in the current Tahuichi offices in downtown Santa Cruz . . . and it seems utterly absurd that the total cost of this project is only $1.2 million.

Yet, strangely enough, I find I have some doubts about the change from rags to comparative riches—from the scuffed ragamuffin surfaces of The Moon to the smooth grass that the Villa will presumably bring.

Progress is a strange procedure. It seems to be definable only after it has happened. It has a habit of taking on a life of its own, of going off in uncharted directions. If it obeys any rules at all, it seems to be wed to the Law of Unexpected Consequences.

I look at the bumpy fields and the lopsided balls, some of them swelling alarmingly into strange bubbles, and I wonder whether they, those very imperfect things, might not be a part of the "secret" of Tahuichi. Whether they might not be the secret itself.

Is it a given that the arrival of more expensive, better facilities will assure the creation of better players? I think not. It may in fact do exactly the opposite. If this sounds pessimistic, or comes across as "standing in the way of progress," it is not intended as either. It is simply an observation that ambition and money change the atmosphere.

I am talking about the Tahuichi club as a producer of exciting young soccer players. But Tahuichi's progress since its founding in 1978 has already led it into other, more serious and—if you like—more meaningful areas. Tahuichi is also an institution that has taken hundreds of kids from the poorest of homes here and given them opportunities and visions that they would never otherwise have had.

Tahuichi can also be said to have had an effect on the consciousness of the entire country. Bolivians will admit, not with any great enthusiasm, that their country suffers under the stigma of being a loser. It has lost all the wars it has ever fought, it has lost huge chunks of territory, it has lost its only seaport and is now landlocked.

A record that has been reflected in the history of Bolivian soccer, which has been one of the least successful in South America. Tahuichi has changed that, at least at the youth level. The under-15 tournament that Tahuichi has recently organized here demonstrated just how strong Tahuichi—and, by association, Bolivia—is at this level.

I don't think any other South American country could have organized so successful an event at the youth level, bringing together top South American clubs, paying all their expenses, and playing the final games in a packed stadium.

On the field we saw superb games, and we saw that the Tahuichi youngsters, those products of The Moon, can more than hold their own with the boys from the pro clubs. The tournament, billed as the South American club championship for under-15s, was won by Tahuichi, which finished top of the final group, ahead of Vasco Da Gama of Brazil, Boca Juniors of Argentina, and Colo Colo of Chile.

The skill level of the players left one's jaw sagging in admiration. Tahuichi's first goal in their 3–1 win over Boca Juniors, for instance. A 25-yard free kick, hit hard and perfectly by Daniel Urgel, curving over the wall and into the top corner of the goal. A world-class player could not have done it better. Or Tahuichi's second goal, coming from a quick exchange of passes, on the ground, between Urgel and Carlos Duran—a move that suddenly, excitingly, sprang Duran free in the area, one-on-one with the goalkeeper. Duran's finishing touch—a brief fake to draw the goalkeeper, then a hard low shot into the net—was once again world-class.

But when the time came, at the end of the tournament, to hand out the trophies, it was not the sturdy Urgel or the tall Duran who took the MVP award. That went to Colo Colo's Claudio Maldonado—a slender, shy wisp of a boy, extravagantly gifted with an almost supernatural soccer talent. We saw Maldonado playing as a center midfielder, as a right flank player, and as a sweeper. He made each position his own, immediately assuming a key role, dominating the play around him with an ease and an assurance that was a delight to watch.

Rarely have I seen such casual confidence in so young a player, such instinctive ability to do the right thing, whether dribbling or short passing or long passing or tackling or simply backing off. In its final game, Colo Colo played without the injured Maldonado, and lost 1–0 to Vasco Da Gama. A key factor, said the Chilean coach Miguel Arellano, was that Maldonado's absence had a depressing effect on the other players.

One moderately sour note. If the skill level of the players was refreshingly high, the tactics adopted by Vasco Da Gama did not go down well with anyone. Said the Boca coach, Ricardo Sotelo, "I'm glad that the title went to Tahuichi, which always took the field looking to score goals, rather than to Vasco, which played defensively, always with a mass of players at the back. This is a Brazilian team, remember—I fear that this defensiveness shows the influence of the World Cup tactics of Carlos Alberto Parreira."

Let us hope not—but the evidence is piling up. The Brazilian team that recently won the South American under-20 championship was composed of relatively big players, and lacked the traditionally skillful playmakers.

Kids do learn, or absorb, from those who play around them. That, too, has been one of the strengths of Tahuichi—that an invigorating, attacking style has been developed, one that excites the imagination of the young players. The close club atmosphere plays its part, allowing the youngsters to meet and mix with their older heroes.

The sight of a group of young Tahuichis besieging Chicho Suarez for his autograph during one of the games told the story. Chicho once played on The Moon, now he plays for the Bolivian national team.

The Tahuichi atmosphere has the warmth of a family, which is exactly what a good club should have. My hope is that Tahuichi can retain that feeling, even as it enlarges, as it expands its ambitions, as it levels The Moon, as it welcomes the sponsors, as it embraces the Tahuichi Way program that brings Americans here to learn the Tahuichi methods.

All those things represent progress, and they should not be resisted. They *cannot* be resisted, because to do so creates an artificial situation. The key question is whether the progress will complicate and distort the original simplicity of the Tahuichi idea.

U.S. Is Simply Not Good Enough

Little Has Changed from Past Teams (Under-17 World Cup-1995)

QUITO, Ecuador—The United States Soccer Federation will have to think carefully about entering any more tournaments in Ecuador. Something goes badly wrong with American teams here. Two years ago it was the full national team that put on an El Stinko act with two losses and a tie with perennial South American doormat Venezuela in the Copa America.

Now the under-17 boys have come up with a repeat performance, losing their first two games in the World Cup here and becoming the first team to be eliminated from the tournament.

It looks like a step backward. After all, in both of the last two under-17 World Cups, in 1991 and 1993, the U.S. has reached the quarterfinal stage.

My feeling is that this team was not noticeably worse than either of its predecessors. In many ways, all three teams were remarkably similar, showing the same strengths and repeating the same weaknesses.

Little has changed, technically.

[*Timeout:* This is permitted, you know, under a soppy FIFA rules experiment in this tournament. Timeout to deal with that word *technically.* A word that gets used a lot in soccer. I find that I use it a lot, but I do so each time with an apologetic feeling—apologizing, I guess, to myself that I cannot come up with something better, something more appropriate to what the word is supposed to describe.

Technically is supposed to describe the area that has to do with technique. Ball skills, in other words: the most natural, the most *personal* of soccer's talents. Yet is there a more *impersonal* word than *technical*? In everyday usage,

Originally published in Soccer America *August 21, 1995. Reprinted with permission of* Soccer America *magazine.*

technical is used to indicate complexity and things that are scientific and measurable. If human experience can be broadly divided into the intellectual and the emotional, the word *technical* belongs firmly on the intellectual side.

But the learning of soccer ball skills should not be—cannot be, in my opinion—an intellectual exercise. If the skills are to be anything more than mechanically reproduced drills, then their learning must involve a love for the game, a feel for the ball. There must be warm emotion involved, the young player must be excited by contact with the ball.

Yet we use that cold, bloodless word *technical* to summon up the image of young boys having fun learning to make friends with a soccer ball. I'll try not to use it again—at least in this column. End of timeout.]

So—the ball skills of our young players have not noticeably improved over the past four years. I will extend that: I don't believe that there has been any significant improvement over the American team that played in the first of these under-17 World Cups in China in 1985.

Ten years of burgeoning youth soccer all over the United States, 10 years of improvements in coaching (that's what I'm told), and there is no clearly discernible improvement in the ball skills of our young players.

On the current team, Francisco Gomez stands out as the one player who always looks comfortable with the ball, who has a distinctly personal look and style to his play. A player I would unhesitatingly say who has a shot at making it in the pros.

I would not want to make that prediction for any of the other boys. Not because they are bad players. Not because of the *level* of their ball skill, but because of the *nature* of their ball skill. They show me a presentable level of technical skills, but they show me too few natural skills.

Obviously, this is not their fault. They are products of a coach-dominated youth system that has consistently tried to *teach* young players how to do everything, rather than encouraging natural development.

You can see glimmers of unusual skill in several of the players: Ryan Trout, Grover Gibson, and Carl Bussey all showed—occasionally—exciting talent. But it looked almost like frightened talent, scared to come forward and be recognized. Natural ability kept too tightly in check by technical rigidity.

I am reasonably satisfied that Glenn Myernick's team was representative of what the U.S. has to offer at this level. "Manny Schellscheidt and I looked under every rock and stone to find players. Every weekend we were at club games, tournaments, following up calls—we looked at 82 players."

Yet Myernick admits that this team, which certainly had as good a preparation period as any of the others here, is simply not good enough to compete at this level.

Myernick keeps a manual in which, after each game, he rates his players and records his feelings about the game. These were his comments after the first game here, the 0–2 loss to Ecuador: "A look at the players' ratings and our weaknesses quickly reveals that we are not good enough to be in contention for a medal in this competition. While we are organized and competitive, we are not good enough in the areas that decide games—namely, finishing, and quality at every position."

Speaking to some of the American players before that game, I got the sort of answers that were predictable and, yes, correct. All were confident of going far in the tournament. Gomez, Steve Pedicini, and Kevin Knott all said the U.S. would get to the final. Ryan Trout, logically enough, said "What's the point of saying we'll get to the final? We're gonna win it."

Had I been talking to the Ecuadoreans or the Japanese or the Ghanaians, I would doubtless have gotten similar answers. If you don't think you've got a chance to win it, why bother to turn up?

Nonetheless, I believe there is a difference between the attitude of the Americans and that of *all* the other teams. During all six of these under-17 World Cups, I have had many conversations with young players from Argentina, Germany, Chile, Qatar, Russia, Nigeria, Mexico, Brazil, Saudi Arabia, Portugal, etc., etc.

Yes, they're always confident—but I have *never* found them arrogant. They always show a decent respect for the ability of whoever their opponents may be. Not a fear—but a respect.

Sadly, I have found that the American confidence is far too often of a different order. There is an undermining element of mindless superiority.

In 1991, shortly before the U.S. was to play Qatar in a quarterfinal, I visited both teams within an hour. In the Qatar hotel, I had a serious talk with some of the players, who had studied tapes of the American team, who knew the names of the best American players, who praised them for being good players, who said it was going to be a tough game, but, yes, they were confident of winning.

In the American hotel what I got was this: "You've been talking with Qatar? Are they nervous? Well they should be, we're gonna kick their ass." Coach Roy Rees was well aware of the problem. He had shown the team tapes from the 1989 under-17 World Cup—in which his team beat Brazil 1–0 and then, brimming with American superiority, was wiped out 5–2 by East Germany in its next game. The ploy didn't work; the Americans lost to Qatar.

The problem is no doubt cultural: this attitude that it's a wimpy thing to do to make a realistic, intelligent assessment of what you're up against, that the bludgeon is the only weapon necessary, that kicking ass will show who's who. That attitude may be fine in high school but it's fatal at the level of a world championship.

Myernick, like Rees before him, admits that there is a problem. He says: "Yes, it is cultural. Take the Argentine kids—they know that big teams can be upset by the little teams, they see it in their pro league games. Our kids don't see that. Maybe the more humble pie they eat, the more prepared they are. That's why about 70 percent of our preparation games were against teams that were older and better than us. If I had to do it again, I'd do the same thing.

"Look at the members of the senior national team now. The way they carry themselves, the way they talk to the press—with overseas experience, they've become members of the international soccer brotherhood.

"The kids on this team are just discovering that there's a whole other level of the game out there that they're deprived of on a daily basis. Now they go back to American club soccer."

The implied criticism of club soccer didn't sound strong enough to me— I asked Myernick to be more specific. He pondered the matter, then measured out the following: "We will never be in contention for a medal at the U-20 or the U-17 levels until, when you see a roster of our players, their names are affiliated with a pro team."

A more pithy response came from one of the players. We had been chatting about what comes next for these players. One of them smiled wistfully and said, "Well, I guess it's back to crap soccer."

Is There a Doctor in the House?

Heal Us of This Sickening Shootout

NEW YORK—To start at the end. That benighted shootout. That nasty, painful excrescence that festers up on the rear end of tied MLS games. An ugly, embarrassing, suppurating, reeking carbuncle that is supposed to be the answer to—well, frankly, I forget what it is supposed to do.

Anyway, does it matter what the intentions were? The thing itself is now what counts, and anyone with eyes to see and a nose to smell can see that it is a childish, rancid nonsense. It mocks the game of soccer and stinks of the worst overripe excesses of the marketing/sponsor/TV/PR nitwits who daily dig their greedy claws ever deeper, ever more damagingly, into soccer.

In case you were wondering, perhaps I should explain. I do *not* like the shootout, either as a "spectacle" or as a way of deciding games.

It is a "spectacle" only in the sense that it allows, maybe encourages, players to make a spectacle of themselves. And, like all tiebreakers except corner kicks, it is utterly synthetic.

The blatant unfairness and cruelty of the shootout is fresh in my mind as I write. Having just watched John Harkes fail in his shootout attempt and thus hand the MetroStars a thoroughly undeserved "victory" over DC United.

That's what the shootout does. It allows the simpletons to see, without having to do any tiresome thinking, just who lost the game. Poor Harkes made matters worse by tripping over the ball and barely even getting off his shot.

What a travesty! As it happens, Harkes had been one of the best players on the field, he had done what he is supposed to do, he had played soccer.

Originally published in Soccer America *May 27, 1996. Reprinted with permission of* Soccer America *magazine.*

When the stand-up comedy routine arrived, he fell down. And I can feel nothing but sympathy for him, and scorn for the idiots who have inflicted this indignity on him.

Why does the MLS feel that it needs to have a tiebreaker anyway? Well, Americans won't accept ties, that's well-known, just as they will never buy German automobiles or Japanese cameras. Hogwash, in other words.

What Americans, quite rightly, will not accept is boring games. Are ties necessarily boring? No—but they have become increasingly so because of modern tactics. Tactics that call for coaches to play for a tie on the road. To play cautiously, defensively, and boringly. The shootout tiebreaker, we are told, stops all that.

Which is also hogwash. Cautious, defeatist coaches, scared that they cannot win the real 90-minute game, are perfectly capable of playing defensive soccer in search of a shootout win.

There is absolutely no guarantee that the shootout will do what it is supposed to. And turning to the specific case of the MLS—why should it be necessary at all?

Before the season started, a meeting of all the MLS coaches made it very clear that they didn't feel the need for any rule changes to encourage attacking play or goal-scoring. Which surely amounts to a pledge from those coaches that they will play attacking soccer, and will not immerse themselves in the mire of negative play.

Observations so far suggest that the coaches have stuck to their word. I've now seen, live or on TV, all 10 teams. None of them seemed flagrantly defensive. Bob Houghton's Colorado Rapids with their tedious reliance on the offside trap (which, if not a defensive tactic, is certainly an anti-soccer ploy) can, for the moment, have the benefit of the doubt.

The three tied games that I've seen were not in any way the result of deliberate defensive play. There would have been nothing wrong, no injustice would have been done, in awarding each team one point. But the shootout knows nothing of justice, does not even know that these very same players about to be stretched on the tiebreaker rack have just given their all for 90 minutes in a real game of soccer.

Bah, forget all that. On with the show. Here come the officials raising and dropping their flags, directing the sterile traffic to nowhere. And here come the players to play their sorry role in this farce.

And sadly, not many of them look very good. When the North American Soccer League introduced this shootout thing, in 1977 if memory serves, they came out with the usual guff to justify the unjustifiable. How much better than regular penalty kicks, they crowed, here you see real soccer skills at work, here the goalkeeper has a chance.

Consider the irony of this. The MLS, which says, which knows, that it needs lively, goal-scoring games, believes that it must have a tiebreaker. The first mistake. It then rejects regular penalty kicks, which would certainly ensure that the ball goes into the net more often than not—mistake number two. Followed by number three: it goes for the 35-yard shootout, which—by "giving the goalkeeper a chance"—ensures that it will get fewer goals.

I don't have any stats to hand to tell you what percentage of NASL players scored in their shootouts, but I'd take a bet that it was at least 50 percent. In the three MLS shootouts that I've watched, it's been 21 goals in 51 tries, or 41 percent.

More irony. It's almost as though the MLS has designed a test to showcase the technical limitations of far too many of its players. Some of the efforts to score have been frankly pathetic. An understatement—*most* of the attempts have been laughable. Which means that the goalkeepers have been made to look good. They should be glowing red with embarrassment to get credit for most of these "saves," in which the striker, in a panic to get his shot off in time, has blindly banged the ball into the goalkeeper's body.

The shootout goals, when they do come, are rarely particularly exciting—no hard-hit shots bulging the net as the goalkeeper dives spectacularly. More likely, the ball is tapped into an empty net, or rolls slowly over the line as striker and goalkeeper stand watching.

At least with regular penalties you have the satisfaction of hearing the ball struck firmly. If the ball goes in, it's likely to do so with power. And if the goalkeeper makes a save, it's likely to be spectacular.

Of the 21 successful attempts I've seen so far, just one leaves an impression: Mark Chung's satisfying chip over San Jose's Tom Liner. Intelligent, skillful, delightful. None of the other 36 players I've watched going through the shootout horseplay has managed anything like that; very few have even tried it. The list of failures includes Eric Wynalda, Leonel Alvarez, Preki, Giovanni Savarese, Peter Vermes, Roberto Donadoni, and the unfortunate John Harkes.

I suppose what happens now is that valuable coaching time will have to be spent practicing this asinine routine, teaching strikers and goalkeepers how to count up to five, so that they will know how much time is left for a shot or a save.

The argument that this is a typical soccer situation, a simulation of a breakaway, is nonsense. In a true breakaway there is no time limit, the attacker will usually have teammates in position for a pass, and the goalkeeper will have defenders steaming to the rescue.

But the shootout assumes an importance it should never have, and begins to overshadow the game itself. When the game reports and the box scores come in, you'll find the game ignored, and the shootout recounted in detail. Players of the game? The goalkeeper who, probably by luck, got in the way of most shootout attempts, and the striker who, probably by luck, scored the winning shootout goal.

It's a pity there are so many lawyers at the MLS. A doctor or two would be more useful in getting rid of this fetid pimple on the ass of American soccer.

MLS Fans Fashion Triumph from Disaster

Players and Supporters Weather Storm for Thrilling Final

FOXBORO—It could have been, probably should have been, a disaster, a total fiasco. When you look out of your hotel window at 7:00 in the morning and it looks like midnight and you can see nothing but rain, rain, rain, and ugly, bulging gray clouds sitting right on top of the trees, when you can hear the wind slamming against the glass, you know that this is not the day to be out and about.

When you reach the hotel elevators and you find nine large plastic buckets scattered about the carpet trying to catch a mini-Niagara pouring through the roof, you sort of give up.

Beautiful day—if you're a duck, used to be the expression.

You check the weather every hour, and it just gets worse. Pity the MLS, its season climax about to be ruined by Noah's flood. They were talking about a sellout crowd, but who in his right mind is going to turn up now?

Even if the fans do come, what are they going to see? What's the point of even trying to play soccer on a field that's bound to be one huge puddle? They should call it off, but you know that they won't, they can't.

We're going to get the world's most farcical final, on a par with that Intercontinental Cup a few years back in Tokyo, when they played in a snowstorm. There's a thought . . . could it snow in Foxboro?

You keep trying to kid yourself that it's getting lighter, that the rain's easing off, but it's actually getting worse. Gloom, gloom, gloom.

You get to the stadium early, you get soaked walking the few hundred yards from the car to the press entrance. But on your way in you have to

Originally published in Soccer America *November 4, 1996. Reprinted with permission of* Soccer America *magazine.*

maneuver through a large group of fans, all covered in plastic (ponchos? they're going to need snorkels before this is over). Smiling, happy, noisy fans who've come all the way from Washington, waiting for the turnstiles to open, fans who don't seem to understand that we're on the edge of a catastrophe here. What kind of nuts are these?

You look down from the dry safety of the press box onto the sad, empty stadium and you see nothing but shining wet benches, and saturated tarpaulins being removed to expose . . . a saturated field.

Hordes of kids race all over the field in the pregame stuff, and you can see the water splashing up everywhere. This is ridiculous. Soccer in a rice paddy. Put the ball in the air and the wind will blow it every which way; keep it on the ground and the mud will make sure it doesn't go anywhere at all.

Forget it—this is almost criminal. How can you ask the teams to play in this? They're going to break the rules, too; it's the referee who's supposed to decide if the field's playable or not, and you know he's not going to have any say in the matter at all. The higher authorities—like television and commissioner Doug Logan, with his high-powered posse of sponsors—may not be able to control the weather, but they can pretend it doesn't exist. Play on, they command.

So the teams splash, squelch, and slosh their way onto the field and here comes Mud Cup '96. But what's that noise? Fans cheering? Where did they come from, all of a sudden? You realize with a shock that there are masses of them—the stadium must be two-thirds full, they've snuck in and you've been too depressed to notice.

Now there's something else to notice. Little Mauricio Cienfuegos, looking for all the world like a bubbly 15-year-old, is actually dribbling and swerving and cutting like this is a normal surface, and John Harkes is racing about like there aren't ten tons of mud trying to slow him down.

You have to check the weather at that point, and yes, the tempest yet rages, the rain is still coming down in torrents, the wind is still whipping up the flags . . . but, preposterous to say, we seem to have a real soccer game going on.

How these guys are doing it, heaven knows, but they're not slipping and sliding and falling over everywhere, there's ball control, there are dribbles and passes . . . and quickly, there's a goal.

Cienfuegos does the clever stuff, no one challenges him, he measures his cross, and Hurtado soars out of the gluepot to head home. Now this is beginning to get real—an early goal, exactly what any game needs. Strangely, unbelievably—is it miraculously?—the monsoon, as violent as ever, fades into the background.

But not for DC United, who are having trouble adapting. For 20 minutes, Cienfuegos runs the show. Then the weather asserts itself again, and the game

Boston, 1996: Despite a field better suited for aquaplaning, or even deep-sea diving, MLS Cup '96 turned into a triumph for the league. Amazingly, the players of the Los Angeles Galaxy and DC United produced a marvelous game to enthrall the 34,643 fans who defied the monsoon conditions. *Photo by Simon Bruty of Allsport Photography*

sags into mediocrity. When Chris Armas opens the second half with a neat second goal for the Galaxy, you sense that it's all over.

One thing, though. The most consistently menacing player on the field belongs to DC United. Jaime Moreno, who has mastered the conditions and proved he has the beating of any Galaxy player who has challenged him. Marco Etcheverry has been having problems getting his passes on target, but Moreno solves that for him. Twice the Galaxy have to foul Moreno to stop him. Two free kicks out on the left, perfect for Etcheverry. Both of them end up as goals.

In overtime, it's Moreno again, outsprinting the defense and winning a corner kick for Etcheverry to take, and for Eddie Pope to transform into the winning goal.

An extraordinary finish to a totally unreal day. That soccer could be played at all on that field is remarkable enough, but that it should be so enthralling, so skillful, and so dramatic is downright astounding.

You get soaked again, and you don't even notice, going to the press conference. Where there's another minor miracle waiting for us.

Why would anyone from DC be there? They're all celebrating. Why would anyone from the Galaxy hurry along? They're all in despair. But the first person to show is the Galaxy defender Robin Fraser. Who treats us to a truly beautiful performance—answering everything articulately, patiently, courteously, honestly, making no excuses, praising DC United, and managing to smile while doing it. This was pure class and it was wonderful to watch.

The DC United locker room is full of youngsters, many of whom are delightedly weighing into a huge crumbly soccer-ball cake. It's difficult to sort out the United players, many of them not much more than youngsters themselves.

Moreno says, quietly, that he did the best he could, which seems a bit of an understatement. But then Bruce Arena appears, locks him into a bear hug and tells him "You were a fucking handful all afternoon, you know that? A fucking handful!" That's a bit more like it.

I suppose there was some sort of MLS celebration that night, and they had every reason to feel good. The weather had been vanquished. The players had conquered the soggy field, while the fans had defied the nightmare conditions—over 34,000 of them soaking up drenching rain for three hours. MLS surely knows how lucky it is to have such support.

But I seriously wonder if MLS understands the true extent of its luck on this incredible afternoon. They should bow down in fawning gratitude to the Moreno-Etcheverry-Pope combination, the trio that saved them from the embarrassment of a shootout. Already a supremely fatuous way to end a final, the shootout would have sunk even lower, to utter slapstick, under these conditions.

It didn't happen, but a pretty powerful warning was posted. We wait, without any great hope of sanity prevailing, for MLS to respond to that.

For the moment, the league can rightly feel proud of what it has so far achieved, and can revel in the memory of what is going to be remembered as one of American soccer's great occasions: the memory of an afternoon when 24 soccer players and 34,643 fans fashioned triumph out of disaster.

Can College Soccer Redefine Itself?

The Reemergence of the Pro Game Forces a Reality Check

NEW YORK—A quarter of a century ago, on January 2, 1972, *The New York Times* ran a long and gushingly enthusiastic story about the NCAA Division I championship.

Subheaded "Hope for U.S. Pro Soccer Envisioned in Growing Strength of College Game," the article ended with a stirring prediction by the author: "When the next millennium for pro soccer is announced, it will not, as so often in the past, have both feet planted firmly in mid air, it will have them firmly grounded in the college game."

Talk about getting it wrong! And I had better talk about it, because I was the author of that article and that misguided prediction. Obviously, back then, I had swallowed the notion that soccer in America would fit into what was held to be the traditional American way of organizing sports.

Looking back, trying to fathom why I was so far off-target, I think it comes down to this: there had been, around that time, a substantial leap in the quality of the college game. I took that upgrading to be something that would continue . . . indefinitely, I suppose.

The first time I ever saw a college game was in 1959. Just off the boat from England, I trotted off to see Columbia University and was duly horrified. Two referees wearing Newcastle United's black-and-white stripes? Kick-ins instead of throw-ins? Quarters instead of halves? Substitutions? Not to mention the abysmal skill level.

Originally published in Soccer America *September 1, 1997. Reprinted with permission of* Soccer America *magazine.*

I fled and saw very little college soccer for the next 10 years—a few Long Island University games, which were certainly better, but still had a weird, distorted atmosphere about them.

In 1971, college soccer tried for the big time, and moved its Division I championship game to Miami's Orange Bowl. I went along, was appalled by the empty stadium, but much impressed by the quality of the soccer from Howard (the winners), St. Louis, San Francisco, and Harvard.

Six years later, I had emerged from my infatuation. In an October 1980 "SoccerTalk" column headed "Is There Any Hope at All for the Colleges?" I had this to say: "The future looks like this: the really promising young players will join the pros from high school, but the pro clubs will have to make a much greater commitment to their development than they are doing at the moment. College soccer will live quite happily without those players. The general standard is rising slowly anyway, but without some sort of expansion, it will surely stagnate."

A reversal of my previous view, and a much more accurate prediction. The pro clubs I was talking about then were those of the old North American Soccer League. That league had its college draft and talked about mandating reserve teams, but never did. By the time the NASL collapsed in 1984, it required that five Americans (they included green-card holders, I think) be on the field at all times.

Most of the Americans were ex-college players, and it was painfully clear that very few of them were up to scratch.

For years I had been listening to the college coaches—an amiable, personable crowd—telling me how their sport was growing by leaps and bounds (true enough, as far as numbers were concerned), how the National Collegiate Athletic Association was enthusiastic about its future, and about all the reforms that were coming to upgrade its importance and to shift its eccentric rules closer to the game that the rest of the world was playing.

The coaches were living in a fool's paradise. For a while, I was right there with them. But reality was too harsh to be ignored. The college players were not good enough, and it is barely an exaggeration to say that *none* of the vaunted NCAA reforms ever happened. Quite the opposite. Changes in the college game tended to be restrictive.

But these were realities that never seemed to strike home to the college guys. They pressed merrily on, increasingly divorced from the real world of soccer. In the mid-'80s came an event that encouraged them to a complete break with reality. The collapse of the NASL left the colleges as the only really *organized* soccer that there was.

What looked like a triumph for the colleges was, in fact, the worst thing that could have happened to them. Convinced that they held the key to the game's future in the U.S., virtually unopposed by any alternative view (in particular, by the pros), college coaches and college mentality took over the game.

Naturally, and calamitously, in their self-appointed role as teachers they came to dominate the United States Soccer Federation's coaching schools. Theory was their strong point, and clinics, seminars, and workshops sprouted on all sides. The sport was buried under an avalanche of plans and charts and diagrams and pseudoscientific studies.

But the supposed strength of college soccer was nothing more than a flimsy house of cards. The giveaway was that whenever the NCAA cracked its whip, the college coaches jumped headfirst through the hoop. These guys weren't even in charge of their own sport, could barely even change the rules of the game without approval from NCAA functionaries who knew nothing about soccer and didn't give a damn anyway.

That was yet another reality that was excused, or ignored, by the college coaches. The house of cards collapsed as soon as pro soccer reappeared last year. Major League Soccer wasted no time in setting up its Project-40 scheme, which is designed to keep promising young players out of college soccer. The extent of the colleges' defeat is underlined by the fact that P40 is backed by the USSF, never before known to oppose the colleges on anything.

The fact that the colleges are now tasting the bitter fruits of their own shortsightedness is no cause for celebration. Common sense demands that they—with their organization, their facilities, their traditions—play a role in the development of the game in this country.

Defining that role is not going to be easy. The colleges can continue along their present route, acting basically as a means of providing the sons of middle-class white families with a free education—an aim not to be sniffed at, but hardly one that helps the sport.

The alternative is a broad change in philosophy designed to get rid of the silly-clever theoretical excesses of so much college coaching, to bring college soccer into line with the rest of the world, and to make it representative of the American soccer scene. Which means: coaching that pays more attention to the realities of the game on the field, and less to diagrams in the classroom; adopting FIFA rules; and a concerted effort to recruit beyond the comfortable confines of suburbia.

College soccer is in limbo right now, looking for a direction. Leadership is needed. I imagine a gathering of the top college coaches hammering out a

Charter for College Soccer, setting realistic goals for its future. I imagine it—but I know it won't happen.

On the hopeful side: Bruce Arena, in his years at Virginia, showed that college soccer can be played at a high level. And last year's impressive final between St. John's and Florida International was anything but a typical college game, coaches Dave Masur and Karl Kremser having recruited decidedly atypical and unfashionable players. Was that an aberration, or does it represent the future?

No Hiding Wide Skill Gap

Europeans Insist There's No Cause for Alarm (Under-17 World Cup–1997)

CAIRO, Egypt—To my eyes, the most striking conclusion to be drawn from the just-completed under-17 World Cup here concerns the difference in skill level between the Europeans on one side, and the Latins on the other.

The difference has always been there. The Latins show more ball artistry, and that fact is at the heart of the difference in style between the two major schools of soccer, the European and the South American.

But *European* is a misnomer. What is meant is Northern European. The Southern European countries—France, Italy, Spain and Portugal—are much closer to the South Americans than they are to the likes of Germany or Sweden or England.

Looking at the teams present in this tournament, I'm talking about the skill levels of Germany and Austria as compared to those of Brazil, Argentina, and Chile, plus Mexico and Costa Rica, and Spain.

The evidence is that we are no longer talking about a mere difference in the level of skills. So wide has the gap become, that the skills themselves no longer seem better or poorer versions of the same thing, but appear almost as totally different skills. Extrapolate that from the individual to the team level, and it can sometimes look as though it is not simply the *style* that is different—it looks like two different games.

This was certainly the case when South America's number-one team, Brazil, met Europe's number-two team, Austria. The 7–0 scoreline greatly

Originally published in Soccer America *October 6, 1997. Reprinted with permission of* Soccer America *magazine.*

flattered Austria, which was repeatedly saved from further damage by good goalkeeping.

The technical level of the Austrians was frankly abysmal. The night before that rout, the Germans had been similarly exposed by Chile. With a big difference. The Germans summoned all their "traditional" qualities of discipline and fitness and fighting spirit, got a hefty dose of luck, and came away with an unlikely 1–0 victory.

What does this skill gap mean for the future of world soccer? Brazilian coach Carlos Cesar mused that "maybe it means that the good players will come from South America, then Africa—with Europe in third place."

"No," said Paul Gludovatz, coach of Austria, "not in the future. Now. That is the reality now."

Asked about the skill level of his players, German coach Bernd Stoeber said "We're closer to Austria than Brazil. But remember, it is not our main job to develop just skillful players. You need also players with other strengths—discipline, defensive work, goal-scoring."

Which really does beg the question: why not all those strengths *plus* high skill? When Stoeber uses a favorite word—*effective*—it can sound as though he is judging ball skill to be of secondary importance.

Anyway, he does not believe that what was seen here has any great significance for the future: "It is the same thing you see in the professional World Cup. You see Brazil and Mexico, they look nice. They are *playing* football. You see a German team, well, we are *working* at football. But is the South American style more effective?"

Evidently, it was more effective here, to say nothing of vastly more attractive. Surely, that means something? Possibly not, not to convinced Northern Europeans.

Such as England's Bobby Robson, former coach of Barcelona, here as an observer, who picks his words carefully: "The evidence is that, from a broad perspective, Brazil and Ghana seem to have a better technical merit than other countries. But some of those countries, e.g. Germany, have some individuals who are at the same level as Brazil and Ghana."

David Will, the Scotsman who is chairman of FIFA's Referees Committee, says "I see no cause for alarm, we've seen this difference too often before at this level. You can say the future for Germany and Austria looks worrying, but that's not the way it works out. For some reason the non-Latin players develop a little more slowly. Germany, and possibly Austria, are still going to be footballing powers at the senior level."

"This difference in skill levels is not new," says Jean-Pierre Morlans, coach of the French under-16 team, here as a member of FIFA's Technical Study Group. "A few years ago, yes, Ghana was a surprise, but not anymore.

Certainly, the difference is now more marked, at this age level. But I'm not sure what this means for later age levels."

A key point. I have raised before the suspicion that the under-17 World Cup might not be at all useful as an indicator of future talent, and this seems to be the thought that comforts the Northern Europeans.

Bernd Stoeber is not exactly a fan of the tournament: "Sometimes I have this feeling that it would be better *not* to play a world championship, that it is not a good way to develop players. Of course it is good to play teams like Mali, Egypt, and Brazil, but I think it would be better if they were friendly games. Too much pressure to win, too much mental pressure is not good for development."

FIFA spokesman Keith Cooper downplays the problem of pressure: "Pressure from where? I think teams generate their own level of pressure, a lot of it comes from within. Some teams are more worried by it than others. They should look to themselves rather than to external influences.

"Obviously, to put young players under exaggerated pressure is not a good thing. But these boys are in the fast track for a professional career in the game. This is part of the learning experience."

Coverage of the teams here is very slight, so there is little or no pressure from the media, and none from fans. With the obvious exception of the home team. After Egypt had tied Germany 1–1 (a loss for Egypt would have meant their first-round elimination), Stoeber went over to the Egyptian coach Mohamed Aly and "I saw his face and his eyes, and I was glad that his team had qualified—he was near to breakdown."

But that sort of pressure—on the coach—is exceptional. As far as the players are concerned, it is difficult to disagree with Cooper: pressure is something they have to learn to live with.

Of course, the boys get upset and are likely to cry when they lose. But my own observations suggest that the vast majority of the kids can handle whatever pressure there is. The overall level of behavior and sportsmanship on the field is incredibly good, much better than at any senior tournament. A group of four top referees here admitted during a FIFA fair play panel discussion that dissent at their decisions was virtually nonexistent.

There is another argument advanced by the Europeans to explain why the South Americans and Africans keep coming out on top. "Brazil and Argentina are the top South American countries," says Robson. "But in this tournament there is no Holland, no France, no England."

The short answer is that those teams simply failed to qualify (England, typically, does not even enter). Then we get the standard comeback that no European country really takes this World Cup very seriously. There may be something in that—Jens-Uwe Boening, the German national team's secretary, calculated that 200,000DM ($110,000) had been spent on preparation—a pretty insignificant amount.

Even so, there are just too many explanations and excuses here. The huge gap in skill level between the Northern Europeans and the Latins cannot be ignored—"it's light years," said Liverpool's youth director Steve Heighway, after he had watched Brazil crush Austria. Another inescapable fact is that rich European clubs spend a lot of money buying up top South American and African players.

In the face of that evidence, it seems dangerously complacent for Europeans to maintain that things are as they have always been, and will presumably so remain.

How MLS Avoided
Its Worst Nightmare

Think About It–
It Could Have Been Clash vs. MetroStars

NEW YORK—Last season, you may recall, Major League Soccer got lucky. It got the final that it wanted, its two best teams, DC United and the Los Angeles Galaxy. It got even luckier when over 34,000 hardy fans sat through the monsoon and turned an appalling afternoon's weather into a PR triumph for the league.

So far, things have not turned out quite so happily this year. The Galaxy, the Mutiny, and the Wizards—three of the more attractive teams in terms of playing styles and stars—succumbed immediately without much of a struggle.

Suddenly, with the Burn and—particularly—the Crew and the Rapids advancing, the playoffs have a decidedly blue-collar look to them. As I write, there is even the awkward possibility of a Columbus-Colorado game.

More likely than Col × Col is that the final will feature DC and Colorado. Colorado's presence in the final would reflect a great deal of credit for Glenn Myernick—they were, after all, quite the worst team in the league last year.

DC was quite the best last year, and is even more clearly the best this year, the class of the league. Unacceptable though it may be for Crew fans, the truth is that the MLS, not to mention the sport of soccer in the U.S., needs DC United in the final. Not just because their presence will ensure a good crowd, but above all because of the quality of their soccer.

Originally published in Soccer America *October 27, 1997. Reprinted with permission of* Soccer America *magazine.*

The MLS, as a league fighting for acceptance, needs its showcase game to feature its best soccer. That means, without any argument, DC United. None of the other three semifinalists can match DC for skillful, attractive, attacking soccer. Which is not to say that they can't beat DC.

I'm talking here about the MLS image. For the climactic game atmosphere, a packed stadium, and high-level, competitive soccer are necessary. A Col × Col final would surely be competitive, but it would fall short on the other three counts.

On the bright side, things could have been a lot worse. Given the fact that every MLS team has an 80 percent chance of making the playoffs, just think that with a couple of different results here and there, we might have got something like this . . . .

Over in a quiet corner of the VIP box, MLS deputy commissioner Sunil Gulati was frantically chewing on his Carlos Valderrama wig. Chairman Alan Rothenberg was revising his postgame speech for the umpteenth time, deleting all references to the desirability of the shootout.

Only a few minutes earlier, commissioner Doug Logan had suddenly started behaving as though he were the Queen of England, and had been carried out on a stretcher shouting "Come on lads, we call it football you know, pip pip . . ."

Down on the field, the MetroStars and the Clash were battling it out, trying to decide the winner of the MLS Cup. No goals had been scored . . . indeed, the army of MLS statisticians that occupied the press box (the media had been moved to the roof) had fallen asleep, as there had also been no shots, no saves, no corner kicks, and only one block.

The game was now in the 473rd sudden-death round of the shootout. The ABC commentators were still injecting breathless excitement into each attempt, blithely unaware that they had been bounced off the air over two hours earlier to make way for a documentary on women's mud wrestling.

Excitement was not exactly hanging in the air. The last kicker had barely reached the ball on his run up when he slumped to the ground in exhaustion. "Another near miss for the MetroStars!" panted the commentators as they analyzed the replay provided by a special ABC camera artfully situated on a twelfth-floor balcony at the relatively nearby Sheraton Hotel.

Complementing that expertise was the usual flow of urgent sideline interviews. Carlos Alberto Parreira said he thought the MetroStars' possession game, particularly during the shootout phase, had improved by about

4.7 percent, which was encouraging. Peter Bridgwater said that the Clash had plans for Spartan Stadium to be widened, but that it might take 35 years as it inevitably involved narrowing the city of San Jose.

The spectators—there had been 127 of them—had long since departed. Yet the cheering and the singing of Olé! Olé! Olé! went on, as the loudspeakers wafted waves of tinny sound down on to the empty seats.

Another journalist had fallen off the roof of the press box, or maybe he had jumped.

The Alan I. Rothenberg Trophy that, at the beginning of the game, had been proudly displayed on the sidelines, was nowhere to be seen. Toward the end of the regular 90 minutes of pulsating center-circle action, it had occurred to someone (none dare speak his name) that the desperately lack-luster play might be the result of neither team wanting to be seen dead with this prize. The deterrent had been quietly stashed away in the ball bag under the fourth official's table.

Well after the chimes of midnight—they had no effect on the VIP area, where everyone had long ago turned into pumpkins—things were resolved, and the game's hero emerged. By now it had been agreed that each shootout kicker should be allowed 10 minutes to score. Tony Meola, twisting and turn-ing as he dribbled forward on his fiftieth attempt, was overcome by an attack of giddiness, and set off for the opposite end of the field. Pausing only to berate the officials about an offside call four and a half hours earlier, Meola hit a wicked 40-yarder that ju-u-u-u-st made it into the net.

Before anyone had time to consider the implications of this, Alan Rothenberg had raced onto the field to pronounce the MetroStars the win-ners and to heap praise on the wonderful shootout that allowed such an exciting ending—hey, where did it say in the shootout regulations that you were limited to scoring at one end of the field only? What the hell kind of stu-pid rule would that be? Soccer had *always* allowed goals at both ends of the field, and MLS was not in the business of altering FIFA's rules, and had posi-tioned itself clearly as a pro-scoring league . . . it was vintage, upbeat Rothen-berg and, considering the circumstances, not a bad effort.

Rothenberg then presented Tony "Wrong-Way" Meola (forget about "The Wall") with the game MVP, top scorer, fair play, and best-dressed goal-keeper awards. Meola and his teammates were getting ready for the victory lap when it hit them that something was missing. Meola, fully recovered from his game-winning vertigo, was suspicious: "So where's the MLS Cup?" he wanted to know.

The VIP pumpkins had by now straggled onto the field, and the MLS season officially closed as they launched into a listless chorus of "For he's a jolly good chairman" while league minions were scurrying frantically hither and yon trying to locate the mysteriously missing Alan I. Rothenberg Trophy.

Of course, MLS Cup won't happen like that this year—well, I can't speak for the ABC television part of it—but I'm keeping my fingers crossed that it won't be Col × Col.*

Note:

* It wasn't. DC United beat the Colorado Rapids in a very good final, and won their second consecutive championship.

Index

Numbers in italic indicate photos.

239

241